THE TRIALS OF ALBERT STROEBEL

Caitlin Press Inc.
8100 Alderwood Road, Halfmoon Bay, BC V0N 1Y1
www.caitlin-press.com

Text design by Vici Johnstone
Cover design by Monica Miller
Cover photo courtesy The Royal BC Museum and Archives B-04092
Printed in Canada

Caitlin Press Inc. acknowledges financial support from the Government of Canada and the Canada Council for the Arts, and the Province of British Columbia through the British Columbia Arts Council and the Book Publisher's Tax Credit.

Library and Archives Canada Cataloguing in Publication
The trials of Albert Stroebel : love, murder and justice at the end of the frontier / Chad Reimer.
Reimer, Chad, author.
Canadiana 20190225238 | ISBN 9781773860206 (softcover)
LCSH: Stroebel, Albert—Trials, litigation, etc. | LCSH: Trials (Murder)—British Columbia.
| LCSH: Murder—Sumas Prairie (B.C. and Wash.)
LCC KE228.S77 R45 2020 | LCC KF223.S77 R45 2020 | DDC 345.711/02523—dc23

THE TRIALS OF ALBERT STROEBEL

Love, Murder and Justice at the End of the Frontier

CHAD REIMER

CAITLIN PRESS

CONTENTS

To Shannon

A page from the Sears catalogue of 1898, which reveals how easy it was to buy handguns at the time and thus how widespread they became. The revolver Stroebel obtained from a friend most closely resembled the one in the centre of the catalogue page, with its five rounds and low price. Sears, Roebuck &Co., *Consumers Guide* (Chicago, 1898).

DEATH IN SUMAS

Ira Airheart peered out his cabin door, squinting into the darkness. A bank of leaden clouds slid over the moon and the last of the stars, and a light drizzle began to fall. Airheart muttered a curse: more rain. Since he had arrived two months ago, all it had done was rain. The trapper thought of home, back on the farm in Iowa, where the winters were harsh but the spring thaw came fast and fresh, and you could get onto your fields. Here it was the third week of April, a month past winter, and a penetrating chill hung in the air, cutting through your warmest clothes. A wood fire crackled behind him in the cabin, sending steam off the woollen clothes hung over it to dry.

Silence lay heavy and still over the prairie. Then the wind changed, and Airheart heard frantic barking from his neighbour's property, half a mile away. He thought it peculiar, because it was not like Marshall's dog to make a fuss, and he toyed with the idea of going to check. It could be a bear, caught in the steel trap he had set between his and Marshall's place, but Airheart shivered at the thought of venturing back into the night. He owned neither watch nor clock, yet figured it to be about nine o'clock. He had spent a long, frustrating day seeing to his traps on the northern fringes of Sumas prairie, had just sat down to a late supper when he first heard the dog's bark coming through the cabin walls, and had gone to the door to check. Now, standing at the threshold, he decided things could wait until morning. Damn the beast, he muttered again, as he turned back into his warm cabin, undressed and slipped into bed.

Just after dawn the next day, Airheart strode toward the property of his neighbour, John Marshall. His gumboots squished on the soggy

1

trail, and rain pelted off his rubber slicker as he approached his trap, Winchester rifle at the ready. Airheart saw the jagged jaws were empty, and he continued on to Marshall's, figuring he would get some milk for his own ailing setter. He rounded the corner of the house and was met by the barking of his neighbour's dog, which stood over a dark heap on the cabin veranda. The trapper frowned as he crept nearer, then stopped short with a gasp—the heap was Marshall himself, lying on his back. The farmer's head was propped up against the doorsill, and his feet dangled over the front of the veranda; his face was a mess, the nose smashed in, the forehead covered with cracked blood. He was, most certainly, dead.

Airheart staggered back, slipping in the heavy mud. He found his footing, turned and headed for the railway bed that ran in front of Marshall's property, then hurried down the line to Huntingdon station, two miles south, to raise the alarm. Within hours, scores of men had descended upon Marshall's farmhouse nestled among the scrub, trees, swamp and grassland of Sumas prairie. The authorities arrived soon after, and an autopsy, coroner's inquest and investigation followed.

Two days after the discovery of Marshall's body, a local handyman and part-time barber named Albert Stroebel was arrested for the murder. Stroebel was an unlikely killer; short, lean and crippled in the right leg and foot, those who knew him found him obliging and reliable, a harmless "boy" who seemed much younger than his twenty years. Likewise, John Marshall was an unlikely murder victim. A spare man with dark features, the Portugal native was generally respected for his hard work and thrift. With his halting, heavily accented English, Marshall was reserved with strangers, but the reserve dropped with those he got to know and a sociable, even jovial, side came out. He and Stroebel had known each other for years and the younger man was a regular visitor at his farm. Now, with Marshall dead and Stroebel charged with his murder, local residents tried to make sense of it all. Many were convinced a serious mistake was being made: the harmless, crippled boy they knew was not capable of murder, and he certainly could not have killed a man who welcomed him into his home.

Yet something went tragically wrong that gloomy night of April 19, 1893—unravelling the mystery would take nine months and two lengthy trials. The first trial ended with the jury hopelessly dead-locked, coming within a hair's breadth of releasing the accused; the second found him guilty and set an impending date for his execution. The drawn-out legal drama seized the attention of local communities on both sides of the Canadian-American border, splitting them into pro- and anti-Stroebel factions. Newspapers devoted page after page of coverage to the trials, providing their readers with detailed reports of the witnesses' testimony and lawyers' arguments. Throngs of spectators squeezed into the courtroom galleries, rubbing shoulders with reporters and members of the province's legal profession. The proceedings were conducted by the heaviest hitters of British Colum-bia's political and legal establishment: the two trial judges were for-mer premiers and Attorneys General, the Crown counsel the current premier and Attorney General, the defence counsel an up-and-coming legal star and future Supreme Court justice.

When the second trial ended with a guilty verdict and death sen-tence, many in the public howled in protest, convinced that a young man had been condemned to die for a crime he did not commit. How-ever, the dramatic events would not stop there. With the condemned man sitting on death row, the case would take more twists and turns as Albert Stroebel tried desperately to dodge the hangman's noose.

❖

Sumas prairie is located forty miles east of Vancouver, just beyond the bedroom community of Abbotsford and south of the Fraser River. Its western edge is marked by a dramatic escarpment that rises more than a hundred feet above the prairie floor, the farthest limit of the last great ice sheet. To the north looms Sumas Mountain, a three-thou-sand-foot peak that separates the valley from the Fraser River; to the south, the prairie continues over the border into Washington state, stopping short of the Nooksack River. Until a century ago, the prairie spread east to the shores of Sumas Lake, a shallow body of water that stretched from the international border at Vedder Mountain across the valley to Sumas Mountain. Every year, Sumas Lake expanded with the spring freshet, flooding much of the prairie.

In its natural state, the prairie's wet, temperate climate fed a cover of lush vegetation. Thick grasses flourished on the land flooded annually by Sumas Lake; west of this, stands of cedar, fir, maple and cottonwood alternated with dense bush, with openings of wet prairie and swamp squeezed in between. Multitudes of fish filled the streams and lake, waterfowl darkened the skies, while bears, wolves, elk and deer stalked the land.

For countless generations, the prairie has been home to the Sema:th and Nooksack peoples—the former north of today's international boundary, the latter south. Sumas prairie, lake and mountain provided the first peoples with a wealth of resources, from edible plants to fish, waterfowl and game. The earliest White immigrants arrived with the Fraser gold rush, when thousands of prospectors made their way from Bellingham Bay to the Fraser River along the Whatcom Trail. In the wake of the gold rush, modest numbers of White settlers stayed on the land, grazing their herds of cattle and horses. The White population grew slowly through the nineteenth century, and by 1890, only a few dozen farmsteads dotted the landscape. As the newcomers took over the land, the Sema:th were dispossessed, pushed onto a pair of reserves at either end of the prairie.

At the beginning of the 1890s, as the Victorian era neared its end, Sumas was still a frontier settlement. Few of the White immigrants had been there more than a decade. They built their houses and barns from half-timbered logs or home-milled planks. They toiled on their quarter-section lots (160 acres, a quarter of a square mile), the closest neighbours anywhere from half a mile to a mile away. Roads and trails over the swampy ground were sparse, and the few that existed were rendered impassable by rain and flooding. Before 1891, nothing that could be called a town existed north of the border. South of the line, a settlement known as Sumas sported a handful of stores and services. When Canadians on the prairie needed to buy anything or required the services of a doctor, dentist or barber, they travelled to Sumas town. The borderline was invisible for prairie residents; they travelled freely back and forth, often several times a day, giving little thought to the fact that they were moving from one country to another.

These, though, were the last days of the frontier on Sumas prairie, although the end was slow to come. In 1891, the Canadian Pacific Railway (CPR) extended a spur line from Mission, across the Fraser River, to a newly built station at the border it named Huntingdon. At the same time, the Bellingham Bay and British Columbia Railroad was built, linking the Canadian spur line to a terminus in Bellingham. The railway boom sparked both a population and an economic boom. The American town of Sumas was incorporated as Sumas City, and an influx of people was accompanied by the frenzied building of hotels, saloons, real estate offices, banks and brothels. The city itself had much of the Wild West about it, with a locally appointed marshal dispensing rough justice to an unruly population. On the Canadian side, the town of Huntingdon's growth was much more modest. It gained a post office but, aside from the railway station, the

The Canadian Pacific Railway station at Huntingdon, erected when the line was built in 1891. The building housed the offices of Bosnell McDonald and James Schofield, along with the telegraph office. Passengers used the raised boardwalk in front to board and detrain, and freight was loaded and unloaded here. Reach Gallery Museum, P8262: "Canadian Pacific Railway Depot"

only other major building was the Huntingdon Hotel, a three-storey structure with covered verandas running the width of its façade on each storey. Meanwhile, the law was a distant force, the closest police and court in New Westminster, a three-hour train ride away.

By 1893, when our story unfolds, the boom years had given way to bust as a global depression took hold. The frontier remained, as did the CPR line that ran directly in front of John Marshall's farmstead, continuing due south past Albert Stroebel's hotel two miles away. That rail line would play a central role in the drama surrounding Marshall's death: it was the main highway for locals, as well as for countless transients travelling through. And it linked together the tragic events that would lead Stroebel to the shadow of the gallows.

UNLIKELY FRIENDS

If it were not for the violent death of John Marshall, his name and that of Albert Stroebel would have passed unnoticed into history. The two men lived ordinary lives on the edge of a closing frontier, different in the details but not in the generalities of those lived by millions of others. Only on such a frontier could the fates of these two men come together. Both were very far from home and largely on their own. One was a middle-aged Portuguese farmer who spoke only rudimentary English, and who had been born on a small dot of an island in the east Atlantic Ocean. The other was a young American from the Midwest, the fourth of eight children whose restless parents had brought them to the very edge of the continent. Despite their differences, the pair shared the belief that the frontier land they now called home—a world still in the making—offered them the chance of a better life, more prosperous and secure than the one they had left behind.

Of course, the reality of the frontier often failed to live up to its promise. For many, dreams of prosperity and security were dashed by the realities of poverty, broken lives and violence. This was true of the frontier on both sides of the border. Our cherished myth of the peaceful Canadian frontier—so different from the violent American one—was and is a fable, smug, comforting, but false. The murder of John Marshall was just one of a string of violent homicides that took place in southwestern BC during the late Victorian era. The crime that bound together the fates of Marshall and Stroebel can be seen as many things—sad, tragic, monstrous—but it was no exception to a rule.

❖

Some of the most basic facts of John Marshall's life remain a mystery to us. For one, we do not know the name he was born with—John Marshall was the name he adopted as a young man upon his arrival in North America. From the documentary fragments we do have, we know that Marshall was born in 1855 on the tiny island of São Jorge in the Azores archipelago, a thousand miles off the coast of Portugal. Although protected by the same patron saint as England—São Jorge is Saint George in Portuguese, and the saint slayed a dragon in both languages—the tiny Azorean island possessed little of England's wealth. Most Azoreans were poor, and many found it necessary to emigrate, something that was relatively easy to do since the islands were a port-of-call for ships travelling to the Americas. Sometime in the 1870s, Marshall joined a small wave of islanders who set out for the United States.

By 1880, the newly christened John Marshall had made his way to the gold mines of Esmeralda County, Nevada, midway between Las Vegas and Reno on the edge of Death Valley. Through hard work, thrift and some luck, Marshall pulled together a modest pool of capital. Tiring of the punishing heat and dizzying altitude, Marshall moved north in search of a more temperate climate, somewhere he could realize his dream of buying some land and starting a farm.

In 1884, he found what he was looking for just north of the US-Canada border, on Sumas prairie. The lush grassland of the prairie was ideal for livestock, and while a handful of dairy operations were up and running, much of the land had not yet been claimed by White immigrants. He and a partner settled on a lot two miles north of Sumas town. The unnamed partner left a few months later, but the Azorean continued to work the land. By the time he officially registered the property in early 1888, his holdings had grown to two hundred acres. On this he had built a two-room house, a fifty-foot barn, a dairy shed and various solid outbuildings; the buildings alone were valued at $750. He also had begun the back-breaking work of clearing and draining the soggy ground, and sowing small parts of it with vegetables and feed crops. By the early 1890s, Marshall had paid what was owed on his land, a

$260 investment (only a handful of Sumas farmers had paid what they owed). His herd of dairy and beef cattle had grown to some twenty head, he owned half a dozen horses for ploughing and riding, and a large flock of chickens provided meat and eggs for himself and for sale. Thus, as he looked forward to his fortieth birthday two years away, Marshall found satisfaction that his dream of a better life was coming true: his own land, a productive farm. A lean man of modest height with ropy, work-hardened muscles, he had the dark eyes, dark hair and olive skin of an Azorean. His spare look, dark complexion and decades of outdoor labour made him look years older than he was. After his death, his neighbours described a "jovial" and "hospitable" man, on good terms with everyone. No doubt, those neighbours felt the natural impulse to speak well of the dead; passing comments slipped through that he had a temper and could act the braggart on occasion.

In this declaration dated February 18, 1888, John Marshall recorded an official claim to his 200-acre lot, describing the improvements he had already made to the property. His house, barn, outbuildings, fences and ditching were valued at $750. Portuguese by birth and unable to read or write English, Marshall signed the document with an 'X'. Royal BC Museum and Archives, GR 312

Despite living in Sumas for nearly a decade, though, no one seems to have known him very well or to have become a close friend. Part of this was due to Marshall's own personality: affable on the surface, the Azorean preferred keeping himself to himself and keeping others at a safe distance. And part was due to the temper of the times: most of Marshall's neighbours were even more recent arrivals than he was, and they were Anglo immigrants—British, American or Canadian—who claimed whatever new land they settled as their home. To them, Marshall was a "foreigner," a dark-skinned Portuguese with no family who spoke only halting English.

The person who saw Marshall the most in the years before his death was the man who would be arrested for his murder. Albert Stroebel was born on January 12, 1873, in Evansville, Indiana, into a relatively comfortable working-class family. His father, George Sr., was a master baker from Bavaria who had been swept up in a wave of German immigration to the United States in the 1850s; his mother, Elizabeth, was a farmer's daughter from neighbouring Illinois.

At the outbreak of the American Civil War, George Sr. enlisted in the Union Army, one of many German immigrants who hoped signing up would provide a swift path to American citizenship. After three years of war, George Sr. returned home to marry Elizabeth, and the new couple moved to Evansville, where George opened a bakery with his brother. The bakery prospered, and the family grew over the next decade, but even as the war receded further into the past, George found it increasingly difficult to settle into civilian life. Risky business ventures, alcohol abuse and restlessness plagued the Stroebel patriarch.

In 1877, hoping for a new start, George moved the family out west to Petaluma, California, a small town forty miles north of San Francisco, where he worked as a hotel manager. The family was on the move again two years later, this time to LaConner, Washington. It was here that Elizabeth gave birth to their eighth and final child, Louis, in 1881. At the time, the Stroebel children included August (fifteen years old), Amelia (twelve), George Jr. (ten), Albert (eight), Ida (six), Hattie (three) and William (one). Over the next few years, Elizabeth kept the family together in LaConner while George Sr. continued his wandering ways, seeking opportunities north of the border in BC.

Over the summer of 1885, it appeared that George had found what he was looking for when he moved onto an empty 160-acre lot in Aldergrove that straddled the Yale Wagon Road eleven miles northwest of Sumas. His family joined him there a year later. In August 1887, George Jr. staked out his own claim on Sumas prairie, a quarter-section sitting midway between the border and John Marshall's property. George Jr. was only sixteen at the time, too young to stake a legal claim, so the Stroebels were trying to bend the law to get their hands on another property. While Elizabeth remained in Aldergrove with the younger children, George Sr. divided his time between Aldergrove and Sumas. George Jr. and Albert stayed in Sumas, working on their claim and hiring themselves out to local farmers.

As had been the case at several points in the past, prosperity seemed within reach for the Stroebels. But then the ties keeping the family together frayed to the breaking point. The eldest daughter, Amelia, married and left; consumption took the life of son August; and, most devastating of all, mother Elizabeth died in the New Westminster hospital in autumn 1889. No official record of her death has survived; however, it was most likely consumption that struck Elizabeth down, the same disease that had already killed one son and would later take another. The Stroebel matriarch had been the family's linchpin. With her death, grief and the burden of single parenthood were added to the demons George Sr. already carried within; he became a fleeting presence in the children's lives, absent more often than he was present.

This left George Jr. and Albert—eighteen and sixteen years old in 1889—with the daunting task of providing for the family and keeping it together. The four younger siblings moved into the brothers' Sumas cabin, but the elder Stroebels struggled to bring in enough to support the family. Seduced by the profits others seemed to be making from rising property values, George Jr. borrowed against his Sumas claim to play the real estate market in Vancouver. George's dreams quickly turned sour: he lost the Vancouver and Sumas properties in 1892 and the siblings were forced to move, scattering in different directions. Albert stayed nearby, moving on his own into the City Hotel in Sumas City.

During his years on Sumas prairie, from 1887 until his arrest in 1893, Albert's limping gait and off-kilter grin were common sights in the small farming community, on both sides of the border. He was obliging and respectful, a "good boy" always willing to lend a hand, whether he was paid or not. He and Marshall struck up an unlikely friendship during this time, and even after Stroebel moved from the family cabin to Sumas City, he continued to visit his Portuguese friend, helping with domestic chores and on the farm. The Portuguese farmer's tidy house became a second home for the young man, yet the relationship between the two was never one of equals: it was more like one of nephew and favourite uncle.

The only photograph we have of Albert Stroebel, taken in the Victoria Gaol on January 9, 1894. Stroebel wore a faded tuxedo jacket, lent to him by one of the guards, over his regulation prison uniform. Royal BC Museum and Archives, F-08396

Even as Stroebel passed his twentieth birthday, the hard-working farmers of Sumas continued to think of him as "the boy." The young man's unassuming, ungainly appearance contributed to this. In the one photograph we have of him, taken while he was in prison, Stroebel's mousy hair, grey-blue eyes and light skin give him an oddly washed-out look. From a distance, his expression appears good-natured, a slight smirk on his open face; but moving in, we see a tension about his mouth and a look of apprehension in his wide-set eyes.

Stroebel's prison warders recorded his height at 5'4", which was short even for that time, and a crippled right leg made him shorter. We do not know the cause of Stroebel's disability, which a doctor told him was an "inflammation of the bone"—it may have been rheumatoid arthritis or one of a number of degenerative bone diseases causing osteomyelitis. The inflammation caused him pain daily, his knee was permanently bent and his foot turned out, and he used a blackthorn cane to walk. Despite his disability and modest stature, he was a hard, adept worker, and he had the broad hands of a working-man to prove it.

The abiding impression of Stroebel as a boy was due to more than his physical appearance—his intellectual and emotional growth also seemed delayed. He did not receive much formal schooling. As a working-class youth and the son of an absent father, he was thrown into the labour market at an early age by the necessity to provide for his family. Stroebel was able to read and write, though with difficulty, but numbers and higher concepts eluded him. He could be clever within his own limits, as we shall see, but he found it difficult to see the larger picture, to realize the significance of events or the gravity of a serious situation.

The first two decades of Stroebel's life contained more than its fair share of trials and tribulations. A broken family, lack of material resources and a meagre education left him ill-equipped to navigate these trials. His biggest asset was an offbeat optimism: again and again he tried to escape the life he seemed destined to live, but too often his actions and decisions would only make matters worse.

A New Year, 1893

Late Victorians greeted 1893 with high hopes. The year promised to be yet another in an unbroken chain of economic, technological and even moral progress that stretched back decades. The bullish optimism of the time was put on full display at the World Columbian Exposition, which opened in Chicago that spring. The exposition showcased the latest wonders of the modern age—from the miraculous capabilities of electricity, used to power a dizzying array of gadgets big and small, to George Ferris's spindle-like wheel, 264 feet high and able to carry 2,160 riders in its thirty-six revolving gondolas. Over in the Arts Pavilion, a young professor named Frederick Jackson Turner rose in front of an audience of historians to declare the American frontier closed. A short distance away, the frontier was very much alive as Buffalo Bill's daily Wild West shows attracted more spectators than any other attraction.

However, outside the magical city of light on the shores of Lake Michigan, the year brought dark clouds of anxiety. That summer, the original Wall Street stock-market crash triggered a row of falling dominoes that, as they dropped, dragged the world into a deep economic depression. What seemed so assured in January—another year of uninterrupted progress and prosperity—was dismissed as naïve optimism by December.

Thousands of miles from the great centres of capitalism, Sumas prairie was not immune to the vertiginous ups and downs of the global economy. Entering 1893, the prairie was still riding the boom fuelled by the building of the railway spur lines. Sumas City was in its heyday and a wildness was in the air: alongside family grocers and button-down

A panoramic photograph of Huntingdon and Sumas City, taken in 1905 from on top of the hill that rises on the western edge of the towns. The photographer stood right on the 49th parallel and looked due east, with the border marked by a wide swath cut into the trees. The bright white building was right at the border, on the American side. One block south, the planked Harrison Road travels east; the long, two-storey building just south of this was the City Hotel, owned by Margaret Bartlett. LAC, PA-037655, Online Mikan No. 3308436

merchants rose a dozen saloons, countless gambling dens, and brothels housing some seventy sex workers.

Prostitution was illegal but tolerated—as was smuggling, an enterprise for which Sumas City was renowned. Opium was a favoured contraband commodity. Illegal in the US but not in Canada, money could be made moving it south across the border, and because of their location and topography, Sumas City and prairie became a much-used crossing point for smugglers. A reporter dispatched by the *Seattle Post-Intelligencer*—the leading newspaper in Washington state—described the sophisticated network that was built to move the drug across the unguarded line: "The smuggling routes are divided into stations, and a different man handles the 'dope' at each new station arrived at. Some of the pioneer ranchers are interested in the business, and those who are not smile blandly." Alcohol was another, more traditional commodity, with Kentucky bourbon moving north and Canadian rye carried south.

With the economic crash of spring 1893, the white and black markets on Sumas prairie plummeted. In Sumas City, saloons and hotels were shuttered, businesses failed and people left. Although it did not stop altogether, smuggling slowed down as the market for illegal imports shrank alongside the market for legal ones. What remained on Sumas prairie was very much like what had come before: an economy and way of life firmly planted in the frontier past, in which a dispersed population wrested a modest living from the land. The early 1890s had provided a brief glimpse of the prosperity and growth the future might hold, but people would have to wait longer for them to arrive.

Like so many others, Albert Stroebel was optimistic as he ushered in 1893. Despite the daunting trials life had thrown his way, he had always possessed a hopeful nature. Now, with the new year, Stroebel had reason to believe that the worst of the struggles and hardships were behind him and a brighter future lay ahead.

For one thing, he had found love—right at his own doorstep. In November 1892, a few months after leaving the family cabin on Sumas prairie, Stroebel moved into a sparsely furnished room on the second floor of the City Hotel, in Sumas City. A two-storey, wood-framed building sporting the signature false front of western frontier towns, the hotel was conveniently located a block away from the border on Railway Avenue, the town's main street. The new north-south rail line ran down the middle of the unpaved avenue. The twenty dollars a month Stroebel paid in rent got him a bed, closet and nightstand in a shared room, along with morning and evening meals. The finest feature of the room was the view from its north-facing window: a sweeping panorama of Sumas prairie, Fraser River and the snow-capped Coast Mountains rising off into the distance.

The City Hotel was owned and run by Margaret Bartlett, matriarch of the sprawling Bartlett family. Her husband, Charles, was a part-time resident of the household. Sometimes he would crawl into a spare hotel room for the night, but just as often he slept in whichever saloon he had been drinking the night away. The Bartletts had moved to Sumas City from British Columbia three years earlier. In the decade and a half prior to that, Charles switched back and forth between farming and managing hotels, first in Yale, then in Chilliwack. Margaret was kept busy giving birth to and raising their growing brood of children, eight in all by the time the last was born in 1889. The following year, the Bartlett hotel in Chilliwack burnt down and a hapless Charles discovered he had neglected to buy fire insurance, leaving him nothing but ashes and bills. Margaret took charge then, moving the family south of the border and opening a new hotel with her name on the deed.

Immediately upon moving into the City Hotel in late 1892, Albert Stroebel felt he had found a new home. The Bartletts were a mirror image of his own family: cursed with an unproductive father, but blessed with a strong-willed mother and a string of sisters and brothers. The Bartlett children filled some of the emptiness left by his own scattered siblings. The eldest, John, was a year younger than he, and Stroebel shared a room with the next son, eleven-year-old George. In between the sons were three daughters, Mary, Levina and Elizabeth, and the youngest three Bartletts were six, four and three years old.

Predictably, Stroebel soon developed more than neighbourly feelings for one of the three sisters. The trio shared the never-ending work of cooking, cleaning and child-tending for hotel and family, and Stroebel bumped into them every day. Awkward, unattractive and young for his age, Stroebel fell for the youngest of the three, twelve-year-old Elizabeth. Before long, he and Elizabeth could be seen stepping out for walks along the sidewalks and streets of Sumas City, not hand in hand or arm in arm, but obviously smitten with each other.

The young couple's favourite walk took them down the only planked street in town. Harrison Road ran parallel to the border, starting at Railway Avenue just feet from the City Hotel and stretching a mile eastward into the woods. There were just two houses on the road, and as they strolled between the trees, bush and stumps of empty lots, Alfred and Elizabeth could be alone, away from the prying eyes of adults and the constant demands of Elizabeth's younger siblings. On one such walk the topic of the couple's future came up. With his heart in his throat and stumbling over his words, Albert brought up the prospect of marriage. Elizabeth was swept away, her girlish dreams of romance coming true.

It is not clear how far along the couple's plans for marriage had gotten before the tragic events of April. The engagement was talked about among the Bartlett family, although mother Margaret would later claim that no formal commitment had been made. Elizabeth herself insisted that everything had been settled, except that Stroebel had yet to buy her a ring. Stroebel's arrest for Marshall's murder dashed these youthful dreams. Today we might think that surely the couple could not have married, even without the murder, for Elizabeth was too young. The girl's real age, though, was not known outside the Bartlett family. During Stroebel's trials, she claimed to be fifteen years old, while local residents, the press and Stroebel himself put her age at fourteen.

Government records show that in the spring of 1893 she was indeed twelve. Assuming she would have had to produce official proof of her age at any wedding, could she still have married Stroebel? The answer is yes, probably. In Washington state, where Albert and Elizabeth resided, the legal age for women to marry was eighteen years, but the eighteen-year rule applied only if the bride's parents lodged a legal complaint opposing the marriage of an underage daughter. If the parents did not protest, an underage girl—even one as young as twelve—could marry. Would the Bartletts have lodged such a complaint if Albert and Elizabeth had tried to wed? After some initial misgivings, Margaret was won over to the couple's side. Charles may have wanted to protest, but given his alcoholism and the fact that his wife ran things in the household, it is unlikely anyone would have paid any attention to him.

Albert and Elizabeth would never test Washington's marriage laws; the important point here is that, as far as the young couple knew, there were no legal obstacles to their marrying. However, the law was one thing, money another, and Stroebel realized that to be able to support a wife and future family, he needed a steady income. After moving to Sumas City, Stroebel picked up odd jobs here and there, earning just enough to get by. His plan, though, was to train as a barber and eventually set up his own shop. Work as a barber would not be as taxing on his crippled leg as most of the other jobs available, which involved hard physical labour. In fall 1892, he signed over ownership of his one asset—a horse—as payment to a Sumas City barber named Larsen to take him on as an apprentice. But Larsen failed to deliver on the promise of regular training and work; his shop had just the one chair, and he gave Stroebel only minimal hours on the job. When Larsen's shop burned down in February 1893, the barber left town and Stroebel had nothing to show for his brief apprenticeship.

Stroebel did not let his barbershop dreams go that easily. In March 1893, he approached another Sumas City barber, Frank Carpenter, and offered to buy his shop, equipment and a few household furnishings. Carpenter set the price at $250, which Stroebel agreed to, saying he was getting married soon. According to the barber, he and Stroebel talked daily about the deal, right up to the time of Marshall's death. What was more, both Margaret and Elizabeth Bartlett knew all about the discussions and Stroebel's plans.

Carpenter never saw any money from Stroebel and asked the same question we might ask: Where could the young man get that kind of money? Stroebel reassured the barber that he had $500 in a New Westminster bank. He made the same claim to Margaret and Elizabeth Bartlett in an effort to prove to them he would make a good husband. Of course, there was no $500 tucked safely away in a bank, yet Stroebel was not lying exactly, for he sincerely believed he had the money, or at least was owed it. He claimed that some years earlier, he had owned forty-seven acres in the Huntingdon area. Being underage, he asked his brother George to sell the land in small pieces; Albert believed the sales netted around $500, which George supposedly deposited in his own bank account. When George then transferred the deeds for two lots in Vancouver to his younger brother, Albert saw that as payment of the $500 he was owed. In Stroebel's mind, the $500 he claimed to possess sat in the deeds to those two Vancouver properties.

The whole scenario might have worked for Stroebel if it had been based on facts not fantasy. For one, there is no evidence that Albert ever owned acreage in Huntingdon. His older brother may have promised him he would get a piece of the Sumas prairie claim eventually (even though George himself never cleared title for it), that these were the acres Albert thought he owned. For another, the two Vancouver properties were already fully mortgaged and could not be counted as assets toward Stroebel's net worth.

The story of the Vancouver lots was messy and convoluted. In spring 1892, George Jr. used the deeds he held on two Vancouver city lots as collateral for a $143 loan from the Sumas City Bank. George promptly lost the money speculating in the local real estate market, which was notoriously fickle. When George failed to repay the loan, the bank's president signed the mortgage over to his friend and partner Charles Moulton, proprietor of the Huntingdon Hotel. As a BC resident, Moulton could file a suit against George in provincial court, which he did. George never showed up for the court date that fall. Instead, he transferred the Vancouver deeds over to his younger brother, thinking that would make it impossible for the bank to collect its debt, which had ballooned to $250. Moulton responded by filing a suit against Albert, who at first agreed to assume the mortgage. Then the younger brother changed his mind and handed the properties over to the bank as payment for the loan. This cleared the loan and settled the matter, but Albert could not understand how he had given up two properties and received nothing in return. He was convinced the bank had stolen the lots, and that it still owed him the money for them.

Moulton had clearly run circles around Stroebel, whom he knew was in over his head. And the Sumas City Bank's profit—75 per cent in just nine months, yielding a yearly interest rate of 100 per cent—was something one might expect from a mafia loan shark, not a registered bank. Worst of all, the actions of his own brother were the root cause of the financial mess Albert was drawn into. George Jr. foisted his own steep debt upon his unsuspecting brother. When George transferred the Vancouver lots to Albert, the latter believed it was payment for the Huntingdon properties George had supposedly sold earlier, in his name. Albert clearly did not understand that a mortgage was being held against the properties. George may not have intentionally misled his brother about this, but even if he did not, he had to have known that Albert possessed only the vaguest understanding of the financial facts of life.

❖

During the early months of 1893, the high hopes and grand schemes which Albert Stroebel nurtured for the new year were falling by the wayside, one by one. As if the trials of his young life were not already enough, the fates also sent Stroebel his own personal nemesis—a teenage imp named David Eyerly. Given the roiling animosity and open hostilities that developed between the two, it is ironic how much they had in common. Both were from the American Midwest, the poorly educated sons of large, working-class families that had pulled up roots and moved to the far northwest of the country. The greatest irony would come later though, when the two youngsters were arrested and imprisoned together as alleged co-conspirators in the robbery and murder of John Marshall, facing the charges in court as co-defendants.

David Eyerly was born on May 25, 1878, in northwestern Illinois, the first child of Orrin and Harriet Eyerly. David was two years old when his parents moved the family north to a farm in Wisconsin, where Orrin struggled to wrest a living from a land of wet prairie and bushy upland. After a decade of back-breaking work, Orrin yielded to the inevitable, surrendered his farm and moved his family west to Sumas City. By 1893, the Eyerly clan had grown to seven children, ranging in age from newborn Lydia to fourteen-year-old David.

In April of that year, Harriet took ill and was moved to a hospital in Tacoma. The four Eyerly daughters moved in with family friends in Sumas City while the sons—David, Oscar (thirteen years) and William (eight)—stayed with their father. Orrin had turned his hard-working hands to carpentry, and he was kept busy with a steady stream of jobs around town. With his father working and mother away, David was burdened with domestic chores, from fetching firewood to preparing each day's meals. David did not attend school, nor did he have to hold down a job as his father made enough for the family to get by. Oscar was given the task of looking after William, so between his chores, David was permitted to run free.

And run free he did, free and wild. In only his second year as a teenager, David had earned a reputation as a young hellion. Some in Sumas City dismissed his actions with a "boys will be boys" shrug, but others saw something more sinister. For one, the boy was already a practised liar, able to smoothly spin yarns big and small. Eyerly was perfectly willing to implicate others in his tales of deeds and misdeeds, not caring what the consequences might be for himself or for others. For another, he was a thief, and his loot was not just candy from the general store. A month prior to Marshall's death, he stole a water pump from a local sawmill owner named Kennedy, then had the cheek to sell it to Margaret Bartlett, who installed the pump in her hotel. Eyerly was found out the very night of Marshall's murder. Confronted with the evidence, he tried to deflect guilt by claiming that Stroebel—who, unlike Eyerly, was of legal age—had been a partner in the crime. In the days after the murder, word spread of Stroebel's alleged part in the theft, adding fuel to the suspicions that led to his arrest.

Eyerly also showed his mischievous nature and willingness to court danger in the things he did for fun. Eyerly's house was separated from the City Hotel by a muddy alley sixteen feet wide and forty feet long, a favourite haunt for David and his closest friends. On occasion, he and his friends turned the alley into a makeshift firing range. The boys fashioned a crude cannon from a foot-long piece of water pipe, closed at one end with lead. They then gathered together as many gun cartridges as they could from the ample supply that circulated about Sumas City, extracted the gunpowder and tamped it down into the pipe. They threw in shell casings, nails and anything else they could find, then fired off the improvised cannon. To improve their aim, they attached a target to the side of the City Hotel, at the back end of the alley. Stroebel's window overlooked the lane, and he would have heard each blast at full volume. Nobody else in Sumas City—neither residents nor authorities—seemed to care about the makeshift cannon going off in broad daylight, in the middle of town.

David Eyerly's favourite pastime, though, was tormenting his hapless neighbour. Like all bullies, Eyerly had a sharp eye for weakness, picking on Stroebel because of the latter's crippled leg and the fact that the twenty-year-old had few friends or allies of his own in town. Stroebel later explained with impotent rage: "He was after me all the time. I could hardly go out in the street without getting hit on the side of the head with a rock or a brick." Unable to stop David because he could not catch him, Stroebel talked to Orrin Eyerly a number of times, pleading with him to rein in his wayward son. When Orrin proved unable or unwilling to step in, Stroebel approached Phillip Lawrence, a lawyer and the town's mayor, asking for his advice on whether the authorities could do anything to protect him and punish his harasser. Eyerly, though, was never stopped or punished, and the violent harassment continued.

Stroebel's fruitless meeting with Mayor Lawrence occurred the first week of April, following an incident that very nearly escalated to serious harm. Early one evening in late March, Stroebel and Elizabeth Bartlett set out for a romantic walk. As the couple passed by the corner of the hotel, Eyerly stood lurking in the alley. The boy moved out of the shadows and launched a piece of broken brick at Stroebel, who reflexively stepped out of the way. The brick hit Elizabeth on the leg just as Eyerly called her a vile name. Stroebel ran at the boy, swearing "to knock the face of him off," but David was too fast for his hobbled victim, and he escaped up the hill that overlooked Sumas City. By the time Stroebel made it to the top of the hill, Eyerly was already back down in town. Collapsing on a nearby tree stump, Stroebel reached into his coat pocket, took out a revolver, loaded it and fired two rounds into the air.

The echoing shots carried Stroebel's rage across the valley below. They also warned his tormenter that his anger had reached a boiling point, and that he now had the means to do something about it. The appearance of the revolver raised the stakes in the game he and Eyerly were playing. Stroebel's gun was a .38 calibre revolver that held five rounds, a cheaply made "trade gun" (meaning not a brand name) that was the most common type of handgun around.

The gun had come into Stroebel's possession by chance. Bill Rowe was a long-time acquaintance of Stroebel's who held the claim on a quarter-section of property on Sumas prairie. Rowe was a rogue, a self-proclaimed "free thinker" on religious matters who never amounted to much as a farmer, so while land-rich, he was constantly cash-poor. In January 1893, he borrowed two dollars from Stroebel to buy a train ticket so he could check out a job opening in Washington state. As a form of collateral, Rowe offered Stroebel a rusty revolver, loaded with five cartridges. Stroebel refused to take the piece at first but gave in when Rowe said the gun could be sold, suggesting it might fetch four dollars. Instead of selling the revolver and netting a two-dollar profit, Stroebel got into the habit of carrying it around—he liked the feeling of power and protection it gave him. On leaving his hotel room, he would slip the gun into the right-hand pocket of his coat and the cartridges into the left. When he was in his room, or when he left the hardware behind, he hid the revolver and bullets under the blankets of his bed.

This was no way to store a firearm and its ammunition, especially since his hotel room door was never locked. A confrontation between Stroebel and Charles Bartlett in March showed just how dangerous it could be. One evening, a heavily drunk Bartlett managed to get his hands on Stroebel's revolver. Either Charles had stumbled into the young man's room himself and picked up the handgun, or he got his son George, who shared Stroebel's room, to lift the piece. Either way, Bartlett staggered into the kitchen and flopped down on a chair, where he began loading the gun with a couple of his own cartridges as Margaret and Elizabeth looked on in wide-eyed fear. Stroebel walked into the room just as Charles snapped the revolver shut and was moving the chamber into firing position. The young man strode over and calmly took the gun away from Charles, who blinked stupidly and did not resist.

Charles's behaviour was alarming, but it did not come as a surprise. According to the accounts of both Stroebel and Margaret Bartlett, on a number of occasions Charles had threatened to kill his wife, his daughter Elizabeth, and Stroebel himself. Charles resented the power his wife wielded in their marriage, and he suspected Margaret was scheming to marry off Stroebel and his daughter behind his back. Either he refused to accept the engagement between his twelve-year-old daughter and twenty-year-old tenant, or he resented the fact that he was given no say in the matter. Resentful and enraged, and emboldened by alcohol, murderous thoughts burned through his mind. When a weapon slipped readily into his hands, these thoughts came dangerously close to being carried out.

SPRING, 1893

The spring of 1893 was wet, dark and unseasonably cold. Even for
those accustomed to the region's three seasons of perpetual rain and
leaden skies, that spring stood out. "I don't think anybody in the province will ever forget it," recalled one old-timer, who had lived through
three decades of Sumas weather. "The spring was cold, wet and cold.
We had two months of summer, last July and August. Otherwise it
has been raining for twelve months, more or less. It left the ground in
a very bad state."

Sumas valley was a wet environment to begin with. Along with
the rain, residents had to deal with a high water table, the presence
of large swamps and marshes, and clay-rich soil that trapped water.
Then there was the yearly flood cycle: from summer through winter,
the shores of Sumas Lake sat along the northeastern edge of upper
Sumas prairie, spanning the four miles from Vedder Mountain to Sumas Mountain. Every spring, the lake grew with the Fraser River
freshet, doubling in size and flooding much of the valley. Residents
watched anxiously as the waters rose, sometimes to their doorsteps.
In exceptionally high years, the waters stretched all the way south of
the border, chasing cattle from the fields and people from their homes.

The wet soil and yearly flooding made it difficult for immigrant
farmers to make a living on the prairie, and many left. John Marshall
stuck it out and, after a decade of hard work, was beginning to reap
the rewards of his labours. No doubt he occasionally felt a pang of
homesickness, especially in the early years. While it rained a lot on the
island of São Jorge in the Azores, it was warm rain, subtropical. The
island's fields and mountain slopes remained a lush green, and after

26

the rain, the Atlantic winds quickly cleared the skies, turning them a dazzling blue. At Sumas, the damp cold penetrated to the bones, no matter how many layers of wool you put on, and some mornings Marshall's knees and back ached so much it was hard to get out of bed.

As Marshall pondered another wet spring, he felt an even heavier burden—loneliness. He had made a home in Sumas, but he was thousands of miles from his mother and childhood friends, with no wife, family or close friends of his own. Marshall had gotten used to being a bachelor, and it had been advantageous in the early years, when he was moving about trying to establish himself. Lately, though, he found himself thinking it might be time to take a wife, someone to do the housework and keep him warm at night. There were few eligible women on Sumas prairie and no Catholics that he knew of, but there were daughters—a little young, but still of marrying age. Like Elizabeth Bartlett, he thought, who looked like a children's doll. The last few times he had visited Sumas City for groceries, he had walked past her in front of her hotel and exchanged smiles. She was young, only fourteen as far as he knew, but back home that was when girls got married. She was not Catholic, but she came from a big family and knew how to cook, clean and take care of children. He had money, a big farm and was not too ugly—she could do much worse than him.

Through April, as spring struggled to gain a foothold on Sumas prairie, Marshall tried to put away his domestic musings and turn to more practical matters. Late one morning, a fortnight before his death, he sat nursing a cup of coffee when the barking of his dog announced the arrival of the man he had been expecting. Marshall got up and went to greet his young visitor on the veranda, then walked with him to the barn. Frederick Raith had travelled from New Westminster to check out a couple of dairy cows Marshall was trying to sell. The two men went into the barn and emerged fifteen minutes later. Marshall's sales pitch had not worked, and after thanking the farmer for his time, Raith headed back to the rail line empty-handed.

The missed sale put a dent in Marshall's plans, but he could not dwell on it since he had other work to attend to. For one, it was time to get going on the year's ditching, even though the ground was still soggy. Marshall had made progress over the past decade, with nearly a mile of ditches carrying water off his property, but the work was painfully slow. He tried to remember the saying in English: two foots in front, one foot in back. The government was paying the bill to connect its ditches with his on the southern edge of his property. His neighbour William Porter got the contract for the job; Marshall knew he was a dependable, hard-working man. Most of the ditching work, though, he needed to see to himself, and it was always difficult to find hired hands to help him. There were not enough White workers around, and those that were just wanted to do their own farming. So like other property owners, he hired Chinese hands. The Chinese laundryman in Hunting-don also acted as an employment agent, and Marshall decided to visit him the next time he went into Sumas City to arrange some help before his neighbours snatched up all the Chinese hands.

Another pressing job was ploughing his fields, a task Marshall nev-er trusted to anyone else. He had just bought a new steel plough, and his neighbour to the north, William Blair, had come over to help put it together. Marshall's first project had been to break ground on a new vegetable garden. The previous year, he had fenced in a flat, relatively dry piece of property a quarter of a mile east of his house, and this was where the new garden would sit. Through early April, he had made a start on the plot with his two-horse team pulling the new plough, but the soil was heavy and stubborn, the horses often getting bogged down and refusing to move. He could use some help, and he decided to ask Porter.

Late one morning in the middle of April, Marshall was thinking of just that—getting some help around the farm—as he came in from the back field for lunch, the dog following at his heels. The farmer rounded the corner of his house, and the dog ran ahead, barking. A man was seated on the steps of his veranda, dressed in a rough wool overcoat, shapeless hat and old boots. He was a wanderer—what the neighbours called a tramp. Marshall had seen his share of them walk-ing up and down the rail line, and a good number had come to his door, asking for food or work. He knew enough to be wary, and he never let them inside his house. There had been many thefts, and neighbours talked about the tramps as dangerous—they could kill you as easily as rob you, some said. Marshall, though, did not want to judge a man too harshly just by his looks.

The man greeted Marshall and explained he was a carpenter by trade, travelling through the area looking for work. Marshall worked the toothpick in his mouth as he remembered the leak in the barn roof, the broken window on the dairy shed, the rotted door on the root cellar: all things he did not have time to take care of. He agreed to give the man a try for a day or two and see how his work was. Marshall brought the man some cheese, bread and milk for his lunch, explained to him what needed doing, then left him to it. Half an hour later, Marshall headed back to his ploughing, the tramp-carpenter eyeing him from atop a ladder propped up against the barn.

❧

Sunday morning, April 16, Albert Stroebel was woken by a heavily-accented voice in his room. George Bartlett was sitting up in his bed, and their friend George Hilliard stood a few feet away by the window. Seventeen-year-old Hilliard had come to collect Bartlett so the two could go fishing across the line on Sumas prairie. Hilliard was a recent immigrant from Britain, whose father ran a freighting operation out of Sumas City, and his thick English accent seemed strange in the little room. Stroebel sat up at the foot of his bed, trying to clear the night's cobwebs; as his eyes focused, they were drawn to the revolver in Hilliard's hand. The young Englishman was aiming the pistol out the window, pretending to fire. Stroebel knew the gun was loaded. One chamber was tight from rust, so he had been unable to extract the cartridge from it the evening before. Alarmed, Stroebel demanded to know how Hilliard had got the piece.

"It was lying on the floor by the side of your bed in the corner. Don't worry, I turned the cylinder round so it won't go off," Hilliard answered innocently—and to prove his point, he pulled the trigger.

The cheap revolver jumped two cylinders and exploded. The bullet whizzed between Stroebel and Bartlett, punching a hole through the thin wall behind them. All three froze, stunned into silence. Stroebel was the first to move. Jumping to his feet, he seized the gun and quickly stashed it under his bed. Hilliard and George Bartlett snapped out of their trance, grabbed their fishing gear, and rushed downstairs, slamming the front door as they exited the hotel.

The accidental shooting did not disrupt the plans the two young Georges had for that day. By mid-morning, the pair were standing on the banks of Marshall Creek, two and a half miles north of the border, their fishing lines breaking the surface of the slow-moving water. The creek ran behind the farmyard of John Marshall, after whom it was named, flowing north and east of his house before making its way to Sumas Lake. The creek was known for its mountain trout, but April was not the best time of year, and after a couple of hours of fishing, Hilliard and Bartlett were skunked. The pair packed their gear and headed home, stopping in at Marshall's cabin for a drink of milk, like they had done many times before.

Wanting some company, the farmer insisted the boys stay for lunch. As the three sat down at the kitchen table, Marshall got to talking about "his girl." Egged on by Hilliard, the farmer announced triumphantly: "My girl, I'm going to buy her a new dress. And I got the money to buy it with, too!"

With that, Marshall pulled a buckskin pouch from his pocket and tipped half a dozen gold coins into his palm. Hilliard and Bartlett's eyes widened as they stared at the twenty-dollar pieces. Marshall smiled at the look on the boys' faces, pleased with himself, then one by one, he returned the coins to their pouch.

Walking home, all the youngsters could talk about were the coins. The other events of the day—Stroebel's revolver, the accidental shooting and the fruitless fishing—were chased away. That evening, back at the City Hotel, they brimmed with excitement as they told Stroebel about their visit and the lustrous gold pieces. No doubt, Hilliard also mentioned Marshall's boasting about "his girl." The farmer had mentioned no names, but both Hilliard and Stroebel would have had a good idea which girl he was talking about.

Unlike her young son and his friends, Margaret Bartlett did not forget about the Sunday morning shooting. She had been downstairs in the kitchen making breakfast when the shot rang out, followed moments later by Hilliard and her son racing down the hallway and out of the hotel. Monday afternoon, while changing the linen on Stroebel's bed, the revolver tumbled onto the mattress, and she quickly slipped it into her apron pocket. Returning to the kitchen, she hung it on a nail hammered into the pantry wall. When Stroebel returned for supper and noticed the gun missing, he asked his landlady if she had seen it. Bartlett admitted she had, and when pressed, reluctantly returned it.

On Tuesday, April 18, the revolver made another appearance. Just before 5:00 p.m.—her afternoon chores completed and her sisters taking care of preparations for supper—Elizabeth Bartlett stepped out with Stroebel for one of their regular walks along Harrison Road. David Eyerly was out behind his place, chopping wood for the family's stove. Stroebel eyed him warily, but the boy was too busy with his chores to cause trouble, so the young couple passed by unmolested. As they neared the end of Harrison Road, Stroebel pulled the revolver from his coat and offered it to Elizabeth.

"He wanted me to shoot. But I said 'No, I don't care to'," the girl recalled later. Stroebel pressed his fiancée, who would not take the gun, so he sighted down the barrel and pulled the trigger.

For Elizabeth, there was no rhyme or reason for Stroebel's actions. She tried to dismiss the gunplay as just something her fiancé did to pass the time, but there was something unsettling about it. We can see that Stroebel was trying to impress his wife-to-be, to show how manly he could be: that he owned a gun, carried it with him and was willing to use it.

We can also see an ominous pattern emerging, an escalation in the young man's behaviour. At first, Stroebel had not wanted the revolver at all, but he took it and kept it, even though the four dollars he could have earned selling it would have come in handy. He quickly fell into the habit of walking about armed, not all the time but often enough that it became something of a habit. And within the past weeks, he had fired the gun in public, then later tried to get young Elizabeth to do the same. Finally, he was careless in how he stowed the piece and, as is its nature, an unguarded handgun begs to be picked up. An angry, drunken Charles Bartlett had gotten hold of it, as did an irresponsible George Hilliard. The revolver—cheap, rusty, lethal—had developed a life of its own.

WEDNESDAY, APRIL 19

John Marshall began the last day of his life like any other. He awoke at dawn, slipped into his work clothes and lit a fire in the kitchen stove. After drinking his breakfast coffee, he put on his coat and boots and headed outside to do the morning chores. The low sun poked through some scattered clouds; it promised to be a fine day. Marshall walked into the barn, milked his dairy cows and pitched hay into their hopper, then collected the day's eggs and was outside casting feed in the chicken pen when William Blair walked into the farmyard. Blair stooped to pet Marshall's dog, which had stopped barking when it recognized him.

"Just came over for some milk for my dog. She's still sick," the visitor said, nodding a hello. Blair was thirty-three years old, a native of Ontario who lived on the quarter-section just north of Marshall. He and his young American wife had no children, and for three years after his arrival on the prairie, he taught at Upper Sumas school, the younger Stroebel children among his pupils. Blair was now having a go at farming and knew that to survive he had to live by the code of the frontier farmer: neighbours helped each other out, sometimes with the heavy work of ploughing, ditching and the like, sometimes exchanging milk, eggs, vegetables and other farm produce.

"Yes, you go get yourself some milk," Marshall replied to his neighbour's request. Blair entered the barn, filled his bucket halfway with thick whole milk, then thanked Marshall on his way out.

"William," Marshall started in his accented English, "can you come later? Help me ploughing?" Blair answered that he could, saying he would come back just after lunch. Marshall completed his chores over the next hour, then carefully packed two dozen eggs into a large bucket and set off down the railbed. In Sumas City, he bartered the eggs for some groceries at the general store, and, on his way back north, stopped in Huntingdon at the Chinese laundry and arranged for Sam Lee, a Chinese labourer, to come up to his place to work on a ditch he needed dug. The pair agreed to terms, and Lee promised to be at Marshall's in an hour to start work.

The sun was still low in the sky when Marshall arrived back home. Slipping into his house shoes, he washed his hands and started making bread. As he mixed the ingredients, he heard his dog bark and thought Lee had come early, but when he opened the door, he found Albert Stroebel petting the dog, its tail wagging furiously in a friendly greeting.

"Morning, Mr. Marshall," the young man said, straightening up. "Can I bother you for a glass of milk?"

Marshall had known the lad since the Stroebel clan had moved to Sumas prairie when Albert was just fourteen, and the farmer had taken a liking to him, treating him like a nephew. Stroebel cheerfully helped out with the household chores or hung around just to keep him company, and despite his twisted leg, the boy could do a man's share of outdoor work. Marshall felt sorry for the boy, what with his family situation and his disability, and there was a feeling of kinship stemming from the fact that neither of them really fit into the community around them. Still, there was always something a little off with Stroebel, something Marshall could not put a finger on. Maybe it was that Stroebel seemed no older now than when he had first arrived on the prairie, or that even after all his hard labour, he was no closer to working his own farm or finding himself a paying vocation. Marshall shrugged the thoughts away as he kneaded the bread dough.

"Play something on that new mouth organ of yours," he said over his shoulder to Stroebel.

A lively tune filled the air and soon Marshall was pounding out the beat in the dough. The dog's bark broke over the song, and this time Marshall was sure it was Lee. Forming the dough into loaves, he told Stroebel to watch over the rising bread while he was gone, then met Lee outside and led him to a swampy patch at the eastern edge of his property, where Marshall explained what needed doing. The farmer lent a hand with the ditch for half an hour, then returned home to clean up. He slipped the bread loaves into the oven and turned to a pile of laundry. Stroebel stood there, grinning proudly after cleaning the two-room cabin from top to bottom

"Good work, Albert. Why don't you go fish in back? I call you for lunch."

Later, the smell of freshly baked bread filled the kitchen as Marshall and Stroebel sat down to eat. As they were finishing up, the dog's barking announced another visitor. Marshall and Stroebel joined William Blair outside. The trio walked to the barn, hitched two horses to a sled and hauled the plough to the garden plot in the back field. While the two older men rehitched the horses to the plough, Stroebel walked off a ways to where William Porter was working on a ditch. For the next two hours, Marshall and Porter coaxed the team back and forth across the wet field, the steel plough biting and sinking into the heavy soil.

Shortly before four o'clock, Blair begged off, saying his wife was expecting him home. Marshall worked another half-hour before calling it a day. He returned the plough, sled and horses to the barn, brushed the animals down and fed them. He tended to the cows as well before heading out to fetch Sam Lee. This improbable pair—a Portuguese farmer and a Chinese labourer who had come together on this unbroken field from homes ten thousand miles apart—walked awhile before they came to a shortcut that led across a boggy pasture to the rail line.

"Goodbye, Mr. Marshall. I see you tomorrow," Lee said with a slight bow.

"Yes, Lee, tomorrow," Marshall nodded, then turned down the path leading to his house. The tired labourer shaded his eyes against the lowering sun and watched the farmer trudge away. Lee figured it to be around six o'clock. Based on testimony collected over the following days, it was the last time anyone admitted to seeing John Marshall alive.

❧

Two miles south, across the border, Albert Stroebel's day started like any other as well. He awoke around seven o'clock, pulled on his pants and shoes and stood over the wash basin. He splashed cold water on his face, dried it with his shirttails and tucked them into his waistband. He limped down the stairs, out of the hotel and to the barbershop to catch any news he might have missed from the previous day. Returning to the hotel for breakfast, he blushed when he caught Elizabeth's eye as she worked over the kitchen stove, then again when she brought in his coffee, buttered bread and eggs. He lingered in the warmth of the dining room, dreaming of the new life he would soon have: his own business, a pretty young wife, and in no time, children, lots of children. Elizabeth's sister Mary came in to clear the dishes, and Stroebel rose awkwardly to his feet, feeling for his walking stick. His leg was stiff most mornings, and the damp air only made it worse. He climbed back up to his drafty room, slipped on his coat and stashed the revolver and cartridges in its pockets.

Stroebel struck out for the rail line and headed north, his bent right leg walking the track, the left leg the gravel bed, his cane tapping a beat. The clouds were clearing, and he figured it might be a good day for fishing. By force of habit, he made his way toward Marshall's place, and just as he reached the gate, decided to go in for a glass of milk. He took his usual seat at the kitchen table and stretched his sore leg, the heat of the stove slowly chasing the stiffness away. At his friend's request, he took out his mouth organ and started into his favourite tune, casting his eyes about as he played—George Hilliard's tale of Marshall's sack of gold had stuck in his mind, and he could not get rid of it.

When Marshall left a short time later to show the Chinese man where to start ditching, Stroebel got to his feet and started cleaning the house. He took special care over every spot, lifting things to dust underneath, but when he finished the cleaning, he had found no sign of his old friend's pouch of gold. When Marshall returned, Stroebel headed out back to fish, with no luck, and after his host called out that lunch was ready, he took his place at the kitchen table.

William Blair showed up half an hour later, and the three went to the barn, collected the team of horses and set out to plough the back field. Stroebel spotted William Porter working on the municipal ditch and decided to see if he needed help. The thirty-one-year-old Porter, born in Kentucky, lived half a mile to the south with his young wife and newborn son. He had not claimed or bought any land yet, so he picked up paid work where he could. He reckoned the municipal ditch would take a hundred man-days to complete and the Kentuckian was glad to have the contract.

"You are ditching, are you?" Stroebel asked Porter with a grin.

"I am."

"Well, I'll just help you for a while." Stroebel picked up a spade and jumped into the ditch. After a few shovelfuls of the mucky soil, he shed his coat and tossed it onto dry ground, then threw his revolver on top of it. Porter caught the glint of the gun as it arced onto Stroebel's coat. He was more amused than disturbed by the sight of the revolver. Back home in Kentucky, pretty near every man—every White man at least—carried a pistol, but up here in Canada they were downright scarce, and the crippled Stroebel was the last man he expected to carry one.

Between pants of exertion, the pair got to talking. Stroebel wanted to go into partnership with Porter on the ditch contract. The lad had worked for Porter a number of times before, ditching and haying, and had shown himself to be reliable and not afraid of hard labour. As far as being equal partners, though, the Kentuckian knew that was beyond Stroebel's abilities.

"Okay, we can work on the project together," Porter replied. "But how about I pay you two dollars a day and give you room and board?"

Stroebel considered the offer: he would end up with a hundred dollars and save the twenty dollars a month he now paid at the hotel. His barbershop plans looked to be dead in the water, so the ditching contract could get him started on his own. But the thought of leaving Elizabeth's place, of not seeing her every day, pained him. More importantly, they would be married soon and they could not live with the Porters after the wedding, so the offer of room and board would not help any. Besides, being married, he would need to move up, be his own man and not just some hired hand. Stroebel told Porter he would have to sleep on the offer.

The late afternoon air was abruptly split by the whistle from the northbound train to Vancouver, and the pair looked up to see William Blair heading home from Marshall's field. Marshall followed half an hour later, leading his tired team. A half-hour after that, at around five o'clock, Porter called it a day, and he and Stroebel stashed their shovels, picked up their coats and headed back toward the rail line. Porter had tied his milking cow just inside the fence that ran along the railway grade so it could graze on the grass there. With Stroebel holding its collar, he milked it and handed the full pail to the younger man for a drink. Famished, Stroebel drained a quart of the warm, heady liquid.

Wiping his mouth on his sleeve, he said, "I'll just get through the fence here, wash my hands and go home." As the lad started off south for the fence opening, his cane sinking into the wet ground, Porter grabbed hold of the rope dangling from the cow's neck and headed home. Looking west toward the sun, he figured it to be 5:30 p.m., although the position of the sun in the unfamiliar northern sky still threw off his sense of time.

❈

Elmer and Frank Jesseph spotted their new friend Albert Stroebel below the railway grade, milking a cow, and they called out a hello. The brothers had spent the afternoon in Sumas City, picking up sugar, coffee and other groceries and were making their way back home along the rail line. Elmer (twenty-four years old) and Frank (twenty-seven) had lived on Sumas prairie for only a month, travelling from their home in Kansas to take up work on the farm of their uncle, Asa Ackerman. Half a mile north of where they saw Stroebel, they were about to turn onto the wagon road that led east to the Ackerman spread when they met a stranger. The man was tall, fair-skinned and dressed rough, with a loose coat and suspenders used as a belt around his pants. He was one of the many tramps the brothers saw travelling up and down the line.

"Hey, boys, do you know what time it is?" the man smiled and asked in a heavy accent the brothers had never heard before.

"I reckon it's after five o'clock, somewheres after five o'clock," Frank replied.

The man looked at the sun, nodded, then asked, "How far into Sumas City?"

"A couple of miles," Elmer replied. As the Jessephs turned east and the tramp south, the brothers glanced over their shoulders at the man's retreating back.

Less than half an hour later, a strange, spider-like vehicle sped south along the railway and over the wagon road crossing. The vehicle was a velocipede, a three-wheeled, single-seat car that straddled the rail tracks, powered by the driver pulling and pushing on the see-saw handle. The driver was Archie Baxter, section man for the ten-mile stretch of the new CPR spur line from Mission to Huntingdon. The thirty-nine-year-old Scotsman had spent that day shoring

A velocipede being driven by an unnamed driver on Sumas Prairie. Archie Baxter used one just like this in his job as section man of the CPR line from Huntingdon to Mission. Royal BC Museum and Archives, C-04099

up ballast on the railbed north of Abbotsford and had stopped work at 5:30 p.m. exactly: he was one of the few men in the area to carry a pocket watch, which he wound and set each morning as he left the Huntingdon station. Packing his gear, he climbed atop the velocipede and started south.

At 5:45 p.m., Baxter rounded the bend and moved onto the long, straight stretch that headed to the border. As the car gained speed down the incline onto Sumas prairie, the section man passed a man walking south. He did not get a good look at him, other than to tell he was tall and roughly dressed, and Baxter figured he was one of the steady stream of tramps using the rail line as their own highway, men without homes, looking for work or a handout. The velocipede slowed as it neared the trestle just opposite the gate to John Marshall's place, and Baxter spotted a second tramp. This man was standing on the trestle, and as the car passed by, he lowered his head as if to hide his face, but Baxter had already gotten a good look at him. The man was of medium height, with dark hair and a heavy mustache; he wore a square-cut coat over blue overalls and carried a bundle over his shoulder.

Baxter had had little time to think about this second man when he passed Albert Stroebel, two hundred yards south of Marshall's trestle. The young man was walking north, making good time with his cane. The ever-punctual Baxter pegged the time at 5:55 p.m. Ten minutes later, he pulled into the Huntingdon station.

❧

According to the government meteorologist, the sun set at 7:03 p.m. on Wednesday, April 19. Clouds had moved in from the west, thick and low, so it was fully dark half an hour after that. The rain had held off all day, but by 9:00 p.m., a cold drizzle had started to fall, and the temperature was dropping dangerously close to freezing. The chill cut through David Eyerly's threadbare coat, shaking his slender frame as he stood facing an angry man on the bridge across Johnson Creek.

Eyerly feared no one, but he knew most everybody else in Sumas City was afraid to cross the owner of the Kennedy sawmill. The boy was trying to convince Kennedy of his innocence. He did not know the pump was stolen when he got it and then sold it to the Bartletts; it was all Albert Stroebel—he took the pump and passed it along, Eyerly swore to God it was. But Kennedy was having none of it. He knew the boy's reputation, knew he was lying. The sawmill owner had been looking for the stolen water pump for weeks, and it had just been found that night, installed at the City Hotel. He was going there now, but before stalking away he warned the boy the law would be coming for him the next day.

Eyerly watched as Kennedy strode toward town. Out of the corner of his eye, he saw the door of the Dunn and Warmsley saloon open, and his father walked out. David hit the darkened streets at a half-run, determined to make it home before his father did. Still breathing evenly, the boy rushed into the chilly house, took off his coat and boots and stuffed them under his bed. Just as he climbed under his blankets, he heard his father come in. Orrin Eyerly paused at the doorless entry to David's bedroom, lantern in hand.

"Are your brothers in bed, boy?" Orrin asked, his face hidden in shadow.

"Yeah, pa, they is," David answered, faking a yawn.

Eyerly sighed with relief when his father turned and headed for his own bed. But David was too keyed up from the night's excitement to sleep. One thought chased another, of how he could dodge his latest troubles, of new opportunities he might go after, of different ways to torment that sad sack-of-shite, Al Stroebel. David loved the night, how you could lose yourself in the dark, hide your actions from prying eyes. He lay back and let the sounds of the night come to him: the rustle of raccoons under the house, the screech of an owl as it struck its prey, the howl of a distant coyote, and the squish of footsteps on the muddy streets outside his window. He knew the town would not sleep for a while—he itched to be out there keeping it company.

Sometime later, just before ten o'clock by his own reckoning, Frank Warnock approached the front of the City Hotel, its lights shining out from gaps in the curtains. Warnock had spent the evening doing the books at Paden's general store, three hundred yards south of the border, and was making his way to his small cabin on the Canadian side of the line, outside Huntingdon. Stepping past the light escaping from the hotel, he saw a small figure approaching. From the uneven gait and walking stick, he could tell it was Albert Stroebel, walking as quickly as his cane would allow. The two passed each other at Harrison Road, without exchanging a word, and Warnock proceeded home.

Stroebel had seen Warnock's dark form coming his way and huddled deeper into his coat. Wet and chilled to the bone, he turned into the warmth of the City Hotel and walked down the half-lit hallway, passing the front parlour where Charles and John Bartlett sat talking.

"I thought you'd been lost today," John called out to him.

Stroebel gave no reply and continued on to the dining room, smiling nervously when he saw Elizabeth clearing some cups and saucers from the table. Half an hour earlier, the girl had served coffee as the sawmill owner, Kennedy, and the part-time constable, Hall, met with her parents and older brother about a water pump that had been stolen. Margaret Bartlett had bought the machine from David Eyerly, and the two men had come to retrieve it. Charles was drunk again, but Margaret convinced Kennedy and Hall that she had not known the pump was stolen, and the matter was closed when the men left with it. Elizabeth had hovered about anxiously, as she had heard the men accusing Albert of helping Eyerly in the theft. Now, leaning over the dining room table, Elizabeth was startled when Stroebel appeared suddenly in the doorway. She had not seen him since breakfast, and the last time she had looked at the clock before his return, it was 9:30 p.m.

"Al, it's you," she said. "You must be hungry. Do you want anything to eat?"

"No, thanks, Lizzie." The couple talked for a spell, then carried the cups into the kitchen, where Margaret Bartlett was getting herself a drink of water at the sink.

"Hello, Al, what you been doing?"

"I didn't do anything," Stroebel answered sharply. Margaret shrugged, put down her glass and left the kitchen for the rooms behind, where the Bartlett women and girls slept.

Albert and Elizabeth returned to the dining room where they sat and talked for half an hour. Rising, the young couple walked over to the foot of the stairs, and Albert climbed up to his room, a lit candle in his hand. Elizabeth turned back to her own bedroom, next door to her mother's. The back of the kitchen stove warmed the room, yet her sheets were still damp and cold. She lay awake both happy and fearful, thinking of the bright future ahead and the unseen dangers that could so easily ruin it. The only sounds were the uneven ticking of the clock and the muffled voices of her father and brother coming from the front parlour.

Thursday, April 20

Dawn came slowly that Thursday morning, without drama, the clouds simply turning from black to dull grey. Wednesday's veil of mist had changed to rain showers during the night, and the thermometer at Huntingdon station hovered just above freezing. A steady rain would continue through the day and the temperature rise only a few degrees.

In the pale light, Ira Airheart jogged clumsily down the gravel bed of the railway toward the Huntingdon station. The world was silent around him, the only sounds his rasping breath and the rhythmic thud of the Winchester rifle against his back. A stream of cloud shot from his mouth with each breath, like the panting of a slow-moving steam train. The trapper stumbled as he hit the stairs to the station platform, found his footing on its boardwalk and fell upon the depot door. It took a minute of frenzied knocking before the door was opened by the customs officer, Bosnell McDonald.

Sleepy and irritable, McDonald stepped back as Airheart pushed into the room. McDonald knew the man by sight only, and what little he had heard had left him suspicious: an American, supposedly a trapper, two months on the prairie and squatting in someone else's cabin. The customs officer turned to Airheart, who took some time to catch his breath and wits.

"I went down to John Marshall's this morning—thought a bear was in one of my traps," the trapper said, pausing for more air. "And there he was, lying by his front door, murdered. He was hit in the face with a club, his nose all broke up." McDonald looked on in disbelief as Airheart continued, "I heard his dog barking last night, at nine o'clock or so. It must have been then."

It took a moment for the news to sink in, then McDonald jolted into action. He rushed through the office door and out back to James Schofield's house, returning with the station master a few minutes later. A native of Ontario, twenty-seven-year-old Schofield had been hired to run the depot three years earlier, when the Huntingdon depot was built. Schofield checked the story with Airheart, then got on the telegraph and sent an urgent message to the New Westminster police station; the nearest constables were in the city, and the station master had no authority to act. New Westminster replied that Superintendent William Moresby and the coroner, George Pittendrigh, would be summoned immediately and would arrive as soon as possible.

While it would be hours before the authorities could make it to Sumas, word of Marshall's death spread quickly, and local residents converged on the depot. Huntingdon's postmaster, Thomas Trusswell, put together an informal posse and led them up the line to Marshall's. Another group followed half an hour later, led by Ira Airheart and Bosnell McDonald. With people trampling all over Marshall's farmyard and house, Trusswell realized he needed to do something to keep people away until the proper authorities could arrive. He posted men at Marshall's gate and erected a sign telling people to stay off the

The interior of Huntingdon railway station. Station master James Schofield (far left) posing in his office with two friends. Schofield was appointed special constable in the Marshall murder case. City of Vancouver Archives, AM54-S4-2: CVA371-1041

farm. He then dispatched William Blair—who had seen the commotion at his neighbour's and come down to investigate—to the home of Asa Ackerman, a mile to the east.

Thirty-eight-year-old Ackerman was the reeve of Sumas municipality and a justice of the peace, and as such was the closest thing to the law in the area. Ackerman and Blair set out for Marshall's, and upon arriving, saw more than a dozen men milling about. A number stood on the veranda, forming a circle around Marshall's body; others were in the house, haphazardly sifting for clues. Still others walked the grounds, searching for tracks or other signs of the killer's presence. Ackerman declared that he was taking charge, and while doing little to seal off the crime scene, he carried out a more systematic search of the house and grounds.

He took a quick look at Marshall's body on the veranda, ordering that a blanket be placed over it, then entered the house and took in the scene. The house was divided in two: a large room for the kitchen and dining area, and a smaller bedroom, which Ackerman could see through an open door. A Winchester lever-action rifle leaned against the corner of the larger room. Two chairs were at the kitchen table, half turned as if their occupants had just got up from them. Two plates sat on the table, empty but for their knives and forks, and two cups were placed beside them, empty but for teaspoons. A large serving plate held leftover potatoes, boiled beef, and bread and cheese, and a pot of potatoes, one-third full, was stranded on the floor between the table and stove. The stove was cold, but an oil lamp still burned on the table.

The household was remarkably tidy, with no signs of struggle or theft. A thorough search uncovered a leather purse, hidden underneath a pair of grain sacks that lay below a window sill. The purse contained ninety dollars in Bank of British Columbia paper tender—a fifty-dollar bill and two twenty-dollar notes. Another purse was discovered in the pantry, buried in a tin of tea leaves; six inches in length and made of black buckskin, it contained four gold coins, each worth twenty-dollars. Peering into the bedroom, Ackerman saw that the bed was unmade, but he could not tell if it had been slept in the previous night.

Outside, Ackerman was led to a small gate on the southern edge of the farmyard, a hundred feet from the house, that led into a soggy field. It was past noon by then and the number of people at the farm had doubled. Boot tracks headed off in every direction, but at the foot of the gate, Ackerman's attention was drawn to a distinctive print made by a riding or "cowboy" boot. It looked to be a men's size six or seven, right-footed, with the heel twisted toward the ball. A small crowd stood behind the reeve, fingers pointing to the boot prints and voices talking over each other, all claiming the tracks must be those of the murderer. Ackerman was not convinced, thinking instead that the print belonged to his nephew Frank Jesseph, who had boots just like that and whom he had seen climb through the gate some minutes before.

The welter of signs and clues at Marshall's farmstead was confusing—it was not clear what had happened, other than that Marshall had been killed on his veranda. No clue pointed to who might have killed him, nor why. The $180 in cash and coins found in the house suggested that it was not a case of robbery, the first motive that came to mind. Ackerman was not trained to sort through the chaos, and he was not fool enough to try. Unsettled by the murder of his neighbour but determined to carry out his responsibilities, Ackerman returned to the house to await the arrival of Superintendent Moresby and Pittendrigh, the coroner.

❖

Just after 7:00 a.m., Albert Stroebel left the City Hotel and set off for Carpenter's barbershop and his morning dose of news. Skittering up Railway Avenue, he bumped into the young telegraph operator from the Bellingham Bay and BC Railroad depot.

"Have you heard?" the boy said breathlessly. "Someone got hisself killed, up past Huntingdon. It was the Portuguese, named Marshall."

"Marshall, oh no," Stroebel stopped dead. "He's a relation, you know, kind of a relation." The boy just smiled in his excitement and scurried off.

David Lucas, sometimes marshal of Sumas City, used aggressive tactics in pursuing those he thought were guilty—including Albert Stroebel. *Roy Jones, Boundary Town: Early Days in a Northwest Boundary Town* (Vancouver WA: Fleet, 1958), p 205

Stroebel turned around and headed back to the hotel, stopping at the kitchen door to ask Margaret Bartlett if she had heard the news about Marshall. She said she had and was about to say more when David Lucas appeared, delivering the morning's milk. The pair fell silent and eyed Lucas warily. The man had served as Sumas City marshal off and on over the past few years, and his heavy-handed methods had made him many enemies. He was not trusted nor liked in the Bartlett household, a hostility Stroebel shared.

After Lucas left, Stroebel slipped on his gumboots and went outside, where he joined a small group heading north up the rail line. As they approached Marshall's gate, the group was stopped by another party coming the other way, led by William Porter, who said that a notice had been posted prohibiting anyone from entering the farm. Porter had arrived at his neighbour's house earlier, and after viewing the scene, he had been posted at the gate to keep people out. He now joined the two groups heading back down the rail line. As they walked, Porter fell into step alongside Stroebel. The Kentuckian had taken a good look at Marshall's body that morning, particularly the wounds to his face, and had seen the table set for two inside the house. He also recalled the revolver Stroebel had been carrying the previous day and the last time he had seen the lad, walking toward the railbed just before supper.

"Say, Al, what time did you get home last night?" Porter asked, trying to sound as casual as possible.

"About five or six o'clock, something like that," Stroebel answered sharply as Porter nodded and held his tongue. Just then, the two men noticed smoke rising from the chimney of the old Stroebel house, now abandoned.

"What do ya think of that, Mr. Porter?" Stroebel asked. "I reckon it's a tramp, making hisself cozy."

Porter agreed and the pair approached the cabin warily. They flung open the door and were hit by the stench of sweat and dirty clothes. A figure crouched in front of the fire, the rumpled bedroll spread out on the floor behind showing he had spent the night. The intruder scooped up his bedding and shot out the door, leaving Porter and Stroebel staring at each other in confusion.

❖

William Moresby was the government's top lawman on the mainland. Warden at the New Westminster Gaol, he was also the ranking provincial police officer for the district, with the title of acting superintendent. Moresby had arrived in BC as a teenager and was meant to follow his father into the law, but the younger Moresby never took to book learning. After trying his luck in the Cariboo gold rush, he returned to New Westminster and secured a dual appointment as assistant jailor and police constable. Ten years later, at the age of thirty-one, he was promoted to warden of the jail, with its accompanying police duties. Now,

William Moresby, police superintendent and warden of New Westminster Gaol. Moresby was known for his doggedness on criminal cases, but overwork led to health problems. New Westminster Archives, IHP 2489

at forty-six, he was finding it increasingly difficult to juggle both roles, and he looked longingly for one last promotion: to become warden of the federal government's penitentiary in New Westminster.

With his heavy responsibilities, Moresby was used to being woken at any hour of the night or early morning to deal with some emergency or another. The telegram he received the morning of April 20 was hastily written and disjointed, but its message was clear enough: a killing had taken place in Sumas, and he needed to come as soon as possible. Moresby immediately sent word to George Pittendrigh, the sixty-year-old coroner of New Westminster. A former sergeant in the British army who had fought in the Crimean War, Pittendrigh was appointed coroner at the beginning of 1890.

Now, as they boarded the train in New Westminster, the coroner and superintendent recollected that they had been called out to Sumas on their very first case together. A farmer named Rutherford had gone mad, believing that his neighbours had been slowly poisoning him. On a snowy evening in January 1890, he set out for his neighbours' houses, shot them dead, then returned home, where he turned the rifle on himself. The coroner remembered the case well because one of the victims was the son of William Hall, a former army corporal who had served with Pittendrigh in the Crimean conflict. The case of Rutherford's double murder and suicide was quickly wrapped up, but it was a gruesome start for Moresby and Pittendrigh's partnership in crime investigation.

Exactly a year later, the pair returned to the central Fraser Valley for a more mysterious case. In late January 1891, a bloated, decomposed body was found snagged along the northern bank of the Fraser River just past Sumas Landing. The victim's head was cracked open, exposing his brain. Half his left foot and the big toe on his right foot were missing, and one end of a rope was tied around his neck, the other around a rock that had weighed him down in the water. Pittendrigh oversaw the coroner's inquest and Moresby began interviewing locals, but nobody could identify the dead man. The superintendent spent the following two weeks scouring the countryside from Sumas to Hope, looking for witnesses and evidence. He was able to identify the victim as Patrick O'Shea, a tramp from Montreal who had been riding the CPR rails. An exhausted Moresby then arrested a Lakahamen First Nation man known—by sheer coincidence—as Shea.

The case went to trial at the spring assize in June, where the Crown laid out the evidence assiduously acquired by Moresby. The defence offered only two witnesses and no closing statement, and Judge Matthew Begbie instructed the jurors that the Crown's evidence was not convincing. It took the jury ten minutes to come back with an acquittal. All of Moresby's hard work had been for naught, and the mystery of Patrick O'Shea's violent death was never solved.

Snow had covered the valley the first two times Moresby and Pittendrigh had been summoned to Sumas to investigate a murder. Now, as the pair changed trains at Mission Junction then headed south onto the prairie, a steady rain had made the April fields wet and muddy. The pair were dropped off north of Marshall's trestle, turning in at his gate just before two o'clock. Catching sight of the crowd huddled on the veranda, Moresby's face reddened with anger. The soggy ground about the house was criss-crossed with tracks from all the people who had descended on the farm that day, and the veranda itself was wet and muddy from countless boots clumping around the body.

Checking his temper, Moresby exchanged greetings with Asa Ackerman, then turned to the body. Ordering the bystanders to back away, the superintendent bent down and pulled back the blanket covering the corpse. Marshall lay on his back, his head propped up against the doorsill, tilting forward, and his feet dangled over the veranda steps. The farmer's nose was smashed, and his forehead had a small hole in it.

"Around the nose, that looks like heavy bruising," Moresby said over his shoulder to Pittendrigh. "And the hole on the forehead, I reckon that's a bullet wound; the skin all around is burnt black with gunpowder."

The superintendent leaned back and surveyed Marshall's clothes. The farmer was dressed in a coat, dark vest and blue overalls, old boots and no hat; his pockets contained some matches, a piece of twine and a plug of tobacco. A pipe stem with no bowl lay on his left-hand side beside a small purse which, upon inspection, was found to contain a ten-dollar note and forty cents in silver coins. Moresby then grabbed the body by the shoulders and turned it over to expose its back. There was no blood, and the only sign of injury was a small hole at the base of the neck.

"Looks like another bullet hole, but no blackening this time," he told Pittendrigh.

Thinking it could be the exit wound from the shot to his forehead, Moresby made a quick scan of the veranda boards but saw no sign of a slug. The superintendent stood with a puzzled look on his face. In his experience, head wounds produced a lot of blood, but there was very little of it about. Marshall's forehead and nose were bloodied, and there was a small, darkening pool of blood on the veranda and a single spot on the floor just inside the door. Other than that, there was nothing.

Having completed his examination of the body, Moresby ordered that it be moved into the house, where it was laid atop boards that straddled two chairs. Ackerman then handed over the two pouches of money that had been found inside, and the superintendent did a quick walk-through of the two-room house, finding nothing new.

The superintendent did not venture out to the south gate to check on the mysterious boot print but focused instead on getting the wider investigation under way. He, Pittendrigh and a small group of men walked down the rail line to the Huntingdon Hotel, where rooms had been reserved for the two officials. Here, at the far end of the dining room, the superintendent set up a temporary headquarters for the investigation. He instructed James Schofield to telegraph Dr. George Boggs in New Westminster, summoning the doctor to Sumas to perform the autopsy. Without a single uniformed officer to help him, Moresby deputized Schofield as a special constable. This gave the station master the same powers as a regular constable to collect evidence, speak with witnesses and generally carry out the superintendent's orders.

Moresby also pulled David Lucas into the centre of the investigation. Lucas was at Marshall's before ten o'clock that morning, and he had spent the following hours going over the crime scene and talking to others there who might have useful information. Upon Moresby's arrival at the scene, Lucas offered his help in the case, which the super-intendent readily accepted. Lucas returned to the Huntingdon Hotel with the superintendent, and the pair now sat discussing the strategy they might follow. Moresby's recruitment of the marshal was a fateful move: over the next three days, Lucas would produce the most damn-ing evidence against the man who had already emerged as the prime suspect—Albert Stroebel.

❧

David Lucas was a character straight out of central casting. With his Wyatt Earp moustache, whisky drinking and plug of chewing tobacco wedged between cheek and gum, he lived the part of a hard-bitten lawman who pursued justice no matter how many laws he had to break. Born thirty-seven years earlier on an old eastern fron-tier—Kentucky—he spent his adult life moving about the cities and towns of a new western frontier, from Mexico north to Canada. After his mother died giving birth to him, his father faded from the scene and the Lucas children were farmed out to family and friends. By the age of twenty, David had followed his eldest brother, Albert, to San Francisco.

Albert Lucas opened one of the first private detective firms in the city, a rival to the more famous Pinkerton Agency. During the 1880s and 1890s—as Albert moved from San Francisco to Los Angeles to Seattle—the Pacific Coast Detective Agency cracked some of the highest profile cases on the west coast. However, Lucas attracted as much publicity for his aggressive, legally suspect methods as for his successes. He was not afraid to flaunt the law in pursuit of his man—he kidnapped suspects, employed known criminals, and played fast and loose with money entrusted to him. He was indicted on a string of charges, convicted of one, acquitted on the rest, and all this time his business continued to thrive.

Off and on through these years, Albert Lucas found work for his eager younger brother. In between jobs that took him from police beats in San Francisco and San Diego to dusty boom towns in Mexico, David was tutored in the black arts of the Pacific Coast Detective

Company. When Albert moved to Seattle, David too went north. In 1890, the younger Lucas settled in Sumas City and opened a boarding house. He was appointed town marshal a year later, just in time for the boom that followed the opening of the railway. Some locals welcomed David Lucas's rough-and-ready methods, believing they were needed to deal with the sudden invasion of rowdy workers, saloon keepers, prostitutes and gamblers. Others despised the marshal's bully-boy ways: his contempt for due process and legal rights, his targeting of the innocent as well as the guilty, and (many were convinced) his willingness to plant incriminating evidence to get the man he wanted.

The economic crash of 1893 hit Sumas City hard, the boom went bust, and the town no longer had money for a full-time lawman. Without his marshal badge, a humbled Lucas had to rely on the occasional lodger at his boarding house and on selling milk from his handful of cows. Lucas still had the power to make the occasional arrest when someone violated a municipal bylaw, and the city would pay him on a piecemeal basis. Thus, when Lucas jumped into the Marshall murder case, he did so on his own, unofficially and without pay; for him, it was a way of getting back into the game. Moresby drew him into the investigation because Lucas was the only experienced lawman on the prairie, and because he could operate south of the border in Sumas City, where their prime suspect lived.

As word of Marshall's murder spread, many locals refused to believe that any of their neighbours were capable of such violence—that the evil deed must have been committed by a passing tramp. However, some started saying that the young, crippled Stroebel had been seen carrying a gun the previous day and that he was one of the last people to see Marshall alive. As Moresby and Lucas huddled at the Huntingdon Hotel, William Porter—the closest witness to Stroebel's movements that day—told the lawmen he had suspected the lad. Lucas eagerly agreed with his fellow Kentuckian, while Moresby nodded sagely at Porter's suspicions.

At around 3:00 p.m. on April 20, Lucas left the Huntingdon Hotel and headed directly for the Bartletts' hotel in Sumas City. He walked down the hall and into the kitchen, where Stroebel and most of the Bartlett family were having tea. Helping himself to some cake, Lucas asked Stroebel to come across the line to identify the Chinese man who had worked for John Marshall the previous day. Stroebel and the Bartletts eyed the marshal warily.

"I don't have to go," the young man finally said.

"No, but it would be a courtesy to Mr. Moresby. He wants to call the right Chinese man for the coroner's hearing tomorrow."

Stroebel thought for a few moments, chewing the rest of his cake, then agreed to go. He put on his gumboots and coat and accompanied Lucas outside. The pair met up with Moresby outside the laundry house in Huntingdon, where Stroebel pointed out Sam Lee. Walking back to Sumas City in the light rain, Lucas stopped within earshot of the City Hotel.

"People been talking that the gun that shot Marshall was a .38," he said casually to Stroebel. "But the doctor examined him and found it was a .44."

The young man brightened, then replied, "Can't be like mine. Mine's a .38."

"Can I see it?"

"Okay, wait here and I'll go get it." Returning from his room, Stroebel grinned as he handed the gun to Lucas. "See, it's a .38, not a .44."

The marshal took the revolver, broke it open and checked the empty chambers, then sighted down the barrel. "Looks like this has been fired not long ago," he said, and he slid the gun into his coat. Stroebel protested that he had no right to take the piece, but Lucas replied he was just picking up any guns he could.

"Weren't you carrying this the day Marshall was killed?" Lucas asked.

"Yeah, but only 'cause it's my habit. I don't mean anything by it."

The marshal nodded and said he would return the piece the following day. With Stroebel still protesting, he walked back up Railway Avenue and headed for the Huntingdon Hotel. Lucas stepped onto the hotel veranda, shook the rain off his coat and hat, and entered. Finding Moresby at their usual table, he sat down beside him and described his conversation with Stroebel that afternoon, then retrieved the revolver and broke it open.

"See here," he pointed with tobacco-stained fingers. "Two chambers have been recently fired, and two cartridges taken out without being fired. And the last chamber hasn't had anything in it for some time." Moresby took the gun and moved it into better light, nodding as he inspected each chamber.

The pair was too deep in conversation to notice that the room was filling up as suppertime approached. The diners were as hungry for news as for food, and their separate conversations soon merged into one rising din. A pair of reporters could be spotted among the local crowd, their rumpled suits and city shoes giving them away. Just then, Dr. George Boggs walked in the door. Flushed with cold and brandy, as ill-tempered as the night, he pushed his way across the room toward Moresby's table.

Outside, cold rain continued to fall and an inky black pressed down from above. Two miles north, Asa Ackerman settled in for his all-night vigil at the death-house of John Marshall. He was relieved that the body had been moved into the bedroom, out of sight. That left no place for him to lie down, but Ackerman doubted he would be getting any sleep that night—as for Marshall, he had nothing but sleep ahead of him.

FRIDAY, APRIL 21

At 9:30 Friday morning, Asa Ackerman looked up from his coffee as the front door to John Marshall's cabin opened and three men came in out of the rain. Ackerman recognized James Schofield and William Moresby, but he had never met the third visitor, a well-fed man in expensive overcoat, gloves and hat.

"Dr. George Boggs," the stout man said, as he looked about for a place to put his outerwear, a soft Maritime burr clinging to his words.

"Yes, of course, the autopsy," Ackerman responded, rising to greet the doctor.

Boggs was forty-eight years old, a physician and surgeon who had moved to New Westminster from his native Nova Scotia two years earlier. A graduate of the Faculty of Medicine at McGill University, Canada's oldest medical school, Boggs had earned a reputation as a surgeon who was not afraid to take on tricky operations. Boggs's skill with the scalpel was useful on the dead as well as the living, and he performed his share of autopsies. Forensic medicine—the application of medical knowledge and procedures to solving crime—was in its infancy and Boggs had no specific training in it. So, like other doctors of the late Victorian age, Boggs had to rely on his traditional training to answer questions unique to cases of suspicious death and murder. What was the exact time of death? How can you tell where bullets were fired from? How did bullets behave once in the body? What do other injuries on the body show? With a confidence that was second nature to surgeons, Boggs was not troubled by the limitations of the methods he and his colleagues used.

Freed of his coat, hat and gloves, the doctor strode into Marshall's bedroom and saw the body laid out, still in the clothes it had worn the previous morning.

"I'll need him moved to the table in the kitchen," he ordered. Once on the table, the doctor went to work quickly and without speaking. He examined the broken nose, noting that it had been struck with enough force to separate the cartilage from the bone, then moved to the wound above the left eyebrow, where the hair was burnt off and the skin deeply blackened. From his black leather bag, Boggs retrieved a steel rod the size of a large knitting needle and pushed it into the opening. The probe slid along the track of the wound, travelling at a downward angle for three and a half inches before coming to a stop against something hard.

Removing the probe and stepping back, the doctor had the body turned over, and he immediately spotted the ragged hole directly above the base of the neck. Wondering whether this might be where the bullet from the frontal wound had exited, he inserted the probe. When the rod stopped after an inch and a half, he took a scalpel and cut through the soft tissue of the neck, exposing the spinal column. A bullet was embedded in the spinal column between the first and second vertebrae, which were splintered and crushed. Boggs grunted with exertion as he worked the slug out with forceps and handed it to Moresby, who wrapped it in a handkerchief and slid it into his jacket pocket.

The doctor stepped back and ordered the body turned onto its back again. He peeled the skin from the scalp and sawed through the top half of the cranium. Removing the skullcap and brain, he discovered that the bullet entering from the front had travelled downward from the eyebrow, skirted the underside of the brain and embedded itself in the bottom of the skull. Wielding hammer and chisel, the doctor chopped into the skull and extracted the bullet, a piece of bone embedded in the deformed lump of lead. The second slug joined the first inside Superintendent Moresby's handkerchief.

Boggs replaced Marshall's skullcap and skin and moved to the sink to wash and dry his hands. "I'm all finished here, Superintendent. Shall we?" He, Moresby and Schofield donned their outerwear, left the house and struck off down the rail line to the Huntingdon Hotel, where the coroner's inquest awaited them.

❖

The dining room of the Huntingdon Hotel was filled to capacity. All but one of the tables had been removed, and extra chairs had been brought in. Dozens of men filled the chairs, and more stood with their backs against the walls, all of them talking excitedly. Against the far wall, a line of seven men sat facing the crowd, spread out behind the room's lone table. The tall windows were shut against the morning cold and the air was stuffy and hot, with the press of bodies adding to

The Huntingdon Hotel, completed just after the building of the CPR line. The hotel was the largest building in Huntingdon for some time. Guests stayed on the second and third floors, and had access to a full-length, covered balcony on each floor. A large dining room, smaller saloon and backroom (often used for cards) shared the first floor with the manager's office and kitchen. Reach Gallery Museum, p7066: "Huntingdon Hotel"

the heat coming from the two wood-burning stoves. Gas lights were reflected against the fogged window panes, casting a yellow glow over the proceedings.

At 9:30 sharp, George Pittendrigh raised his voice over the din, calling to order the coroner's inquest into the death of John Marshall. The previous evening, as required by law, Pittendrigh had selected a jury of six from among the men milling about Marshall's house. Among the six were CPR lineman Alexander Baxter and postmaster Thomas Trusswell, who was chosen foreman. The coroner had ordered the men to take a close look at Marshall's body, keep the picture in their minds, then be present Friday morning at the official inquest. The jurors now sat facing the restless crowd, trying their best to look serious, but uncomfortable under the gaze of so many eyes.

The crowd hushed at Pittendrigh's command, but a stream of whispers rose when the first witness was called. Albert Stroebel took a stand in front of the coroner's table, his pale, broad face set in an expression of sincere concern. He described his movements on Wednesday, April 19: arriving at Marshall's house at 9:00 a.m., baking bread and cleaning house, fishing out behind the cabin before lunch, walking with Marshall and Blair to the back field to plough, and turning to help Porter dig a ditch.

"I stayed until about half past five o'clock," he concluded. "At about half past four o'clock, Mr. Marshall passed us on his way home. That was the last time I saw him on that day."

Up next, William Blair spoke of visiting Marshall early that morning, then returning to help plough in the afternoon; he recalled seeing Stroebel and Porter ditching nearby. When Pittendrigh asked whether his neighbour kept large amounts of money in the house, Blair replied, "I saw him with money occasionally, quite a little roll of bills."

Young George Hilliard followed. He recounted the Sunday visit he and George Bartlett had made to Marshall's, describing the half-dozen gold coins the farmer pulled out when the conversation turned to Marshall's girl.

The principal witness of the morning was Ira Airheart, who testified that he first heard his neighbour's dog barking at around 9:00

p.m. on Wednesday. The trapper moved on to his discovery of Marshall's body the following morning: "On nearing the house, I saw that the door was open and a man lying on the floor of the veranda, on his back. On going up, I saw it was Marshall with blood on his face." Under Pittendrigh's questioning, Airheart said that the farmer's dog did not usually bark at night and that he "heard no shots fired" before or after the barking.

Sam Lee was the last to testify that morning. Speaking through an interpreter, Lee explained that Marshall had arranged for him to work on the nineteenth. He arrived at the farm at 10:00 a.m., walked out to the east of the property with the farmer, then worked through the day. Lee testified that "at six o'clock, Mr. Marshall came to me at the ditch. He showed me a shortcut home. He said 'Good-bye,' I said 'Good-bye.' I saw Marshall go to his house, then I went home by the rail." Pittendrigh treated the other witnesses with respect, but he grilled Lee with sharp questions which had the sting of accusation in them. Lee was decisive and firm in his answers: he did not go back to Marshall's house that evening, did not see the farmer after 6:00 p.m., and had not come into work Thursday morning because of the rain. He concluded, "I never had a gun or revolver, nor do I carry a stick. I have only a cane to carry my lunch on."

The inquest broke for lunch and on its return took the evidence of Superintendent Moresby and Dr. Boggs. Moresby quickly and efficiently ran through his observations at the scene of the crime: "There was a quantity of blood on the body, a small quantity on the veranda, and one small mark of blood on the floor, just inside the door." The superintendent described the scene in Marshall's kitchen, then laid the evidence he had collected on the table in front of the coroner: the money pouches, coins, bills and two bullet slugs.

Finally, George Boggs presented his autopsy report, describing in detail the nature of Marshall's wounds. "The bullets were apparently such as would be used in a .38 calibre weapon," he stated. "The bullets produced in court are the same ones that I took from the body. The one most twisted out of shape is the one taken from the front wound, and the one least broken up is the one taken from the wound in the neck.

I am perfectly satisfied that one or both of these bullets caused the death of the deceased."

With all the witnesses heard, the jurors huddled awkwardly, returning to their seats a few minutes later. Foreman Trusswell remained standing and read the jury's verdict: on April 19, in Sumas, "a certain person to the jurors unknown... did feloniously, willfully, and of his malice aforethought kill and murder the said John Marshall."

Pittendrigh thanked the jurors for their work, then declared an end to the inquest. A babel of voices broke out, rolling over the sound of scraping chairs as men rose to leave the dining room. The crowd spilled from the hotel and was met by shots of steam and the rumble of iron as the CPR train rolled in from Vancouver. The men hurried to the Huntingdon station, drawn by a rumour that the train carried the coffin John Marshall was to be buried in. Inside the cargo hold, the CPR handlers moved the simple pine box into place, ready to unload. They opened the car doors and stopped short before the ghoulish mob on the platform, too afraid to go any farther.

❖

Murder arouses public interest of all shades, from the politely curious, to the morally outraged, to the perversely morbid. By the 1890s, newspapers and society at large had shed many of the reservations held by earlier Victorians, who thought public interest in and discussion of violent crime was both vulgar and dangerous. Indeed, late Victorians had acquired a taste for murder, both imagined and real. The fiction of Charles Dickens, Edgar Allen Poe and Arthur Conan Doyle found a large, avid readership in Europe and North America. The same readers obsessively pored over news of the gruesome, real-life murders attributed to Jack the Ripper and Lizzie Borden.

Newspaper editors were keenly aware of their readers' tastes, so when a local resident was murdered, they jumped on the story. After John Marshall was killed, the first paper out of the gates was New Westminster's *Daily Columbian*. The largest circulating newspaper on the mainland, the *Daily Columbian* came out in the evenings, so it broke the story the same day Marshall's body was found. Under the blazing headline "FOUL MURDER," the paper reported that "about 5:30 this morning" Marshall was shot through the head while standing in his doorway, "causing instant death." A lamp burned in the kitchen and the dinner table was set for two, which "plainly shows some person took supper with Marshall last night." With no suspects in the case, the paper pointed its finger at a convenient culprit: "this place and Sumas has been infested with toughs lately."

The idea that a passing ruffian had done Marshall in was given greater currency when newspapers in Vancouver and Victoria picked up the *Daily Columbian* piece.[1] In the following days, these newspapers would send their own reporters to cover the story. The *Daily Columbian* stoked the flames further in its Thursday edition. While adding no new facts, the paper declared: "the only theory regarding the murder at present is that it was the work of some one of the numerous toughs who have infested this town of late."

That same day, the *Bellingham Reveille* in Washington state published a substantial piece on the "HIDEOUS SUMAS MURDER." Demonstrating the more aggressive brand of journalism practised south of the border, the article told a much better story—more detailed and dramatic, but all the more inaccurate because of that. According to the *Reveille*, Marshall's body had been found outside his front door by two trappers who had come to buy some eggs and butter. The night before, the farmer "had apparently been called to the door and as he opened it he was shot dead"; the killer then rifled Marshall's pockets for money before disappearing into the night.

The paper also dangled a tantalizing piece of information. Customs officer Bosnell McDonald told the *Reveille* reporter "that a few days

---

1   At the time, each of BC's three major cities hosted two competing newpapers: the *Daily News Advertiser* was Vancouver's only daily paper, the *Daily World* its misnamed weekly counterpart; in Victoria, the *Daily Colonist* boasted the biggest readership in the province, while the *Victoria Times* was a spirited upstart that gave the more established paper some stiff competition, particularly in its crime coverage; and in New Westminster, the *Daily Columbian*'s meek competitor was the weekly *Pacific Canadian*. A fourth city, Nanaimo, put out the feisty *Daily Telegram*.

ago, Marshall told him that he had an assistant on the ranch, a sort of tramp carpenter, who was destitute and had nothing to do. That man has disappeared." This information was accurate, but what the article did with it was rather fanciful. Noting the dinner table set for two, the paper speculated that the mystery carpenter had been eating with Marshall when he slipped out the back door and around to the front, knocked and shot the farmer when the door opened. It was not explained why the purported killer felt the need to sneak out and around the house when he could simply have shot Marshall while they sat at the kitchen table.

The spectre of the passing killer was given more life by Timothy Montgomery, the weather-beaten partner of Ira Airheart. Montgomery was one of the sources for the *Reveille* piece, and he claimed to be the second of the two trappers who found Marshall's body. The old trapper inserted himself further into the story in an interview with Victoria's *Daily Colonist*. Known locally as the "Old Sleuth"—the name of a popular magazine detective—Montgomery claimed he had worked as a private investigator in Kansas City and boasted he could spot clues in the Marshall case no one else could see.

"I think I can run in the man who committed the deed, I'll bet a coon skin," he stated grandly. "Three suspicious characters have been loitering around town and this portion of Sumas prairie. It is evident that more than one was present at the murder." Montgomery based his deduction on the fact that Marshall's table had been set for two. But Montgomery's arithmetic was as weak as his powers of deduction: Marshall and one guest would leave a table set for two, two guests would leave three settings, and three guests four settings.

Rumours and speculation swirled around the case in these early days, in the press and among residents on both sides of the border. Even as more facts became known after the coroner's inquest, some papers insisted on getting things wrong. No doubt covering the inquest from afar, Vancouver's *Daily World* reported that in the wake of the coroner jury's verdict, "a Chinaman has been arrested on suspicion of murder." Some, including David Lucas, had initially considered Sam Lee a suspect, for no other reason than that he was Chinese.

This was as predictable as it was depressing. Because of the rabid racism that permeated every aspect of White society in BC, it was common practice for the public, press and police to automatically suspect any Chinese person who was in the vicinity of an unsolved crime. Painfully aware of this prejudice, Sam Lee was forthright and forceful in his testimony at the coroner's inquest. The authorities were on the verge of making an arrest—fortunately for his sake and the sake of justice, it would not be Lee.

LATE APRIL, 1893

A large crowd turned out for John Marshall's funeral on Saturday morning, April 22. The cold, wet front that had stalled over Sumas for so long had been pushed out overnight, and sunshine greeted the mourners as Marshall's pine coffin was lowered into the freshly dug ground. The grasslands, trees and hillsides glistened in countless shades of green. Spring had arrived at long last, and the prairie was coming to life.

Standing beside Marshall's grave, on the hillside cemetery rising above Sumas prairie, John Silverthorne glanced over the bountiful landscape. Silverthorne was the senior member of the Sumas branch of the International Order of Odd Fellows (IOOF), which counted both Marshall and Albert Stroebel as members. The society was founded on the principle of mutual assistance, giving aid to fellow members in time of need. This aid included seeing to funeral arrangements when there was no family or church available to step in. The vast majority of late Victorian funerals were conducted by clergymen, but no one had ever talked to Marshall about his religion and everybody simply assumed he was a Roman Catholic. Sumas prairie had no churches—Catholic, Protestant or Zoroastrian—and the only clergymen to visit were itinerant ministers.

As the casket came to rest at the bottom of the soggy grave, Silverthorne stepped forward to deliver the simple homily prescribed in the official IOOF guidebook: "We are assembled to render the last office which the living may minister to the dead. Man is born to die. The coffin, the grave, the sepulchre, speak to us in terms that cannot be misunderstood, however unheeded it may be, of 'man's latter end'."

Silverthorne paused as a gust of wind turned the pages of his book. "We now commit our departed brother's body to the grave: earth to earth, ashes to ashes, dust to dust." Silverthorne picked up a handful of dirt and tossed it into the grave, the wet clumps pattering like rain on the lid of the coffin. One by one, the other Odd Fellows present did the same.

Whispers broke the silence when Stroebel stepped forward, cast dirt on the casket and said, "Mr. Marshall, he was a true friend. I do sure regret his dying."

Stroebel's words echoed in the hills as the mourners broke into small groups and began their walk home. Once again, Stroebel found himself walking alongside William Porter, and the pair got to talking about the last day they had seen their friend alive.

"Say, Al, I can't remember, precise-like. What time did you say you got home that night, after we finished ditching?" Porter asked in his slow Kentucky drawl.

Stroebel took a moment to answer. "Oh yeah, Thursday, the night Mr. Marshall got killed. I went fishin' after I left you, so I got home late."

"That's funny, I thought you said you got home 'round six o'clock, thereabouts."

"No, no, I went fishin'."

Before Porter could say more, Stroebel hurried ahead, catching up with a group from Sumas City. The Kentuckian watched the young man go, troubled by what he now believed he knew. Porter recalled the gun Stroebel had flashed that afternoon, what the boy had said Thursday about going straight home after ditching, and other people saying that he was last seen walking north to Marshall's. With mounting suspicion, Porter had kept an eye on Stroebel throughout the funeral. Several times he had caught the lad's eyes darting about, as if fearful that others suspected him. He did not want to think ill of the boy, especially over something so serious, but to Porter that was the look of a guilty conscience.

❖

Throughout that Saturday, the Huntingdon Hotel was a hive of activity. Mourners returning from Marshall's funeral stopped in for lunch; others nursed drinks in the saloon or just milled about, talking excitedly among themselves while waiting for something to happen. It was a rare sunny day, and there was a mountain of work awaiting the men on their farms, but the Marshall murder was the most exciting thing to happen to the community, and locals could not resist its pull. Hotel keeper Charles Moulton scurried about happily as a steady stream of people came and went, rumours and gossip flowing as freely as the beer and whisky.

At their back table in the dining room, William Moresby and David Lucas were deep in conversation. The pair agreed on who killed Marshall; however, the ever-cautious Moresby demanded hard evidence before he moved in for an arrest. Levelling his gaze at the marshal, the superintendent reminded Lucas that their suspect lived in Sumas City, so it fell on him to bring the evidence in. Lucas rose and stalked out of the hotel, turning sharply right for Sumas City.

"I knocked around town," Lucas would later describe that frenetic day. "I walked round town trying to produce some evidence, if I could get any, or catch any news I could hear."

Margaret Bartlett, who saw the marshal a number of times that day, had a different view. "He was running around like a crazy man," she reported.

Lucas first checked out Frank Carpenter's barbershop, hoping Stroebel would be there, which he was, sitting inside talking to friends. With the coast clear, the marshal continued on to the City Hotel to question Margaret Bartlett and search Stroebel's room. Bartlett was in the kitchen with her daughter Mary when Lucas walked in.

"You here to arrest someone, to arrest Al?" she asked uneasily.

"No, why should I arrest him?"

"Well, two days ago, right here in front of the hotel, I saw you take his revolver and heard you talkin' about some cartridges. I seen him with cartridges before. I'm afraid the children will get them."

Lucas asked Bartlett if she was willing to make a statement—about the cartridges, about Stroebel's movements the night of the murder—and she reluctantly agreed.

Neither could read nor write, so Lucas walked over to a friend's

store, dictated a statement to him, and returned to the hotel for Bartlett to sign it.

As he was leaving, the marshal met John Bartlett at the doorway
to the front parlour. Lucas was about to ask whether Bartlett had any
information on Marshall's murder when he caught sight of Stroebel
seated at a table in the parlour, writing a letter. The marshal watched
out of the corner of his eye as Stroebel folded and pocketed the first
letter, then started into another. Not wanting to confront Stroebel
yet, Lucas headed back to his usual table at the Huntingdon Hotel
and sat down to wait for Moresby, who was out conducting his own
investigations.

A quarter of an hour later, John Bartlett nervously approached the
marshal, holding out a rolled piece of paper the size of an index finger. "Mr. Lucas, I found this on the parlour table, after you left. I think
Al wrote it." Bartlett paused. "People are all suspicioned about Al, and
I know you was anxious to scrape up evidence on him."

"Thanks, John, much obliged." Scanning the unrolled letter, Lucas
could guess at only a few phrases—"hell of scrape," "Marshall shot,"
"grand guary"—he smiled and tucked the note into a vest pocket.

Moresby arrived at their table, and as he sat down, the marshal
launched into his argument that they had enough evidence to arrest
Stroebel. The superintendent still balked, burnt by past failures such
as the Patrick O'Shea case. He wanted more evidence, something sure-
fire, such as an eyewitness or physical clue, something that would hold
up in court. Lucas stormed out of the hotel again, his temper at a boil,
cursing that if evidence was what Moresby wanted, then evidence was
what he would get.

Lucas glanced skyward as he returned to Sumas City. The rain
had held off all day and the sun peaked timidly through a gap in
the clouds. The city streets and lanes were a mess, however, muddy and potted with puddles, and the dark clouds banked up against
the mountains promised more rain. Lucas walked the length of the
town, then back, and a singular idea pushed through the swirl of
thoughts in his mind. He turned into the alley beside the City Hotel and emerged a few moments later. He then retrieved Margaret

Bartlett from the hotel and asked her to show him which of the alley windows was Stroebel's.

"Do you see that?" he exclaimed, pointing to a puddle beneath the lad's second-floor window. Two empty cartridges sat atop the muck, one on its side, the other sticking straight up. "I just found these, and didn't have to look much."

Bartlett looked at the cartridges, frowning. "They're awful clean-looking, after being out here in all the rain and mud we been having."

Lucas ignored her and bent over to retrieve the shells. "I just wanted you to see these, where they were. And to see that I have them." Bartlett watched in confusion as the marshal walked out of the alley. A spring in his step, Lucas once again mounted the stairs into the Huntingdon Hotel and went directly to Moresby.

"You wanted evidence, here's evidence." Lucas slapped the shells down on the table and explained how and where he had got them.

The superintendent nodded, satisfied that the time had come to arrest Stroebel—the only question was how to do it. The crime had been committed in Canada, but the suspect was in the US, and Moresby could not simply walk across the line and grab Stroebel. If Lucas had him properly arrested in Washington, they would have to wait while the long, tortuous extradition process worked its way through, and there was no guarantee it would be successful. So the lawmen hatched a plan to lure the young man north of the border and into Moresby's hands.

Lucas headed back into Sumas City, a hungry look on his face. After checking at the City Hotel, the marshal found Stroebel at the Bellingham Bay and BC Railroad station.

"Hey Al, come and take a walk with me," the marshal said casually.

Stroebel eyed him. "You think you got me. You're fixing to get me arrested."

"That's foolishness. Why would you say something like that?" Lucas protested. The marshal drew Stroebel into conversation, throwing out tidbits about his investigation, all the while leading Stroebel north. Lucas stopped short when they reached the Huntingdon Hotel.

"Look here, why don't you come in and have a drink with me?"

"No, thank you, Mr. Lucas, no."

"You had a drink with me and Mr. Moresby the other day. C'mon, I'm buying," Lucas pressed.

Stroebel looked about uneasily, then followed Lucas into the saloon. The marshal had his usual whisky, neat, while Stroebel nursed a glass of raspberry wine, his eyes darting back and forth. Stroebel breathed a sigh of relief as the pair escaped the hotel and started south, the light fading in the west. The relief was short-lived; a few strides later Stroebel felt a strong hand grip his shoulder from behind.

"Albert Stroebel," Moresby's voice rang out deep and ominous. "I'm arresting you for the wilful murder of John Marshall. I advise you not to speak, as anything you do say can be used against you at trial."

"Alright, but I'm innocent of it," Stroebel protested.

"Come on lad, let's do this quietly," Moresby added more gently. Offering no resistance, the arrested man was led back to the hotel and installed in Moresby's room.

Lucas trailed behind, and upon entering the room, asked Stroebel to write a note authorizing him to get some of the prisoner's clothes. Note in hand, Lucas returned to the City Hotel and, with Margaret Bartlett holding a lamp for light, gave Stroebel's room a thorough search. It did not take long to go through the young man's meagre possessions. Nothing was found in the few threadbare clothes in the closet—no gold coins, no paper money, no bullets. Lucas then set upon the bed, and as he wrenched the mattress up, he uncovered two loaded cartridges nestled on the bed slats. Margaret Bartlett gawped in surprise as the marshal pocketed the cartridges, threw Stroebel's clothes into a cardboard suitcase and returned to Huntingdon.

Lucas knocked and entered Moresby's room, deposited the suitcase by the door and backed out. Stroebel was lying on the bed, with the superintendent sitting beside him. The young prisoner could not stop himself from talking about Marshall's murder, trying to convince the older man he had nothing to do with it.

"I was at Mr. Marshall's house that day, you see. But it was earlier...."

Moresby broke in. "That's enough, son. You shouldn't be talking. Anything you say can be used against you in court."

Stroebel was silent for a moment, then blurted out: "But that day Mr. Marshall got killed, in the morning, I left my fishing rod up by his place. And after leaving Mr. Porter's cow, later, I went up to get my rod to go fishing...." Moresby broke in again, sternly warning the prisoner he could only do himself harm by talking now.

Finally, it hit Stroebel that he really was going to trial for the most serious crime of all, and that he could lose his life over it. He fell silent for some time, then he began to weep.

"Will they allow me to see my brothers and sisters before they hang me?" he asked desperately.

"Of course they will," Moresby stirred uncomfortably, then tried to calm his prisoner. "But buck up, son, it hasn't come to all that yet."

The superintendent rose and checked his pocket watch: it was time for Schofield to relieve him for the next few hours. Staring out the window into the night, he said over his shoulder, "Time to get some sleep. You'll see, tomorrow will take care of tomorrow." The face looking back at him from the mirrored window was no more convinced of his words than he was.

❖

James Silverthorne shifted uneasily as he stood outside the door of Superintendent Moresby's room, readying himself to knock. It was early Sunday morning. God made the sabbath for man, and it was usually a time of rest and peace, but Silverthorne felt neither. He had not been sleeping well since the discovery of John Marshall's body three days ago, followed by the talk of Albert Stroebel's part in the murder. Both men were brothers, belonging to the same chapter of the Odd Fellows as he did, and he was duty-bound to assist them if he could. Silverthorne had conducted Marshall's funeral the previous morning, then Stroebel was arrested last evening; he had fulfilled his responsibilities burying Marshall, and now he had a duty to help the farmer's alleged killer. Silverthorne drew a breath, knocked and entered the room.

Moresby rose to greet him. "I'll let you two talk in peace," he said, pulling the door shut on his way out. Stroebel was perched on the edge of the bed, finishing his breakfast, and Silverthorne sat down on the room's only chair.

"Al, how are you faring?"

The prisoner swallowed his food and answered, "Just fine, Mr. Silverthorne, considerin'."

"I've come to help, to make sure you know the circumstances of the case. Superintendent Moresby is going to take you to New Westminster today and will probably keep you there six months or so." The older man paused, keeping his eyes on Stroebel's face. "If you're innocent, you won't have to go to trial. All you have to do is stand before a magistrate and swear you had nothing to do with brother Marshall's death."

"But they won't believe me, Mr. Silverthorne, they just won't."

"They will if you tell them what you did that night, after you left off milking Mr. Porter's cow."

Stroebel perked up. "Yes, after I helped Mr. Porter with the cow. Well, I gone fishing. I went up to get my rod which I'd left aside the railway that morning, and some salmon eggs. Then I fished my way down the creek to Joe McQuee's old place. I sat there, on the bridge, fishing and whittling until before dark. If you go there now, you'd see the whittlings. And then I come back to the railway, got my revolver from the stump, and headed home." Stroebel stopped, breathless, a look of triumph on his pale face.

Silverthorne rose from his chair as the sound of approaching footsteps came through the door. "If that's the whole truth, Al, you just tell them that."

❧

Stroebel took a window seat on the outbound CPR train, his body fidgeting with nervous energy. He gazed out as the morning sun climbed above the eastern mountains and tried to raise his hand to shade his eyes from the low sun, but was stopped by the heavy steel cuffs binding his wrists. Moresby settled in beside his prisoner on the wooden bench, boxing him in, and the pair was jolted back as the train started, picking up speed as it approached the trestle in front of Marshall's house. The superintendent instinctively grabbed Stroebel's arm when the prisoner half-stood and clumsily pointed across to the west side of the train car.

"See there, Mr. Moresby, on the bank. That's where I left my fishing rod last Wednesday morning." The superintendent pushed his prisoner back into the seat and looked over, trying to fix the spot in his memory.

Three hours later, a black carriage manned by two uniformed guards awaited Stroebel and Moresby at the New Westminster station. After a short drive, the carriage pulled onto the crushed gravel driveway of the provincial jail. Stroebel had grown quiet and increasingly tense during the journey from Sumas, but he was relieved by the sight that greeted him. There were no forbidding prison walls in front of the New Westminster Gaol, only a low picket fence that surrounded grounds of lush grass, flower beds and neatly pruned trees. A red brick building rose before him, ivy climbing the three storeys to its roof, with rows of high, arched windows filling its façade. To the outsider, it looked like a private boys' school in rural England—only the sharpest eye could make out the bars hidden behind the glass windows.

Once inside the prison, Stroebel's relief turned cold as his handcuffs were removed and he was ordered to undress. A quick physical examination followed, with his vital information recorded on a prison identification card: twenty years old; light hair, blue eyes, fair complexion; 5'4" tall, medium build, stiff right knee; Protestant; US nationality; unmarried; can read and write; temperate; charged with murder. The new inmate was handed an ill-fitting uniform of rough, grey-brown wool, his prisoner number stitched onto the breast.

Stroebel was then escorted to his cell on the ground floor. The New Westminster Gaol consisted of seventy cells, each nine feet long by six feet wide; they were designed to hold two prisoners, but as the jail population averaged just over fifty men at the time, prisoners enjoyed the luxury of their own cell. The sixty-six units for men were divided evenly over three floors, with a U-shaped balcony running in front of the barred doors that allowed the guards to see the prisoners

The New Westminster Provincial Gaol as Albert Stroebel and David Eyerly would have seen it. The jail and its counterpart in Victoria were built in the mid-1880s along the same design, although the New Westminster grounds were much more pastoral. Unseen behind the building was a 13-foot-high wall, white-washed and made of wood, which encircled the prison yard. Royal BC Museum and Archives, A-03353

at all times. Although the jail was only seven years old, there were no lights or running water inside the cells, and each prisoner was given a bucket to use as his toilet. Prison regulations banned prisoners from speaking to each other at all times, whether from one cell to another, in the mess hall, or out on work details. Punishment for this and a laundry-list of other taboos included a reduction in food (to bread and water or half-rations), solitary confinement and cold-water treatments.

The man responsible for enforcing these rules was William Moresby, who along with his policing duties, was also the New Westminster Gaol warden. Moresby was generally considered a firm, even-handed man, and as long as a prisoner toed the line, he would get a fair shake from him. The warden took no pleasure imposing punishments on his charges, but he never shied away from his duty. Once every two or three years, that duty took him up the steps of the gallows, escorting a condemned man to his death. The task always shook Moresby and he prayed it always would, even though he never doubted it was the just punishment for murder. However, some cases were harder than others: the condemned man was so young, so alone, too slight for the enormity of his crime and the grim finality of his punishment. The warden sensed that Stroebel would be one of those cases.

❖

Fortunately for Moresby, he had little time for this type of reflection. The same day he admitted Stroebel to jail—Sunday, April 23— he was called to the scene of another suspicious death. The body of William Zachary had been discovered in the Fraser River at Port Haney, across from the victim's home at Fort Langley. Zachary disappeared on March 10, the day his empty boat was found caught in a snag on the river. At the time, it was assumed he had accidentally drowned and that the current had carried his body away. When Moresby and Coroner Pittendrigh inspected Zachary's bloated corpse in April, however, they noticed an ugly wound on its head and called in Dr. Boggs to perform an autopsy.

Boggs conducted the post-mortem on Tuesday, April 25, and concluded that Zachary had indeed been murdered. The victim had been struck on the head with a club or some heavy weapon, likely while bending over to launch his boat, and his body was then rolled into the water. The victim still had money on him, so robbery was not the motive. One witness who lived a short distance away remembered hearing a cry that March night, then silence, while others saw a light moving in Zachary's house the night of his disappearance. There was little else to work on, and the weeks that had passed since his death left scant hope that new clues would emerge. Moresby attacked the case with his usual stubborn energy. He raced off to Victoria chasing "one very slim clue," then hurried back empty-handed the next day. There were no other leads or clues, and the team that worked together on the Marshall murder never found the killer of William Zachary.

Thus, it was an exhausted Moresby who received another urgent telegram from James Schofield on Friday evening, April 28. The station master, who still held powers as a special constable, reported a startling development that sent the Marshall case veering off in a new direction. A witness had come forward and confessed to being a co-conspirator with Stroebel in the robbery and murder of the Portuguese farmer. The witness was none other than Stroebel's bitter enemy, David Eyerly.

❖

Schofield stood close beside Eyerly on the Huntingdon station platform as the New Westminster train pulled in. The boy was a tight bundle of energy, as eager and wide-eyed as if he was embarking on a great adventure. Moresby stepped off the train and approached the pair.

"This the boy, Jim?"

The station master nodded and glanced at the small crowd gathering on the platform. "Why don't we take a walk? Better to talk that way."

The trio started up the rail line, and after a few steps, Eyerly blurted out, "I knows all about the murder, Marshall's murder, as I told Mr. Schofield. You see—"

"Hold on, son," Moresby cut him short. "I have to warn you that anything you say will be used in a trial, either against you or against Al Stroebel. One lie from you might be the cause of hanging an innocent man. A boy your age, or any boy, that would swear falsely to a lie—why any respectable man would look on him as a dog." The superintendent paused dramatically. "You can make a statement if you like, but be very careful what you say."

The warning had no effect on Eyerly, who started into his extraordinary tale: "On the night of the murder, I reckon around nine o'clock, I was in bed and Al came up to my window and said, 'Hey, Davey, let's go down and rob Marshall.' I says, 'No, I don't want to get into trouble.' He says, 'We won't get into trouble, I knows where he keeps his money. I'll go and get it and you can wait outside and watch that no one comes. I'll give you a $1.50 if you help me.'"

Eyerly paused and looked at Moresby to measure the effect of his words, then continued: "So we starts down to old man Marshall's, taking the wagon road atop the hill. We comes down to his gate and Al leaves me as lookout, him going into the house. I begins to walk up and down, nervous-like. Then I heard a man yell. A dog barked and there was two shots. I started back down the railroad tracks, real fast. Al musta took a shortcut from Marshall's because he caught up to me. I asked him, 'Did you get anything?' He pulled out a flour sack and a buckskin wallet and poured out a fistful of gold pieces. Musta been eight or ten coins, twenty-dollar ones they was, and some smaller ones. I heard more clinking in the sack. Al said, 'We'll divide these up tomorrow morning.' " Eyerly paused to catch his breath.

"I asked him how he got them, and he said 'I had to hit old Marshall with my stick.' Then I asked him about the shots, and he said he'd tell me in the morning. We walked home quick-like and I snuck into bed." The boy fell silent as the trio turned around and headed back to Huntingdon.

"Did anyone offer to pay you to say these things?" Moresby asked.

"No, sir," Eyerly shook his head.

Moresby nodded gravely and stayed silent for the rest of the walk. For some reason, he did not ask where the money was now, whether the boy had been given some or whether Stroebel still had it all. Arriving back at the station, Moresby ordered Eyerly to put out his hands, slapped cuffs on his thin wrists and told him he was being arrested for the robbery and murder of John Marshall. A crowd of bystanders had gathered behind Moresby and Eyerly flashed them a mocking smile, pleased to be the centre of attention. The smile lasted throughout the train trip to New Westminster and the carriage ride to the provincial jail.

As it had been with Stroebel, upon entering the prison doors, Eyerly was stripped down and his vital statistics duly recorded. His identification card read: David Franklin Eyerly; fifteen years (he was fourteen); 5'5½", slim build; fair hair, light blue eyes, fair complexion; no religion; US nationality; can read and write; temperate; charge of wilful murder.

The prison uniform was too large for his slim frame; Eyerly had to grab hold of his pants to keep them up, and he shuffled awkwardly between guards as he was led to a cell in the women's wing. It was common practice to put boy prisoners in the women's block when it was empty, rather than among the general population. Watching the new prisoner disappear through the door to the cells, Moresby's many years of experience told him this was no ordinary boy. Eyerly may have been a month shy of his fifteenth birthday, but Moresby sensed a devilry there that he had seen only in career criminals twice that age. He knew he would have to keep his eye on this one.

New Westminster Gaol

When news of David Eyerly's confession broke, it came as a shock to a public still aroused by the arrest of Albert Stroebel. In the days following Marshall's death, there had been widespread speculation that a passing tramp had committed the crime, so many residents and reporters were surprised when the seemingly harmless Stroebel was taken into custody. Reporting on Stroebel's arrest, the *Daily Columbian* described him as an unlikely killer: "a young man about 22 years of age, badly crippled in one of his legs, and of a rather unprepossessing appearance." The *Bellingham Reveille* expressed similar surprise, stating that Stroebel "has borne a good character and been well liked in Sumas City. A leading citizen does not believe the boy guilty."

After the initial shock, the press came around to believing that the evidence against Stroebel was strong, if circumstantial. With Eyerly's confession and arrest, newspapers were willing to declare the crime solved, the two youngsters certain murderers. The *Daily Columbian* led the way again, proclaiming "STROEBEL THE MURDERER" on its front page—Eyerly's testimony that his companion shot Marshall for a fistful of twenty-dollar gold coins clearly "fixed the murder on Stroebel." And again, the American papers were even more dramatic. In bold, front-page headlines, the *Seattle Post-Intelligencer* declared: "A MURDER CONFESSED—[David] Eyerly Accuses Albert Stroebel of Killing Marshall—Huntingdon Mystery Cleared."

The story received another boost when the preliminary hearing for Stroebel and Eyerly was held ten days later. The purpose of the preliminary hearing was to determine whether there was enough evidence to take the accused to trial; only the Crown presented witnesses, but defence counsel was allowed to cross-examine them. On May 8, the hearing opened at the New Westminster district courthouse in front of George Pittendrigh, who as a magistrate had the authority to hear the case, acting as both judge and jury. The defendants were represented by Aulay Morrison, a rising young lawyer from Nova Scotia. The courtroom was packed, and one reporter noted the contrast in how the two defendants were bearing up: "Stroebel looked pale and worried, while Eyerly did not seem to mind his position at all."

The Crown presented its witnesses throughout that day and into the next, with Morrison asking the occasional pointed question. When the last witness stepped down from the stand, there was little doubt which way the verdict would go. Pittendrigh ordered the defendants to stand, then asked if either had anything to say about the allegations made against them.

"I have nothing to say," Stroebel replied softy.

"I have nothing to say," a smirking Eyerly echoed.

Pittendrigh cleared his throat and delivered his decision: "This court commits both prisoners to stand trial in the wilful murder of John Marshall at the next assize"—in one month's time.

❀

As May gave way to June, legal preparations for the spring assize of the New Westminster district court proceeded apace. The *Daily Columbian* reported that public excitement was growing over what promised to be "the most formidable session" in years. Three murder cases, involving six defendants; one attempted murder; the seduction of an underaged girl; and a grab bag of lesser cases—all presided over by the legendary justice, Matthew Begbie. So when the assize opened on the morning of June 7 in the main chamber of the New Westminster courthouse, the room was full wall-to-wall.

As Begbie settled into his high-backed chair, he glared at the restive spectators and reporters who wanted nothing less than a good show. Begbie himself revelled in the theatrics of the court, as long as he was the starring player. He displayed a haughty disdain for everyone else in the courtroom, believing they failed to show due respect for what was the highest criminal court in the justice system. Every spring, then in fall, the assize court would sit in each of the province's judicial districts to hear the most serious cases. Sometimes the docket was light, the cases decided inside a week; when the docket was heavy, the assize could sit into a third or fourth week.

The high expectations held for the 1893 spring assize were soon dashed. Judge Begbie's first order of business was to postpone two of the murder trials until the fall assize and dismiss the third murder charge for lack of evidence. In the first case—against two Indigenous Chehalis men charged with murdering the son of George Pittendrigh—the Crown requested the postponement so the trial could proceed under the new Criminal Code, which would take effect the following month. The second case—against Stroebel and Eyerly—was pushed back because Superintendent Moresby had fallen ill and was unable to appear in court. The Crown convinced Begbie that its case could not proceed without the superintendent's active involvement. At the time, the press reported that Moresby had suffered from exhaustion and "a mild sunstroke" while working on the case; he had taken to bed the previous Sunday and was still there three days later.

The superintendent was certainly overworked: on top of his day-job as warden of New Westminster Gaol, his policing duties included investigating all the major violent crimes in the Lower Mainland, with almost no support or backup. His workload was even heavier during a big case such as the Marshall murder, when he spent long hours collecting all the evidence the Crown needed at trial. However, the public explanation that Moresby was suffering from "mild sunstroke" was rather thin. Given his robust constitution and the length of time he stayed bedridden, the illness was likely something much more serious. Moresby would die three years later, an apparently hearty, active forty-nine-year-old, and the official cause of death was given as "inflammation of the lungs," one of those overly broad diagnoses doctors used at the time. We know today that lung inflammation can be caused by angina or congestive heart failure. While doctors routinely missed it, heart disease was a common ailment for late Victorian men, and Moresby was a good candidate. A stocky, well-fed man approaching his fiftieth birthday, he enjoyed the rich diet of his times—high in fat, red meat and cholesterol. Making matters worse, Moresby's job was psychologically stressful and alternated sedentary desk-work with bouts of strenuous physical exertion. The superintendent's 1893 illness could well have been a minor stroke or heart attack.

Whatever its true nature, Moresby's mysterious illness was serious enough to push the trial of Stroebel and Eyerly back five months. Before clearing the case from the docket, Begbie gave the Crown the opportunity to obtain a true bill—an indictment—from the grand jury, which was sitting patiently in the courtroom. A body of up to twenty-three men, a grand jury was empanelled at the beginning of each assize. For each case presented, the jury met in a closed session apart from the main court to hear witnesses presented by the Crown. It then returned to court to notify the judge of its verdict: either to issue an indictment against the defendant or to throw out the charge because of insufficient evidence. In the matter of Reg. v. Albert Stroebel and David Eyerly, the Crown dutifully presented its case *in camera* to the grand jury, which returned late that afternoon with a true bill. And with that, Begbie closed the one-day assize—"the shortest on record," noted a disappointed *Daily Columbian*.

❖

The New Westminster spring assize of 1893 lasted a mere six hours, and that included the break for lunch. Thanks to the short day, the judge, lawyers and spectators could make it home for supper with plenty of time to spare. The fallout for Stroebel and Eyerly was not so timely. No doubt, the pair were relieved that the postponement pushed back any reckoning they might have with the gallows, yet it also added five months onto their time in prison awaiting their day in court. By the time their trial opened in November, the pair would have spent seven months of their young lives in the New Westminster Gaol. The delay also meant their trial would be conducted under the provisions of the new Criminal Code, which for the first time permitted defendants to testify on their own behalf. That change would have a momentous impact on the outcome of both trials in the murder of John Marshall.

For the first half of those seven months in the New Westminster Gaol, Stroebel was kept on the first floor of the men's block while Eyerly was the sole occupant of the women's ward. The isolation did not suit the boy prisoner, who plagued his guards with a stream of one-way conversations. The prison routine was broken the first week of June when Eyerly was visited by attorney Andrew Leamy, who had been temporarily assigned to represent him. After a brief consultation, Leamy called in William Moresby to hear a statement his client wished to make. With lawyer and warden looking on, Eyerly proceeded to recant the confession he had made to Moresby and James Schofield at the end of April. None of the things he had confessed to had happened: he had not met Stroebel the night of the murder; Stroebel had not suggested they go rob John Marshall; he had not accompanied Stroebel down to Marshall's; he had not heard shots fired at Marshall's; Stroebel had not come rushing back with a bag of gold coins.

Moresby glared at the boy. The superintendent was confident that his years of experience dealing with criminals gave him a special ability to tell when a person was lying; he was also someone who did not change his mind easily. Moresby had been skeptical when he first heard Eyerly's statement, but after giving such a stern warning about lying, he came around to believing the confession. Now the young prisoner's life was on the line, and the boy was asking the superintendent to change his mind again. The hardwired pathways of Moresby's brain refused to change course again, and he left Eyerly's cell without saying a word. In the months leading up to the trial, the superintendent remained convinced that Eyerly's confession was the truth, and that it was a decisive piece in the case against both the boy and Stroebel.

The wholesale retraction of his confession gave Eyerly a jolt of excitement, but the buzz was short-lived, and within hours, he returned to the drab routine of prison life. Then, two weeks later, his life brightened when a new prisoner was brought into the neighbouring cell. Ben Kennedy was a lean man in his late twenties, with striking blue eyes, a trim moustache and the easy air of a born grifter. Under the name Jack Myers, he had blazed a trail of crime across Washington state, from theft, to forgery, to prison break. With a bounty on his head and a posse at his heels, he fled across the border, adopted a new name and finagled a boat filled with contraband whisky. He headed north to Read Island, between the mainland and Vancouver Island, where he fell in with a group of loggers who proved eager customers for his liquor. After a night of heavy drinking, the short-fused Kennedy took offence to something Jack O'Connor, one of his new friends, said about his dog. Guns were drawn, shots fired and when the smoke cleared, O'Connor lay dead, his chest torn open by a slug from Kennedy's Colt .44 revolver.

Kennedy was hunted down, arrested and thrown into the New Westminster Gaol. Why he was placed in the women's ward is not clear. Authorities may have taken his cockiness and bragging ways— he boasted the Read Island victim was the fourth man he had killed— as signs of an unstable mind. To Eyerly, though, his new neighbour was a godsend. Here was someone the boy could look up to, someone who flaunted the law, used people as he liked and cared only for himself—it was as if Jesse James himself had walked into the next cell. We do not know what the two talked about as they whiled away the time waiting for their November trial dates, but it is not hard to imagine Kennedy spinning tales of murder and mayhem, the mentor tutoring his young protégé in the darker facts of life.

Eyerly and Kennedy's splendid isolation ended over the summer when the provincial jail received one of its rare female prisoners and the pair were moved to the men's block, with Eyerly placed three cells down from Albert Stroebel. All that separated the co-defendants were two, six-foot-wide cells. One of those units was empty; the other was occupied by Charles Collins, a thirty-two-year-old native of Jamaica serving a four-month sentence for a bar fight. Prior to this, Stroebel and Eyerly had never discussed their case. Guards were lax in imposing the ban on prisoners talking and now that they were near neighbours, the pair took the opportunity to find out what the other was thinking, since their fate might well hang on what the other would say in court. Other prisoners, even guards, caught snippets of what the two said.

"Hey, Al, how do you think we're going to come out?" Charles Collins would later recall Eyerly asking.

"I don't know," Stroebel answered in a stage whisper. "I guess we'll come out alright. All you have to do when you go to court is say you don't know nothing about it all."

"Alright, Al, guess you're right. But you fired two shots, right?"

"Oh, go on to bed. I'll talk to you in the morning."

Guard Richard Lister overheard a similar conversation, even though he admitted he was too far away to hear the prisoners' voices clearly.

"Al, you did fire two shots, didn't you? What did you fire at?" Lister heard Eyerly ask.

"A stump, just a stump."

After another string of questions from Eyerly, Stroebel snapped angrily: "You told a dreadful lie on me! What you done that for?" The rest of the conversation was lost in the noise of the cell block, except at the end when Eyerly threw a crude racist slur at Collins.

Again because of lax enforcement of the ban on conversation, inmates had the opportunity to talk during recess period, when they were taken from their cells and herded into a common area. Charles Brown was a twenty-four-year-old Englishman serving a one-year sentence for drunk and disorderly conduct. He approached Eyerly one recess and asked him what he was in for.

"For telling a lie, on Al."

"What was the lie?" Brown listened with alarm as Eyerly recapped the statement he had given Moresby and Schofield.

"What was your object in telling such a lie?"

"I reckoned Mr. Moresby would fetch me over here. Keep me at the hotel and give me $3.50 a day."

"Don't you have better sense than to swear a man's life away?"

"I'll tell a different story when I get to court," Eyerly shrugged. Brown shook his head in disbelief as the boy prisoner sauntered off.

❧

While Eyerly and Stroebel awaited their trial date, Superintendent Moresby divided his time between his duties as prison warden and police work on a string of serious crimes. The Marshall murder was the most complex of these cases, and the superintendent did his best to produce and preserve the evidence the Crown would need for convictions. This work did not always go as smoothly as Moresby would have liked. As we shall see, key pieces of evidence in the Marshall case would be mislaid or mishandled and important paperwork improperly completed. Illness and overwork hampered the superintendent even more. Moresby was slow to recover from the mysterious ailment that struck him in early summer, and when he got back to work, he was shocked to discover that he had lost his police notebook for the weeks between Eyerly and Stroebel's arrests and their preliminary hearing.

As Moresby gathered evidence for the Crown, the defence was also busy. From the preliminary hearing onward, Stroebel was represented by Aulay Morrison. The young lawyer could not call upon the resources available to the Crown and police, meagre as they were, so he enlisted the help of Oliver Ackerman, the forty-eight-year-old brother of Asa. Born in New York state, Oliver Ackerman was only seventeen years old when he joined the Union Army to fight in the American Civil War, serving one year in the infantry and two years in the cavalry. Following the war, Oliver married and headed west to California, settling in Petaluma, north of San Francisco.

In 1883, he moved his wife and young children to Sumas prairie, where he pre-empted 160 acres along the southeastern border of John Marshall's property. Oliver purchased another 380 acres over the following years, making him the largest landholder on the prairie. Throughout the 1880s, he divided his time between Sumas and New Westminster, where he ran a thriving construction company in partnership with his brother Theron. Asa remained in Sumas, keeping an eye on his brother's properties. From what we can tell, Oliver first met George Stroebel Sr. in the late 1870s, when the two families lived in Petaluma. The Stroebel clan arrived on Sumas prairie just after the

Ackermans, and George Sr. rented Oliver's farmstead before staking his own claim in Aldergrove. During these years, Oliver saw the Stroebel children grow up; after their mother died, George Jr. and Albert frequently worked for Oliver's father, Erastus, and on occasion, for Oliver himself.

Like other locals, Oliver was shocked by the news of Marshall's death, but he could not believe Albert Stroebel had any part in it. Oliver knew more than most about the murder, since his brother Asa was the first to take control of the crime scene and witnessed Marshall's autopsy. Oliver was also one of the first to know of Stroebel's fishing alibi, hearing it from Bettie Boley, his married sister. James Silverthorne told Boley about the talk he had with Albert the Sunday it occurred.

Confident that Stroebel was innocent and acting from what he later described as a "sense of deep conviction," Oliver Ackerman visited the young prisoner at the New Westminster Gaol on two occasions, once just before the preliminary hearing, then again a week later. After each prison visit, Ackerman travelled to Sumas to investigate leads Stroebel had given him, with Aulay Morrison accompanying him on the first trip. The pair examined Stroebel's room at the City Hotel, interviewed Margaret and Elizabeth Bartlett, then inspected the alley where David Lucas claimed to have found the two spent cartridges. The alley was wet and muddy, and there was a shallow pool of water under Stroebel's window. The defence pair were convinced that the two cartridges could not have stayed as clean as they were when Lucas found them if Stroebel had dumped them there, which meant the marshal had planted them. Ackerman and Morrison also interviewed a number of Sumas City residents who testified to the lad's good reputation.

On his second trip to Sumas City, Ackerman crossed paths with Lucas, whom he had first seen at the preliminary hearing. According to his own version of their conversation, Ackerman dismissed the evidence presented at the hearing: "I can't see there was much against Albert."

Lucas scowled back that Ackerman was prejudiced, that Stroebel was guilty, and that the young man had a bad reputation in Sumas City: "I been watching him for some time, before the murder, trying to get a hold of him. I don't know if they have enough evidence to hang him. If they don't, and he comes back here, I'll make it damned hot for the son of a bitch." The marshal then attacked William Moresby: "If it hadn't been for me, Moresby would have made a botch of the case."

Ackerman was shocked by Lucas's comments, which only deepened his suspicion that the marshal was playing a malicious and illegal role in the murder investigation. Given Lucas's questionable past and his reputation in Sumas City, the suspicion was not out of place.

First Trial: The Bloody Assizes

At eleven o'clock on the morning of Wednesday, November 8, Justice John McCreight walked into the main courtroom at the New Westminster law courts, ascended five steps leading up to the judge's bench and took his seat. Before calling the fall assize of the New Westminster district court into session, he paused to survey the scene. A low railing split the high-ceilinged room in two. Behind the railing, the space reserved for the public was packed tight with spectators. In front of the railing and to his left were the empty jury seats, waiting to be filled. Behind and above them, a row of high, narrow windows ran the length of the wall, each with a transom at the top to circulate air when opened. The three long oak tables directly in front of him were occupied by the Crown and defence counsel, along with various court officials. To his right, the witness stand rose two steps off the floor, set apart by a U-shaped railing three feet high. Seats reserved for reporters and members of the bar were bunched against the right-side wall; extra chairs had been brought in and all were filled.

The *Daily Columbian* reported that the morning's crowd was "the largest in the history of the court. The intense local interest in several of the most important cases was no doubt the cause." Vancouver's *Daily News Advertiser* agreed: "No such vital interest has ever been shown in any criminal case here as in those upon the docket of the fall assize of 1893." Five months earlier, the spring assize had failed to live up to the high expectations of court watchers. The disappointing spring session would be forgotten with the opening of the "bloody assize" of fall 1893—an epithet first used more than a decade earlier, during the trial for the murderers of police constable Johnny Ussher, but which more aptly fit the current docket. An unprecedented number of cases involving the most serious crimes appeared on its docket: six defendants were charged with murder in four separate cases of homicide; five other defendants faced charges of rape, kidnapping, physical assault, seduction and escape from prison.

For those who could not attend in person, blanket coverage in local papers fed the appetite for news of the trials. At the height of the two biggest trials—for the murders of Alfred Pittendrigh and John Marshall—nearly one-half of the news pages in issues of the *Daily Columbian* and *Daily News Advertiser* were taken up with coverage of the proceedings.

To newspaper editors in the 1890s, sensational trials involving murder, sex and greed were godsends. They provided inch after inch of copy to feed the insatiable appetite of readers for news, distraction and entertainment. Late Victorians had ushered in the first age of mass media, when mass-circulation newspapers dominated the public eye—and nothing drew that eye's attention as much as murder. Despite the tut-tutting of professional moralists, late Victorians had acquired a taste for murder, both imaginary and real. The novels of Charles Dickens were full of violence and death, as were the writings of Edgar Allan Poe, who carried his readers into the darkest realms. Dickens's close friend Wilkie Collins wrote what many consider the first mystery novel in English, *The Moonstone*; and Arthur Conan Doyle created Sherlock Holmes, the most revered detective in fiction. Penny-dreadfuls and dime-novels brought formulaic tales of murder, mystery and derring-do to ever wider audiences.

Real life provided even greater tales of depravity. In 1888 and 1889, the world was riveted by the horrors of the Whitechapel killings, the murder and mutilation of at least five London prostitutes attributed to Jack the Ripper. Three years later, the story of Massachusetts spinster Lizzie Borden captured the headlines: the grisly axe-murders of her parents, what most considered her obvious guilt, her dramatic trial and shocking acquittal. These were just the two most celebrated cases. Before, in between and after, newspapers and magazines fed their readers a steady diet of violence, death and crime.

On Thursday morning, November 9, British Columbia's "bloody assize" of 1893 opened the first of four murder cases on its docket. On trial was Ben Kennedy, the American outlaw who had been held in the cell next to David Eyerly over the summer. Kennedy was charged with killing Jack O'Connor after a night of drinking in a logging camp off the coast of northern Vancouver Island. The three-day trial took place in the main courtroom, the same chamber where Eyerly and Stroebel's fates would be tried the following week. Attorney General Theodore Davie, ashen-white from illness, appeared for the Crown; Judge McCreight's colleague, Justice Norman Bole, presided.

Davie's case rested on what courts at the time considered direct evidence—the testimony of eyewitnesses. One by one, Crown witnesses who had been in the logging cabin pieced together the events of June 25: the long night of drinking; the argument that broke out between Kennedy and O'Connor over the former's dog; the multiple

The main courtroom in the New Westminster Courthouse, where the first trial for the murder of John Marshall took place. The judge's bench, witness box, defence and Crown tables can be seen. Part of the railing for the jury box is visible on the far right, as is one of the room's high windows. New Westminster Archives, IHP 10001-1428

shots fired; and O'Connor lying dead with a gaping bullet hole in his chest. To corroborate this testimony, Davie called on local gunsmith Samuel Webb, who testified that the calibre of the bullet taken from O'Connor matched the calibre of the defendant's gun.

The defence counsel, Charles Wilson, countered that, even if they had been present during the shooting, the Crown witnesses themselves had participated in the drinking orgy, thus their testimony could not be relied upon. Moreover, the fatal shot was fired during a confused scuffle in a darkened room, with other rounds going off in every direction. Kennedy himself took the stand to tell his version of events. This was the first time in BC that a defendant had been called to testify in his own defence, something the new Criminal Code allowed.

Closing arguments from the defence, Crown, and judge pushed the trial into Saturday night. At 10:30 p.m., the jury retreated for deliberation, returning at midnight with its verdict: "guilty of manslaughter without any recommendation for mercy." Deeply disappointed that Kennedy had dodged a murder conviction, and with that an automatic death sentence, Judge Bole sentenced the American to life in prison, the stiffest penalty he could impose.

Kennedy would serve only two months of his life sentence. In mid-January 1894, a group of inmates was on work duty in the prison yard of the BC Penitentiary. On a pre-arranged signal the inmates rioted, pelting guards with rocks and sticks. Kennedy broke free from the mob and headed for a low point in the prison wall, but was cut down by rifle fire. Gravely wounded, he was brought back to the infirmary where he died a few days later.

❖

The second case of murder on the fall docket lacked elements that had made Kennedy's trial so sensational. There was no brazen outlaw, drunken shootout, dramatic capture and fitting end. The story of Walter Sangster was sad and tragic, a tale of drink, mental illness and free access to deadly firearms. The story of Sangster's victim, Capilano

Tommy, was even sadder, one of random, pointless death. Sangster was a twenty-four-year-old lumberman from New Hampshire who had come west in search of work, but like so many others in the wake of the 1893 economic crash, he was having no luck. After visiting Tacoma and Victoria, he landed in Vancouver in early September, where again he could not find a job. Sangster seldom drank, but on the afternoon of September 11, he bought a bottle of whisky in a fit of despondency and quickly became drunk. Staggering down the street, he came across an Indigenous man known as Capilano Tommy, who was resting on a bench beside the road. Without uttering a word, Sangster raised his revolver and shot the stranger dead. He then fired shots at two other men walking by and at the constable who apprehended him.

When Sangster sobered up in a police cell, he had no recollection of the fatal events. He broke down at his trial, begging forgiveness for his violent deed. Sangster's lawyer presented evidence that the defendant was afflicted with an extreme sensitivity to alcohol, as were his father and mother, so that even the smallest amount made him go mad. (This was the same affliction that had led to the death of author Edgar Allan Poe, decades earlier, a death long wrapped in mystery.) Late Victorian newspapers blamed Sangster's actions on alcohol and put in a plug for temperance, but the needless death would not have happened if the defendant had not had ready access to a handgun. Sangster's remorse and the mitigating evidence were enough for the jury to come back with a conviction for manslaughter rather than murder, and he was given a twelve-year sentence.

❖

The third murder case got underway Monday morning, November 13, in the New Westminster city hall. The trial of Stroebel and Eyerly began that same day in the courthouse's main chamber. City hall was a few blocks away, the nearest building with a room large enough to accommodate another major trial. A father and son from the Chehalis First Nation along Harrison River—identified in the records only as Jack and Peter—were charged with the murder of Albert Pittendrigh,

the twenty-four-year-old son of George Pittendrigh. On a foggy
night in October 1892, a New Westminster constable had stumbled
upon Albert lying face down in the bushes along a trail that led from
the city to the Fraser River. Pittendrigh was barely alive, shot in the
back of the head; he was carried to a nearby hospital where he died a
few hours later, his father at his bedside.

A manhunt for his killer was immediately launched, led by Superintendent Moresby. Peter was arrested the next day in his tent, which
was pitched just below the spot where the body had been found. Jack
was arrested a week later, after Peter's wife, Mary, gave a statement
implicating him in the killing. Father and son languished in the New
Westminster Gaol for a full year before going to trial. Their case came
too late to be included in the docket of the 1892 fall assize, then six
months later, their case was pushed from the spring 1893 session to
the fall. As their trial got underway, Peter and Jack assumed a placid
demeanour that would see them through the proceedings, but the year
in prison had left its mark. The two men had spent their entire lives
working outside; in prison, their copper skin had turned sallow, and
their lean, muscular frames had softened from disuse.

The Crown's case, presented by Deputy Attorney General A.G.
Smith, appeared strong. Weaving circumstantial evidence with eyewitness testimony, Smith presented his version of events for that day
more than a year earlier. In mid-afternoon on October 27, 1892, Pittendrigh had walked from the city to the riverfront in search of a ca-
noe he believed some Indigenous men had stolen. When he returned
up the trail some time later, he was unaware that Peter and Jack were
waiting in ambush. As Pittendrigh passed by, Peter stepped out from
behind a bush, raised a revolver and shot him in the back of the head.

The Crown's key witness was Mary, Peter's wife. Mary testified that
she witnessed the crime as it unfolded: her father-in-law, Jack, loading
the revolver in his tent, father and son crouching behind bushes along
the trail, Jack handing the gun to his son, Pittendrigh walking past
them on the trail, and Peter stepping forward to fire the fatal shot.
Questioned about motive, Mary claimed her husband was convinced
that she and Pittendrigh had been lovers two years earlier, when the

two men had worked at the Harrison River fish hatchery. With his father egging him on, Peter had killed the young man in revenge.

The defence attacked Mary's credibility, presenting witnesses who claimed she had confessed to them that she had killed Pittendrigh when he sexually assaulted her. Peter and Jack took the stand and insisted that Mary had confessed to the killing. Parts of Peter's testimony were contradicted by witnesses for both the Crown and the defence, including his own father. Although the opposing testimony did not cover Peter's alleged role in the shooting itself, the contradictions undercut his credibility.

The case was handed to the jurors on Saturday, November 18, and after half an hour of deliberation, the jury came back with the dreaded words: "We find the prisoners at the bar guilty of the wilful murder of Albert Edward Pittendrigh." The packed courtroom breathed with relief as Judge Eli Harrison handed down the death sentences and set the date of execution for January 15.

New Westminster's White residents applauded the verdict. After his death a year earlier, the press and public had lionized Albert as "a general favorite in a wide circle of acquaintances, without an enemy in the world so far as is known." Despite the fact he had never stuck to one job or vocation, he was depicted as the promising son of a respected city elder, a father who had risked his life for Queen and country. As a member of the local militia, he was given a full military funeral and hundreds turned out when the procession wound through the streets. Not a single voice was permitted to besmirch young Pittendrigh's character or to ask what the young man had been doing so close to Mary's tent. At least publicly, all agreed with the coroner jury's conclusion that "the true evidence proves he was not in the locality for any immoral motives." Of course, the fact that the jury felt the need to explicitly deny that Pittendrigh had any immoral motives demonstrated that some people were thinking that he might have.

The reaction was different up the Fraser Valley, closer to Mary and Peter's home village. Elders at Chehalis and Sumas (where Mary's aunt lived) wrote their Indian Agent insisting that numerous witnesses had heard Mary say she had killed Pittendrigh in self-defence, and that their people believed the confession. Charles Tate, the Methodist minister who ran the Coqualeetza School in Chilliwack, dared to say what others thought: if the two Chehalis men had killed Pittendrigh, "it was because he was where he ought not to have been. This question was studiously avoided on all sides, but the fact of his body being found a few yards from Mary and Peter's tent tells the tale too plainly."

Neither the press nor the defence counsel was willing to dig into Pittendrigh's prior relationship with Peter and Mary—doing so would have put the case into an entirely different light. Peter and Pittendrigh knew each other well, because they had worked together at the Harrison hatchery for some years and had lived in neighbouring houses. The young bachelor sometimes took his shirts to Mary to clean, paying her twenty-five cents per shirt. Peter was furious when he heard this: twenty-five cents was half the price of a new shirt, and Peter was convinced Pittendrigh was paying Mary for sex as well as for laundering.

We cannot know the true story of what happened the afternoon of Pittendrigh's death. Peter may well have been the shooter, thinking—either rightly or wrongly—that Pittendrigh had had a sexual relationship with Mary and was down by the riverfront looking for more. Or Mary could have killed the young man after he assaulted her. What we do know is that the tale became cloudy enough by the time it reached Ottawa that the cabinet and Governor General decided to commute Peter and Jack's death sentences to life in prison.

❖

The trial of the two young defendants indicted for the murder of John Marshall also began on Monday, November 13. An air of excitement filled New Westminster's main courtroom as the legal players took their seats. The cast was a who's-who of BC's legal and political scene: the judge was a former premier and Attorney General; Crown counsel was the current premier and Attorney General; and defence counsel was a future Supreme Court justice.

Justice John McCreight, BC's first premier, presided over Albert Stroebel's first trial with his usual aloofness. When given the chance in the trial, though, he failed to apply the deep knowledge of the law he was reputed to possess. Royal BC Museum and Archives, A-01449

John McCreight was in his fourteenth year as chief justice of the New Westminster district court. Born in Ireland sixty-six years earlier, McCreight had arrived in Victoria in 1860 and became BC's first premier and Attorney General in 1871. In 1880, he was Crown counsel in the trial of Alexander Hare and the three McLean brothers (Allan, Archie and Charlie) for the murder of police constable John Ussher. McCreight's successful prosecution of the notorious quartet led to his appointment to the New Westminster bench that same year. Aloof, often irritable, and hard of hearing, McCreight was known for his extensive legal knowledge and his strict adherence to the letter of the law. In physical appearance, he was perfectly suited to his role: his full, silver-white beard seemed an extension of the thick, cropped wig he wore on the bench, and his black robe fell elegantly over a tall, athletic frame. As he gazed down from the bench, many a witness, counsel and defendant were unsettled by his cold, aristocratic air.

The man who presented the Crown's case against Stroebel and Eyerly was not one of those intimidated by McCreight's gravitas. Just forty-one years old, Theodore Davie had risen quickly to the top of BC's political and legal world since arriving in Victoria as a young immigrant from England a quarter-century earlier. Locally trained, Davie was just twenty-eight when he represented Alexander Hare at the Ussher trial, crossing swords with Crown counsel McCreight.

In 1886, Davie secured his reputation as one of BC's most formidable lawyers when he defended Robert Sproule. Even though his client was convicted, Davie's courtroom performance convinced much of the public that Sproule was innocent. Meanwhile, Davie's political star was rising; he became Attorney General in 1889 and premier three years later, all the while keeping his private practice open.

The punishing workload Davie maintained throughout his professional life occasionally took its toll. During the first week of November 1893, Davie was confined to bed with an unspecified but serious illness. On November 9, he rose from his sickbed to take up the Crown's case against Ben Kennedy. The

Theodore Davie, premier, Attorney General and Crown prosecutor at both of Stroebel's trials. Davie was brilliant and unrelenting, particularly in his cross examination of Stroebel himself. Royal BC Museum and Archives, A-01219

Kennedy verdict came in just after midnight on Saturday, November 11, which gave the Attorney General just one day to rest and refocus before the Marshall murder trial began. As he returned to the Crown's table Monday morning, the effects of illness and hard work still showed on Davie's face—the pallor of his skin made all the whiter against his thick, black beard, itself streaked with grey. Yet as he looked over the crowded courtroom, his dark eyes were as alive and piercing as ever.

The slightest smile flitted across Davie's lips as he locked eyes with his opponent, Stroebel's defence attorney, Aulay Morrison. The Nova Scotia native was thirty years old and had been practising law on the west coast for three years. The Stroebel trial was Morrison's first high-profile case. By the end of his client's second trial, Morrison had caught the attention of the public and press as a rising star in the province's legal firmament. Morrison would go on to a long career as a superior court judge, but he was at his best as a defence lawyer. His quick wit, aggressive questioning and cutting asides made him an effective advocate for the accused. Many of his colleagues, who felt the courtroom was a place for decorum and drily reasoned argument, were alienated by his rough-and-tumble style and willingness to push boundaries. His methods also irritated trial judges, but Morrison never backed down when faced with a hostile justice. In court, Morrison sported a lean, hungry look, his narrow face and wiry body leaning forward as he grilled a witness or drove home an argument. An extravagant walrus mustache hid his mouth, but behind it an amused smirk or dismissive sneer played across his lips.

Seated beside Morrison at the defence table was the counsel for David Eyerly. Louis Ekstein was just twenty-six years old, the only member of the BC bar who had been born in the province (his father had set up a feed store in Victoria in the 1860s). Morrison would take the lead defence role throughout the trial, including the cross-examination of Crown witnesses. Ekstein would call and question witnesses on matters directly related to Eyerly's guilt or innocence; his own client would be one of those witnesses.

❖

Theodore Davie's first move in the trial against Stroebel and Eyerly surprised Judge McCreight and shocked the public gallery. Putting on as cool a front as possible, the Attorney General requested that the true bill issued against the defendants at the spring assize be declared null and void. Audible gasps rippled through the courtroom, and Davie hastened to explain that the indictment in question had not been completed according to specifications laid down in the new Criminal Code. Morrison shot to his feet and demanded that his client be discharged "on the ground that there was no indictment now against him before the court." The Attorney General countered by presenting a newly drafted indictment, asking that the grand jury retire to consider it. McCreight dismissed Morrison's objection and authorized Davie's request; the grand jury withdrew and returned a while later with an approved true bill.

The pool of potential jurors was then ushered into the room and jury selection began. After a half-dozen disqualifications for a number of trifling reasons—for instance, John Tyre was excused for being insane—the required twelve were selected and Andrew Ross sworn in as foreman. The court clerk then stepped forward to read the indictments. Albert Stroebel was charged with "the wilful murder of John Marshall," and David Eyerly with the lesser crimes of "accessory before the fact to robbery, and accessory after the fact to murder." Asked how he pled, Stroebel stammered, confused by the morning's legal manoeuvres; recovering, he managed a shaky "Not guilty." Eyerly looked on with his usual mocking smile, and to the same question replied, "NOT GUILTY!"

Despite Eyerly's cheek, the stakes for the defendants could not have been higher. If found guilty as an accessory to murder after the fact, Eyerly faced a life sentence; conviction on the robbery charge alone would net him up to fourteen years in prison. For Stroebel, a conviction for murder brought an automatic death sentence (although that could be commuted to life imprisonment upon appeal to the federal cabinet and Governor General). Nor would Stroebel find relief if the jury were convinced he had not intended to kill Marshall, but did so while trying to rob him. The most straightforward definition provided by the new Criminal Code stated that the killing of another person was murder "If the offender means to cause the death of the person killed." But in the code, it was also murder "If the offender, for any unlawful object [such as robbery], does an act which he knows or ought to have known to be likely to cause death, and thereby kills any person, though he may have desired that his object should be effected without hurting anyone." Over seven full days, witnesses would testify, attorneys argue, the judge adjudicate and the jury deliberate—with the lives of two young defendants hanging in the balance.

CASE FOR THE CROWN

Shafts of sunlight shone through the high windows of New Westminster's main courtroom as the trial in the murder of John Marshall resumed Monday afternoon, November 13. With the barometer rising and clouds breaking up, the federal meteorologist for New Westminster forecast cold, clear days ahead. While the air outside cooled, the temperature inside rose. The courtroom was packed tight with bodies, itchy and perspiring under thick woollen clothes. The central heating system was modern, something of a novelty: a mammoth, coal-fired boiler in the basement delivered steam to the radiators that lined the walls. However, the temperature was set at the boiler, one level for the whole building with no way to adjust it for individual rooms. As the trial progressed, the air inside the chamber would grow heavy and hot, relieved only when the window transoms were opened to let in gusts of cold air.

At 1:30, Justice McCreight took his place behind the bench and peered down with displeasure at the two defendants. Stroebel was staring vacantly at the coat of arms hanging above the bench, and Eyerly was glancing about restlessly, trying to catch others looking at him. The twelve jurors bent forward, keenly awaiting the start of proceedings. Displayed on a table in front of them was a five-foot-long, ink-on-linen map, prepared for the Crown by professional surveyors, which depicted the territory from Sumas City south of the border to William Blair's house three miles north. The distances between various locations were given and an enlarged sketch of Marshall's farmstead appeared as an inset. Sites of significant events were also noted: the field Marshall and Blair ploughed the day of the murder; where Stroebel and Porter ditched and where they milked Porter's cow; the gate where a mysterious boot print was discovered; the spot on the CPR line where Archibald Baxter saw Stroebel; and the point in Sumas City where Frank Warnock passed Stroebel later that night.

McCreight let the silence in the chamber stretch out before turning his gaze to Theodore Davie and nodding. Davie rose, adjusted his robe over his sloping shoulders, then launched into a brief summary of the case he would present. As he talked, the Attorney General dramatically produced Stroebel's revolver and cartridges and explained their significance. He described "the boot print of the peculiarly shaped foot of a lame man" discovered in Marshall's farmyard, and he noted the confession made by David Eyerly, which implicated both defendants. Stroebel broke in with a scornful laugh at this, drawing a pause from Davie and a menacing glare from Justice McCreight. The Attorney General then concluded that, taken together, the physical evidence and witness testimony presented by the Crown would form an unbroken "chain of circumstantial evidence" that demonstrated the defendants' guilt.

Davie's use of this phrase was neither novel nor casual. Most trials in the Victorian era relied in whole or in part on circumstantial evidence. In an age before forensic science, only the testimony of eyewitnesses was considered "direct evidence," yet most serious crimes were not witnessed by third parties. At the same time, juries were often reluctant to convict a defendant of a hanging offence based on circumstantial evidence alone. In the mid-nineteenth century, the concept of the "unbroken chain of evidence" emerged in jurisprudence to get around this problem. A case based on circumstantial evidence could be made against a defendant by viewing each piece of circumstantial evidence, not on its own in isolation, but as part of a larger chain of circumstances. If each link of the chain was sound, and the links together formed a logical and convincing case, then the jury could return a guilty verdict in good conscience. If any part of the chain was weak, or if the overall case was not credible, then the jury could acquit. There were no eyewitnesses to the killing of John Marshall nor, Davie recognized, was there a singular piece of physical evidence that left no doubt that the defendants had committed the crime. So the

Attorney General needed to forge his chain from the circumstances surrounding the crime, piecing them together link by link.

Moving from his opening statement to his first witnesses, Davie set out to track Albert Stroebel's movements and actions on Wednesday, April 19. William Blair and William Porter were called to the stand, where they repeated the evidence they had given at earlier hearings: Blair helping Marshall with his ploughing, Stroebel aiding Porter in ditching, and the last either saw of the victim and defendant. In the most critical part of his testimony, Porter described seeing Stroebel with a gun that afternoon soon after they started ditching.

"Stroebel pulled his coat off and throwed it down."

"What then?" Davie prompted.

"Well, he threw a revolver on top of it. I don't know where he got the revolver. I just saw him throw one."

Davie held up Stroebel's handgun. "Was the revolver anything like this one?"

"That don't look much like it. I think that one has a longer barrel than the one I saw at the preliminary hearing," Porter frowned, and Davie hurried on to the matter of the milked cow.

When Aulay Morrison rose for his cross-examination, he pressed Porter about the gun: "What was the distance Stroebel threw his coat?"

"Across the ditch, about eight feet."

"Then he would have thrown the coat and revolver *eight feet?*" Morrison asked in disbelief.

"Yes."

Two witnesses were then called who saw Stroebel the evening of the nineteenth. Archie Baxter, the soft-spoken section man for the CPR, spotted Stroebel walking north on the railbed toward Marshall's gate just before 6:00 p.m. Frank Warnock then testified that at 10:00 p.m., he and the defendant had passed each other at the foot of Harrison Road in Sumas City, with Stroebel walking quickly toward the City Hotel. The two men's brief, matter-of-fact testimony was very significant, although few in court realized this at the time. Aside from Eyerly's statement to Superintendent Moresby, not a single witness would say they saw Stroebel between 6:00 and 10:00 p.m., the times set by Baxter and Warnock. Moreover, unlike most of their neighbours, both men carried watches and those watches were set to "railway time," the time set on the Huntingdon railway station clock. Thus, Baxter and Warnock's estimates of the timing of events were more accurate and reliable than those of other witnesses.

The missing hours between 6:00 and 10:00 p.m. were crucial because it was the Crown's contention that Marshall was murdered around 9:00 p.m. that evening. Davie based his estimate of the time of death on the evidence of Ira Airheart. Called to the stand, the trapper repeated his testimony that he had heard Marshall's dog barking at nine o'clock or so while he was having a late supper in his cabin, over half a mile away.

Yet unlike Baxter or Warnock, Airheart did not own a watch, nor did he have a clock in his cabin. He calculated the time of the dog's barking by adding the hours that had passed from the time it had gotten dark, which he testified was around 6:00 p.m.—that is, he estimated that three hours passed between then and the time he heard the dog bark. But the sun set that day at 7:03 p.m., and twilight faded rapidly for another half-hour, which would put the dog barking at ten o'clock or later. The Crown's main evidence as to the time of Marshall's death was far from solid.

❧

The Attorney General turned next to the cause of death, calling up Dr. Boggs. The doctor quickly summarized the findings of his autopsy and provided his interpretation of the results. He identified the two slugs he had extracted from Marshall's body, which were entered as evidence: Exhibit A, taken from the back of Marshall's neck, relatively intact; and Exhibit B, chiselled out of the base of the skull and heavily distorted. As to what caused Marshall's death, Boggs gave the expected answer that the bullet wounds had. He surprised the court, though, when he stated the fatal shot was the shallower one to the nape of the victim's neck, not the deeper one to the forehead.

Justice McCreight broke in, "The back one was the fatal one?"

"Yes, my lord, and death would be instantaneous."

Davie then asked, "Which shot was fired first?"

"My opinion is that the rear wound was inflicted first."

"Will you give us your reasons for that opinion, doctor?"

"I don't know that I could, sir." Puzzled, McCreight repeated Davie's question and received the same response

"I hold that opinion, and still I cannot explain it."

It is not clear why Boggs was so mysterious in his answer, but his evasion did not help Davie's case. Nor did the fact that Boggs's testimony differed from his official autopsy report. The latter had mentioned nothing about which shot had come first and concluded that "one or both of these bullets" caused Marshall's death. The doctor stirred up even more confusion with his response to a question Morrison posed in his cross-examination: if the shot to the back was first, and it instantly killed Marshall, which way would his body have fallen? Boggs answered that if shot from behind, the victim would likely fall forward, if shot from the front he would fall backward.

The jury probably would have accepted the answer if Boggs had left it there. However, the doctor felt it necessary to explain further, veering into speculative psychology to do so: "If shot from behind, the victim would have no apprehension of anything assaulting him. If shot from in front, he would see his antagonist and it would make him naturally throw backwards, which he would not from a shot from behind."

Boggs was even less definitive in fixing the time of death. When asked how long Marshall had been dead from the time of the post-mortem, Boggs replied, "Well, it was a recently dead body. I should suppose less than forty-eight hours."

The autopsy on Marshall began at 9:30 on the morning of April 21, which placed his death as early as 9:30 a.m., April 19. Marshall was seen by many witnesses, alive and well, nearly half a day after that. The doctor provided no help in determining when after 6:00 p.m.—the time Sam Lee left Marshall—the farmer was killed. Davie was disappointed but not surprised by Boggs's answers. Both he and Morrison knew the limits of forensic medicine at the time, and neither made a serious effort to use medical science to determine the time of death.

❖

Davie recognized that Boggs's first-day testimony had been underwhelming, so opening day two of the trial, the Attorney General turned to a more dependable witness to put his case back on solid ground. A respectful hush fell over the courtroom as William Moresby strode purposefully to the stand. Stiff and solid in his well-worn, high-buttoned suit, Moresby was the epitome of British law and order: hard-working rather than quick-thinking; trusting in shoe leather and straight talk rather than deduction and imagination; and above all, honest and incorruptible. Economical and confident from countless court appearances, Moresby described the progress of the case from the time of his arrival at Marshall's house on April 20, through the arrests of Stroebel and Eyerly, to his investigations leading up to the trial. As the superintendent testified, Davie entered into evidence the three leather purses retrieved at Marshall's house: the small bag found on his body containing $10.40, and the two larger pouches uncovered in his house containing ninety dollars in bills and eighty dollars in gold coins.

Davie was finished with Moresby for now, but the superintendent's authoritative presence and testimony re-established the Crown's version of events in the minds of the jurors. Fortunately for Davie, the court was not aware of the chinks in Moresby's investigation of the case. Returning to work after recovering from the mysterious illness that had hit him in early June, Moresby discovered that his police notebook had gone missing. The notebook covered key parts of his frenetic investigations in the two weeks after Marshall's death, so he had to rely on his memory alone in testifying about this crucial period. The superintendent hid this fact—of his lost notebook and extemporaneous testimony—from both the court and the defence counsel.

If William Moresby was the embodiment of the British police officer, then David Lucas was the strutting incarnation of the American

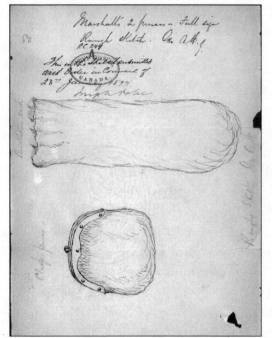

The judge made these sketches of the money purses found in John Marshall's house after the farmer's death, which were then submitted in evidence at trial. The one purse held $90 in banknotes, the other $80 in gold coins. Library and Archives Canada, LAC, RG 13, v. 1428, f. 265A: Statement of Judge Walkem (30 Dec. 1893)

frontier lawman. As Davie called his name, Lucas swaggered across the courtroom and took the stand. His coal-dark eyes darted back and forth across the room, his dense Wyatt Earp moustache twitched with anticipation, and a plug of chewing tobacco bulged between his cheek and gum. He was all coiled nerves and menace, leaning forward as if ready to leap out at his questioner at any moment.

Davie knew there were risks in putting Lucas on the stand, but while he might question the marshal's methods and temperament, the Attorney General could not quibble with his results. It was Lucas who had obtained the key exhibits in the Crown's case during his three days of "knocking about" Sumas City: the revolver he tricked Stroebel into handing over; the rolled note in which the defendant seemed to admit guilt; the two empty shells found in the alleyway; and the two loaded cartridges found in Stroebel's bed. Lucas explained how he had obtained each of these, then described the state of Stroebel's gun when he got it: "There had been two chambers recently fired, two of the cartridges had been thrown out of the gun without being fired, and one chamber had had no cartridge in it for some time." For Davie, the condition of the revolver corroborated the Crown's scenario that Stroebel shot Marshall twice, then back home extracted the cartridges, threw the spent shells out his window and hid the loaded cartridges in his bed.

Lucas greeted Morrison with a smug grin as the defence lawyer approached the witness stand and asked sharply: "When you were 'knocking about' town, trying to produce evidence, you would have left no stone unturned, you having the reputation of hunting up things of this kind?"

Seeing no question there, Lucas mutely stared back.

"Did you search long for the two empty shells in the alley?"

"No, sir, they were right on top of the ground."

"They were .38 calibre bullets. Are those quite common in Sumas City?" Lucas admitted they were, that he himself carried several for his revolver.

Morrison drew out the silence, then snapped, "You did not put these two cartridges in the alley yourself—these shells?"

"No, sir, I did not!"

Morrison smoothly shifted topic. "Did you drink at all during this time you were working on Stroebel in this matter?"

"Yes, sir, I took a drink. I take one, I presume, every day."

"Did you eat on that day, the 22nd?"

"I didn't eat anything that day, for sure."

"You must have been quite dizzy, knocking about so much," Morrison mocked, then shifted to the conversation Lucas had that led to Stroebel handing over his revolver. "Now, Mr. Lucas, you knew you were telling what was not true when you told Stroebel that it was found it was a .44 and not a .38 that was used to kill Marshall? You knew you were lying?"

"I knew there had been no examination made."

"You knew you were lying?"

"Yes, sir."

"You admit it?"

"Yes."

Morrison stood for a moment holding Lucas's eyes, which glared back in anger. He then sat down and after a few secondary questions from Davie, the marshal was released from the witness stand.

As the air in the New Westminster courtroom grew heavy and warm through the first two days of the trial, the correspondent from Victoria's *Daily Colonist* passed an upbeat verdict on the Crown's performance. "The case of Stroebel and Eyerly grows more interesting hourly," it reported. "There appears to be a certainty of conviction, from the quality of evidence adduced." Theodore Davie held a more mixed assessment. Boggs had been a dud on day one and Lucas had taken a beating during cross-examination on day two, yet the pair had succeeded in putting the most incriminating pieces of physical evidence—the slugs from Marshall's body, Stroebel's revolver and cartridges—before the jurors. Davie now had to demonstrate the significance of that evidence.

To do that, the Attorney General called up local gunsmith Samuel Webb to act as his expert witness on guns and bullets. In late Victorian courts, gunsmiths were routinely called upon to testify on gun-related evidence. The craftsmen who fixed and sold firearms were aware that the rifling in a gun's barrel left marks on the bullets fired from that gun, but experts were decades away from the discovery that the pattern of twists and grooves produced was unique to each barrel. In the meantime, Victorian experts used the build-up of rust in a gun's barrel in their efforts to link a particular bullet to a particular firearm. The rusted barrel left marks on a bullet used in a crime; if the same or similar marks were made on a test bullet fired by the gunsmith from the same gun, it was claimed, then the first, offending bullet most likely came from the barrel of that gun.

Webb was well-versed in all this. Over the past two decades, the fifty-two-year-old gunsmith from England had run his own business selling and repairing firearms in New Westminster, and he had acted as an expert witness for the Crown in a number of trials, including the murder case against Ben Kennedy. At Superintendent Moresby's request, Stroebel's revolver, his two loaded cartridges and the two slugs taken from Marshall's body were sent to Webb in early September.

Now on the stand, the gunsmith explained how he had fired one of the loaded cartridges from Stroebel's gun into a sack of flour; the re-trieved bullet had been entered as Exhibit E. Davie produced Exhibit E and Exhibit A (the slug taken from the back of Marshall's neck) and asked Webb to compare the two.

"Do you trace any similarity between the grooves on one of these bullets and those on the other?"

"There is a similarity."

"What was the cause of these grooves?"

"They were caused through the barrel inside the gun being rusty," Webb explained. Davie then pointed to a creasing in both slugs, ask-ing if that meant they were fired from the same rusted barrel.

"Yes. At the same time, it might be caused by firing out of another revolver, one rusted in the same manner as this."

This was not the answer Davie wanted, but he pushed on. "But there is evident indication of both of these bullets—Exhibits A and E—hav-ing been fired out of a revolver which has rust in the chamber?"

"Yes."

Morrison's cross-examination jumped on Webb's inability to defin-itively link the slug from Marshall to Stroebel's revolver. Under stiff questioning, Webb clung to his conviction that he could "see a little groove" in bullet A similar to bullet E, and that each was caused by a rusty barrel. Morrison then moved to the revolver.

"Is not this .38 calibre the ordinary common pistol that is most frequently purchased by people wishing to buy a revolver?"

During the testimony of gunsmith Samuel Webb, the judge made sketches of two bullet cartridges entered as evidence. These bullets were intact, but Webb testified they were the same calibre and make as the ones that killed John Marshall. Royal BC Museum and Archives, GR 1727

"Yes, mostly farmers and ordinary people like that."

"Tramps for one thing?"

"Yes. They buy these very cheap revolvers."

An exhausted Webb stepped out of the witness stand and Davie recalled Superintendent Moresby, hoping to bolster his ballistics evidence. Because of their experience with firearms, police officers also commonly testified on gun matters. Davie handed Moresby the revolver from the exhibit table and the superintendent proceeded to describe the condition it was in when Lucas gave it to him.

"These two barrels here had been fired off; they were quite dark and blackened. These two barrels had had loaded bullets in them which had been taken out. They are free from dust, with some grease in them. The fifth chamber was somewhat black."

On cross-examination, Morrison noted the uncanny similarity between Moresby's description of the revolver and the one given the day before by David Lucas. Moresby replied that he received the gun from Lucas on either April 20 or 21, and that the marshal had explained the condition of the chambers at the time.

"It was he that showed me the pistol and said that two had been drawn and others had been fired. But I satisfied myself that such was the case by personal examination." Once again, Morrison's raised eyebrows showed his disbelief.

❖

Davie kept Moresby on the stand for what he hoped would be the testimony that clinched the Crown's case: the "confession" given by David Eyerly a week after Marshall's death. If the statement stood, it would prove that Stroebel killed Marshall in the course of robbing him, and that he had planned the deed beforehand—and of course, it would implicate Eyerly as an accessory to both the robbery and murder.

"I met Mr. Schofield at the Huntingdon station and Eyerly with him," Moresby began, explaining how the confession came about. "Eyerly then commenced making a statement, but I stopped him and gave him a severe caution to be careful what he said."

Superintendent Moresby then related what Eyerly had told him: Stroebel visiting Eyerly the evening of April 19; the pair walking up the wagon road and across to Marshall's gate; Stroebel moving on to Marshall's house; the two shots fired; Stroebel taking a shortcut to catch up with Eyerly; the gold pieces Stroebel showed him; and the pair's swift return home.

Eyerly's attorney, Louis Ekstein, knew he had to discredit his client's confession and Moresby's acceptance of it as the truth: "Mr. Eyerly has, since speaking to you last April, denied the whole story?"

"He denied it, said he was telling falsehoods. This was at the jail, in the presence of Mr. Leamy, a barrister."

"I notice you said that any boy that would swear falsely to a lie, any respectable man would look upon him as a dog. You had an idea at that time that it might be a lie?"

"I had the opinion that perhaps the boy might have been lying at the time, but after the caution I gave him, I came to the conclusion that it was true."

The news that Moresby himself had initially been skeptical of Eyerly's confession was potentially damaging to the Crown. To lend credence to Moresby's acceptance of the confession, Davie called up James Schofield, the man who had first heard the boy's statement.

"On April 28, I was going up to the post office, and on the road, I met the prisoner Eyerly," Schofield explained. "He said he knew all about the murder, that he had been down there that night with Stroebel." The station master then laid out what the young defendant had told him, the details meshing with Moresby's account.

On cross-examination, Ekstein chipped away at Schofield's testimony. The station master admitted there had been much talk about the murder in the week before the boy's confession, meaning Eyerly could easily have gotten all the facts he needed for his tale from what others were saying. Schofield also admitted that no money had been found on Stroebel when he was arrested, nor was any uncovered in his room.

"What have you heard about the relationship between the defendants?" Ekstein pressed.

"I heard they were really bad friends. And that they stole a pump."

Morrison took over and asked Schofield if he paid or offered any-thing to Eyerly for the story, to which the station master answered no.

"Did you hear he had been asking for pay?"

"I did, yes. After he gave me his statement, I believe he asked Porter if he knew anything about the murder. He offered to tell Porter his story for fifty cents."

"And what have you heard of Eyerly's reputation?"

"I have heard nothing good of him."

On re-examination, Davie tried to show that the defendants had not always been at odds, that they had recently been partners in the theft of Kingston's pump: "You have told us two things about the pris-oners: one, that they were bad friends; and the other, that they stole a pump together. Which did they do first: fall out, or steal the pump?"

"Fall out."

"Fall out, and afterwards stole the pump?"

"Yes, sir, that's what I heard." Stroebel and Eyerly grinned at each other as a ripple of laughter rolled through the gallery.

Judge McCreight tried to clear the confusion: "I should think they stole the pump first, before they fell out."

"I only know what I heard," Schofield replied with a shrug.

Undaunted, Davie moved to corroborate Eyerly's confession with a key piece of outside evidence: the "peculiarly shaped" boot print found at a gate on the southern side of Marshall's farmyard, a hundred feet from his house. That gate opened onto a soggy pasture which, if not too wet, could be used as a shortcut back to the rail line. The Attorney General believed this was the shortcut Stroebel used the night of the murder to catch up with Eyerly, his collaborator.

Ira Airheart, who had milled about the south gate on the twentieth, was called back to the stand by Davie and asked to describe the boot print.

"It was about a No. 6 size, leather not rubber."

"Was there anything singular about the track?"

"It appeared to be round. The ball of the foot appeared to be one way and the heel the other way, like a twisted foot."

On cross-examination, Airheart admitted that it was raining that day, that the ground on either side of the gate was "muddy and marshy," and that he first saw the boot print around three o'clock that afternoon.

❖

"That, my lord, is the case for the Crown," Davie declared, turning to the bench. "I wish now to beg leave that the court go and view the locality of the crime, to clarify points raised in testimony."

In an era before photographic or video evidence, it was common for the judge, jury, counsel and defendants to visit the scene of the alleged murder, if it was nearby. That very day, November 16, those involved in the Pittendrigh murder trial had done so, although they needed to travel only a few blocks down toward the New Westminster riverfront. Morrison objected to the request, but after consulting the relevant sections of the new Criminal Code, McCreight ruled in Davie's favour. Morrison retorted that since the defence was compelled to accept the field trip, then the defendants must be allowed to go.

"Then they must go. In proper custody, of course," McCreight said in a huff before sweeping out of the chamber. In the swirl of bodies left behind, Eyerly and Stroebel glanced about, broad grins lighting up their faces.

RETURN TO THE SCENE OF THE CRIME

At just past 8:30 on Friday morning, a ragged parade started out from the New Westminster courthouse, headed for the CPR station a few blocks west. Leading the way was the dignified form of Sheriff William Armstrong, the sixty-seven-year-old former lumber merchant who was in charge of logistics for the day. The twelve jurors marched behind him, two abreast, the rubber galoshes Armstrong had issued that morning slung over their shoulders. Judge McCreight, Attorney General Davie and defence counsellors Morrison and Ekstein came next, fur hats and woollen overcoats replacing their usual white wigs and black robes. Trailing behind, Superintendent Moresby and four armed guards surrounded the two defendants, who looked about excitedly despite the cold steel handcuffs digging into their wrists. Twenty or so trial witnesses and a handful of reporters brought up the rear. The parade of men assembled on the station platform, talking brightly, glad to be free of the stuffy courtroom that had been their prison for the past four days. The nine o'clock train was waiting for them; an extra passenger car had been added for their use and the four dozen men obediently filed in.

The two-hour trip to Mission Junction hugged the northern bank of the Fraser River, and as the morning fog lifted, the train passed by dozens of sawmills coming to life, massive log booms tied up nearby on the river. The party changed trains at Mission, then descended onto the Sumas prairie. Laid out before them, the sharp ridge of the Cascade Mountains led east to a distant Mount Cheam, its upper slopes covered in fresh snow, blindingly white in the morning sun.

The train slowed to a stop just north of Marshall's trestle and the whole party disembarked. After consulting with McCreight, Sheriff Armstrong led the group to Marshall's farmhouse, stopping at the veranda. Moresby and Ira Airheart pointed out where Marshall's body had been found—bloodstains, deep brown with age, were still visible on the veranda's planks. To a juror's question, the superin-tendent replied he had found no bullet holes on the porch, nor in-side the kitchen. Moresby led the jury, judge and attorneys into the house, where the dinner table and chairs remained in place.

Jury foreman Andrew Ross asked, "Did the same person who supped with Marshall shoot him, or did some other person sup with him and leave before the murder occurred?"

"The same idea has occurred to me and others," Davie answered, without explaining further.

The group then made their way to the south gate of Mar-shall's farmyard, to where the mysterious boot print had been found. The track was no longer there, of course, seven months after it had been discovered. In-stead, the party examined the condition of the gateway and the field it led into. Davie wanted to demonstrate that the gate and pasture were passable, because Eyerly's confession claimed that Stroebel had cut across there

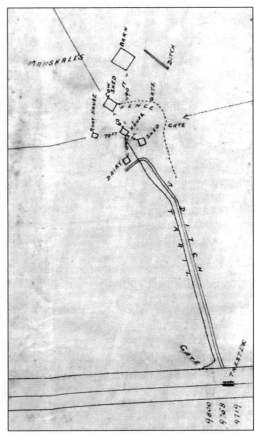

This sketch, drawn by surveyors for use in the tri-als, shows Marshall's farmyard (due north is to the left): the house and outbuildings surround-ed on one side by a fence, with a gate on the south leading to a soggy field. A trail connect-ed the yard to the CPR line, shown at the bot-tom going over the trestle right at Marshall's gate. Royal BC Museum and Archives, GR 606

after killing Marshall. William Porter explained that he had come through the field and fence opening the afternoon of April 20, on his way from and to his house. Now, Porter could not get the gate to open properly, but after a few tries forced it ajar. Stepping through, he commented that the mud hole on the far side had been much deeper in April. Young Elmer Jesseph agreed, telling the party that the pasture had been flooded with six inches of water the day after Marshall's death. The party then picked its way across the field—described by one reporter as "very swampy"—and back to the rail line.

Despite being shackled and closely guarded, Stroebel and Eyerly took everything in with a carefree, even cheerful attitude. One correspondent noted, "The prisoners walked across the whole route handcuffed, and without assistance. Their manner was perfectly unconcerned." Another agreed: "During the trip the prisoners carried themselves with entire *sang froid*." For the two young defendants, the day's field trip was a break from grey monotony of prison life. After seven months in prison, they soaked up the sunshine and took deep breaths of the crisp, fresh air. The trip was also a return home, back to their old haunting grounds, and a chance to catch glimpses of acquaintances and, for Eyerly, family who came out to greet them.

As lunchtime approached, the party reassembled on the railbed and walked down to the Huntingdon Hotel, where they stopped to eat. The men lingered over coffee, catching a last bit of warmth before heading back into the cold, sunny day. Outside, the group split into two smaller parties. The first party included the sheriff, jury, Ira Airheart, William Porter, and long-time local resident Henry Kipp; it headed back up the railway by foot. The second party took to the hilltop wagon road that ran to the west of the railway; McCreight, Morrison, a number of witnesses, the prisoners and their guards crowded into two carriages, while Davie, Moresby and Frederick Hussey mounted their own horses. The reporters and the remainder of those who had set out from New Westminster that morning walked behind their betters.

The first party moved briskly up the rail line and stopped at Marshall's trestle. After some discussion, Sheriff Armstrong walked to

Marshall's house, stepped onto the veranda, unholstered his .38 calibre revolver and fired two rounds into the air. The shots rang out across Sumas prairie and from the trestle sounded clear and close. One of the jurors suggested they do the test again, but this time gather inside Airheart's cabin to find out if the shots could be heard from there.

"Well, you'd have to git all the conditions the same," Airheart equivocated. "You see, I was having supper, the door was closed, and the fire crackling." The trapper did not want the test done in case the party did hear shots while inside his place, which would have raised the question why he had not on the night of April 19. He wanted jurors to believe that just because he heard no shots that night does not mean there were none.

The conversation drifted from there to the question of Marshall's barking dog. Airheart piped up again: "I bin around lots of dogs. I can tell one barking from another. The night Marshall was killed, I heard Ackerman's dog barking in the northeast, Blair's in the west and Marshall's in the south." Jurors shot each other confused looks because, in court, the trapper had said nothing about other dogs barking that night.

Meanwhile, the horses and carriages of the second party worked their way over the rutted wagon road. At one point, the three horsemen tried to pick their way down to the railbed but were stopped by swampy ground, forcing Hussey to dismount and lead his horse through on foot. Some minutes later, reported a weary *Daily Columbian* correspondent, "the revolver shots fired at Marshall's house were heard distinctly by the persons walking with the carriages on the hill."

Just before 3:00 p.m., the two parties met at the point where the wagon road crossed the rail line. With the sun riding low and temperatures dropping, they continued together to Abbotsford, where they caught the train back to Mission Junction, then on to New Westminster. Stroebel and Eyerly squeezed the most out of their day of freedom, "smoking cigarettes with evident relish" on the return trip. The train steamed into New Westminster station at 7:00 p.m. and the tired, hungry passengers disembarked. Judge McCreight, Morrison and other officials returned to warm houses and home-cooked meals;

Davie, Hussey, the jury and the witnesses hurried back to hotel rooms and restaurant food; Stroebel and Eyerly were taken away to their dank cells and cold prison rations.

❈

The residents of New Westminster greeted Saturday morning, November 18, with good cheer as the sunny weather held on for a third day. Inside the city's main courtroom, though, the mood was anything but bright. The previous day of fresh air and sunshine had been exhilarating for the jury, witnesses, reporters and legal officials—the morning after, the hours spent slogging through swampy ground and stumbling over an uneven railbed had left them weary, sore and grumpy. The malaise reached all the way to John McCreight himself, who was known for his fastidious adherence to the rules. The judge had ordered court to resume at 10:00 a.m., yet as the clock ticked toward 10:30 on day six of the trial, he was nowhere to be found.

Reporters filled the time doodling in their notebooks or indulging in flights of fanciful prose. Somehow, this passage from the correspondent of the *Daily News Advertiser* escaped the blue pencil of his editor:

> The jury had a tired look as if they had all been serving a term which no doubt they realise that they have. The court stenographer leaned his forehead on his hand, and had the appearance of wanting to express his views on the immutability of things. The sheriff looked at the bench and the jury box with a hopeless far away smile, and the barristers adjusted their wigs with an air of determination to stay with it or die trying.

The reporter spotted "only a few stragglers" in the public gallery and concluded glumly that "interest in the trial seems to be dying out."

Reaching the end of his patience, Theodore Davie broke the courtroom silence to ask Sheriff Armstrong, "Does his Lordship know that the jury, bar, prisoners and people await his pleasure?" Before Armstrong could answer, McCreight burst into the room. The judge's face—always so calm, pale and grave—was uncharacteristically flushed, his wig slightly askew.

Taking his seat, he frowned absently then turned to Morrison, who had risen and asked leave to present a surprise witness. The judge nodded and Morrison called Henry Kipp to the stand. Kipp was one of the first White immigrants to settle in the central Fraser Valley, arriving in 1864. The fifty-one-year-old farmer lived in Chilliwack, not Sumas, and appeared to have no connection to the case. He had been visiting New Westminster on private business when Oliver Ackerman introduced him to Morrison. The lawyer wanted someone to travel with the party to Sumas, to act as a witness for the defence should anything go awry. Now in court, Morrison's pre-emptive action was about to pay off.

Kipp stood comfortably in the witness box, his intelligent blue eyes contrasting with his rough dress. Kipp explained he had been standing at the edge of the jury party, on Marshall's trestle, when the two rounds were fired from the murdered man's house. After the test shots, Kipp overheard the conversation that took place between Airheart and the jurors: Airheart's explanation of why he might not have been able to hear shots fired the night of the nineteenth and his description of all the dogs that barked that night.

"Was his Lordship, or counsel from the Crown or defence, present?" Morrison asked pointedly.

"I didn't see them. I think they were on the wagon road."

On cross-examination, Davie wanted to know how Kipp came to be with the court party the previous day. "You have had no previous connection to this case?"

"No, sir, I have not."

"Mr. Morrison simply asked you to go on the train, without directing your attention to what you were required to do?" Davie asked in disbelief.

"Yes, sir. I don't know why he wanted me to go."

Davie paused, allowing the jury to puzzle over Kipp's plea of ignorance, then continued. "There is one of the jurymen of your name—Mr. A.E. Kipp. Is he any relative of yours?"

"He is my nephew, and I am proud of him."

Davie raised his eyebrows and looked meaningfully at the jury. Just then Morrison rose and requested that Judge McCreight "reserve the point" as to whether Airheart's conversation with the jurors amounted to jury tampering. A trial judge could reserve a point when a difficult question of law was presented, but he was uncertain how he should rule on it. After declaring the point reserved, the judge would then let the trial proceed. If the reserved point affected the verdict of the trial, it could be taken up on appeal with a higher court; depending on how the latter ruled, the trial verdict would either be upheld or thrown out. McCreight agreed with Morrison that the presence of jury tampering, if proven, was serious enough to be grounds for a new trial. The judge expressed his reluctance to rule that tampering had taken place, so he said he was leaning toward reserving the point.

"My lord," Davie protested strenuously, "based on the evidence already given, if the point was reserved and sent up, the higher court would quash any verdict given by this jury." The Attorney General argued that the evidence the jury had been tainted was clear: first, Airheart had spoken to the jurors, without the defendant, judge or counsel present; and second, Kipp himself was a biased witness, working for Morrison, and his own nephew sat on the jury. Davie's unspoken fear was that, if the present trial reached a verdict that was vacated by a higher court, then the principle of double jeopardy might kick in. That is, the defendants could not be tried again for the same crime, and they would walk away free. Davie demanded that McCreight rule on the matter then and there, insisting the correct course would be to dismiss the current jury, select a new one and start the trial from the beginning.

The Attorney General's arguments failed to sway McCreight, who decided to reserve the point and continue with the trial. Davie knew the issue was pivotal, and that it would cast a shadow of doubt over whatever verdict the trial produced. This was a rare instance where McCreight ruled against the Crown in the trial, but Davie's frustration on the point was understandable. The judge had a reputation for erudition and absorption in the finer points of the law, a reputation he took great pride in. Here was a chance to apply that learning, but he timidly passed it along for someone else to decide. The reason McCreight gave for his decision—that he wanted to spare the public purse the cost of starting the trial anew—was equally tepid.

McCreight's refusal to rule on the matter looks even more timid in light of the fact that he was responsible for allowing Airheart's unauthorized conversation with the jury to occur in the first place. The judge reportedly consulted the Criminal Code when deciding on Davie's request for a crime scene visit, but McCreight must not have read his copy too carefully. The code stated that a trial judge could authorize such a trip, provided he "give such directions as seem requisite for the purpose of preventing undue communication with such jurors." According to the official transcript and detailed newspaper reports of the trial, McCreight gave no instructions to the jury before embarking on the trip. Then, once in Sumas, the court party was split in two for the afternoon, with the jurors allowed to go off on their own; the only official accompanying them was Sheriff Armstrong, whose responsibilities did not include censoring what was said. Meanwhile, the judge, lawyers and policemen stayed half a mile away, preferring to ride rather than walk. Uninstructed in how they should act, the jurors naturally asked questions of the witnesses present; Airheart was the closest thing to an eyewitness in the case, so they were especially keen to hear what he saw and heard.

❧

There was a lull in the proceedings after McCreight's decision to reserve the point on jury tampering as the judge took some time to complete his bench notes on the question. Davie retreated to the Crown's table, allowing himself a moment of pique before putting the matter behind him. He had learned long ago that you had to accept a trial judge's ruling, no matter how muddled. Morrison also returned to his seat, sifting through his papers until he found his notes for the defence's opening statement.

The jurors watched in discomfort, puzzling over the morning's legal wrangling and pulling overcoats atop their legs for warmth.

Glancing at his shivering colleagues, foreman Andrew Ross rose and asked McCreight if the transoms at the top of the high windows could be closed as the air rushing in was too cold. Through the long trial days, the steam radiators drove up the temperature inside the courtroom and on a number of occasions McCreight ordered that the window transoms be opened. The five-foot-high windows ran along the entire length of the left-hand wall. The jurors sat with their backs against the wall and when the transoms were opened, frigid air rushed in and descended upon the hapless jurors. One reporter explained the problem:

> The heat at times in the room was very great. But the way the cold air came in on the windows being opened proved the defective ventilation of the room. Several jurymen were observed wrapping their overcoats around their lower extremities as though taking a sleigh ride in Alaska. When a bell was heard ringing somewhere adjacent the effect was irresistible.

In response to Ross, the judge commented pertly that the court needed as much fresh air as possible. When Davie spoke up, backing the foreman's request, McCreight ordered that the transoms immediately above the jury be closed, and the rest be left open. With this "unsatisfactory compromise" the trial proceeded.

CASE FOR THE DEFENCE

Day six of Stroebel and Eyerly's trial had begun with a weary court: the religiously punctual judge arrived late, the jury was tired and downcast, and for the first time, there were empty seats in the public gallery. With the explosive testimony of Henry Kipp and charges of jury tampering, the case came very close to being declared a mistrial. The morning's dramatic turn of events energized the proceedings and set the stage for the defence case. Jurors and spectators now asked: What did Morrison and Ekstein have up their sleeves? Would they put the defendants themselves in the witness stand?

Aulay Morrison's opening statement was brief and emphatic, lasting a mere three minutes. The defence would provide evidence to refute the cardinal points of the Crown's case, he asserted. All the cartridges fired from Stroebel's revolver would be accounted for; the movements of the defendant from the time he left Porter on April 19 to the following morning would be revealed; and the "confession" of Davie Eyerly would be exposed as worthless.

Morrison then called Oliver Ackerman to the stand, the first of four defence witnesses from the Ackerman family; Oliver's brothers Asa and Theron, along with his nephew Elma Jesseph, would follow. Through the tribulations of the previous year, the Ackerman clan provided Stroebel with the kind of support a young man in trouble usually received from his own family. The fact was that in his time of greatest need, the twenty-year-old defendant was effectively an orphan. Stroebel's mother had died four years earlier, and his father had recently fled to Oklahoma Territory. George Sr. did not return to Sumas, despite his son's desperate pleas and misplaced expectations—

not when Albert was arrested for murder, not while he languished in prison, and not when he was put on trial for his life. Nor did George Jr. step in to fill his father's empty boots, even though he lived nearby, floating between Sumas and Vancouver. There is no evidence he visited his younger brother in New Westminster Gaol, and it is clear he did not attend the trial.

Morrison would have loved to put his client's father, older brother and sisters into the witness stand, if only to humanize his client and give at least the illusion that he was a devoted son and brother from a loving family. The father and siblings could have painted a moving picture of the tragedies and deprivations of young Albert's life. George Jr. could have helped on a number of specific points as well, most notably regarding his botched real estate moves and how they had harmed his younger brother. There can be little doubt that the absence of Albert's own family was noted by the jurors. Surely it was a sign that something was not quite right about the Stroebel clan.

The Ackermans stepped into the void left by Albert's family. The Ackermans had known the Stroebels for years and had watched as the children struggled in the wake of their mother's death and their father's departure. After Albert's arrest, the Ackermans—the largest landholders on the prairie—threw their considerable resources behind the lonesome defendant. They footed the bill for Morrison's services and acted as consultants to the defence attorney, even carrying out their own investigations. Inside the courtroom, the Ackermans put their reputation as one of Sumas's leading families on the line, testifying at length and pitting their word against that of Crown witnesses.

The eldest Ackerman brother, Oliver, was the most active in support of Stroebel. Now, standing confidently in the witness box, Oliver described his personal investigations and his consultations with Morrison, explicitly casting doubt on David Lucas's actions and the evidence he had collected. Oliver also acted as Morrison's expert witness on guns and ballistics, providing a rebuttal to Samuel Webb's testimony for the Crown. Ackerman had served three years in the Union Army during the American Civil War and was a regular hunter, so he had considerable experience with both pistols and rifles.

"If you saw a bullet with indications on it or marks on it caused by rust," Morrison began, "would you undertake to state that that particular bullet came out of any particular revolver from its resemblance to another bullet fired out of an apparently rusty barrel?"

"I certainly should not."

"And is there a very strong similarity between any revolver of the same calibre as to the impressions they would make up a bullet?"

"I should say so. The .38 calibre gun [like Stroebel's] is an ordinary cheap revolver. I have seen quite a number of them round the country. And very few revolvers in the hands of ordinary men are not rusty."

Ackerman also rejected the testimony of Moresby and Lucas concerning the condition of Stroebel's revolver. The lawmen had claimed they could tell two unfired cartridges had been extracted from the gun because grease from them had been left behind in the chambers. While there was grease on new cartridges when they were taken out of the box, Ackerman countered, that grease "is lost in a very short time." Carrying cartridges around in one's pocket rubbed the lubricant away even more quickly. Ackerman also rejected the lawmen's claims that they could see that two cartridges had been fired from Stroebel's gun.

"I don't think you could tell the difference in the condition of a cylinder where an exploded shell had been left for some time and taken out, from a cylinder that had a loaded cartridge."

On cross-examination, Davie stirred up doubts about Ackerman's objectivity and trustworthiness as a witness, given how deeply involved he was with Morrison's defence of Stroebel. Ackerman admitted he had been "instructing counsel here at the trial and giving notes and ideas to him." Curiously, Davie did not go after Ackerman's ballistics testimony, and in particular, the latter's qualifications as an expert on guns. It was a sign of the poor state of forensic ballistics at the time that someone could be accepted as a firearms expert because he had been a soldier three decades earlier.

Replacing his older brother in the witness box, Theron Ackerman testified primarily as a character witness. Theron ran a successful lumber mill in New Westminster and served as chief of the city's

Aulay Morrison, defence attorney for Stroebel and future BC Supreme Court Justice. Morrison's no-holds-barred style, which alienated many of his colleagues, was on full display at Stroebel's trials. Royal BC Museum and Archives, A-02357

fire department. He explained that his wife had known Albert Stroebel's mother, visiting her frequently when Elizabeth fell ill and was admitted to the local hospital.

After their mother's death, he said, "the two eldest boys kept the family together, and they worked a good deal for my father who lived in that neighbourhood. For that reason, we have taken an interest in their welfare. As far as I know, Albert has been a very good boy, very industrious. I didn't feel like turning my back upon him merely because he had been arrested."

The youngest Ackerman brother, Asa—a justice of the peace and municipal reeve—also stepped forward to lend his reputation and standing in the community in support of Stroebel. Asa Ackerman stated he had known Stroebel for seven years and that "his reputation for truthfulness and peacefulness were good." Asa then went through his actions in the two days after the murder: arriving at Marshall's on April 20, taking control of the crime scene until Superintendent Moresby arrived, finding the two purses of money hidden in the house, and observing the misshapen boot print discovered by the back gate.

"Can you describe the boot track?" Morrison asked.

"This was made with a fine boot, with a long heel—what I would call a cowboy's boot, or riding boot. A number seven boot, I should think. The heel was tipped in towards the ball of the foot." Ackerman saw the print around 2:00 p.m. A small crowd that included his nephews Elmer and Frank Jesseph was gathered about the print, and some, like Frank, had even walked through the gate. The reeve believed the track belonged to Frank since his nephew wore the same kind of riding boots.

On cross-examination, Davie asked, "Is your nephew Frank Jesseph lame?"

"No, sir. He walks like anybody else."

"He's perfectly sound on his feet?"

"Yes, sir."

Ackerman's other nephew, Elmer, took the stand next. The twenty-four-year-old knew Stroebel well, even though he had been in Sumas only a short while. Elmer and Frank had arrived at Marshall's just after 10:00 a.m. on the twentieth. They walked over to the south gate in the morning, then again in the afternoon. Elmer explained: "I saw the track that they was all talking about. It was from a high-grade stock boot, what they call cowboy boots. There was a good many tracks by then, in the afternoon. I thought it was my brother's, either his or someone's made afterwards. There was no track when we went there in the morning."

Jesseph then described the ongoing animosity that existed between the two defendants: "Stroebel told me that one time, Eyerly threw a stick at him when he called his girl a son-of-a-bitch." In that incident, Jesseph joined his friend in trying to catch Eyerly, but they failed. Jesseph then saw Stroebel sitting on a stump some ways off and heard him fire two shots into the air.

❖

Jesseph's testimony explained what had happened to two of the cartridges Stroebel possessed. Morrison next called Elizabeth Bartlett to the stand to account for two more. As she made her way forward, her slight frame draped in a hand-me-down dress, Elizabeth glanced nervously toward Stroebel, who smiled brightly back at her. Prompted by Morrison's gentle questioning, Bartlett described her walk with Stroebel the Tuesday afternoon, April 18.

"What happened when you were out?"

"Well, Mr. Stroebel had his pistol with him and fired two shots down Harrison Road." Morrison then turned to the evening of the nineteenth, and Elizabeth recalled Stroebel's return to the hotel sometime after nine o'clock.

Davie was less gentle on cross-examination, trying to shake the girl's account of the events of Tuesday afternoon. He was convinced that the young couple had concocted the story about their walk up Harrison Road and the two shots Stroebel allegedly fired as a way to account for the two bullets that killed John Marshall. He also grilled Bartlett on the details and timing of Stroebel's return home late Wednesday evening.

Elizabeth Bartlett, a month shy of her thirteenth birthday, held up surprisingly well in the face of Davie's cross-examination. Also surprising—at least to us—was the fact that the Attorney General did not ask Bartlett about her engagement to Stroebel. No doubt it was a delicate matter, but it could have cast the defendant in a bad light: Was it not immoral and illegal for a twenty-year-old man to be engaged to a twelve-year-old girl? As we have seen, nobody outside her family knew Elizabeth's true age. Others, including Stroebel, believed she was a young-looking fourteen or fifteen. The Criminal Code set no age limit for marriage, so Elizabeth could have wed in Canada, as she could have in Washington state if her parents did not object. At the time, brides of fourteen or fifteen years old were not uncommon, especially in frontier communities such as Sumas. Albert's younger sister Hattie was fourteen when she married (in August 1893, as her brother sat in jail), while David Eyerly's mother was fourteen on her wedding day and fifteen when she gave birth to David.

Even Attorney General Davie had taken a child bride, though that fact was not widely known. Davie married for the first time in 1874, when he was a twenty-two-year-old solicitor in training; his bride, Blanche Baker, was fourteen. Davie's family was dead-set against the marriage but could not talk Theodore out of it. Tragically, Blanche died two years later of kidney disease. Davie was distraught and remained a widower for eight years before remarrying—his twenty-year-old second bride was a decade younger than he. Given this personal history, it is understandable that the Attorney General did not make an issue of Elizabeth's age and the eight years that separated her from Stroebel.

※

As Elizabeth Bartlett demurely stepped down from the witness box, a hum of excitement rippled through the courtroom. That morning's empty seats were filled, and a restless crowd had formed outside the chamber doors. Morrison stayed on his feet and called the most anticipated witness to the stand. Albert Stroebel was only the second defendant in BC legal history to take the stand on a murder charge. The first was Ben Kennedy, who a week before had stood in the very same spot and testified in his own defence. Prior to the new Criminal Code, which had taken effect that July, defendants were not permitted to testify. The prohibition was a piece of British common law intended to protect the accused: if the defendant could not testify, he could not be coerced into making self-incriminating statements. A defendant could now testify, but he did not have to. If he did not, the judge was to instruct the jury not to interpret that as an admission of guilt.

During the early years the new code was in effect, the defendants in most trials took the stand. The accused testified in all four of the murder trials held during that "bloody assizes" of fall 1893. The reason was that jurors expected to hear from the accused now that he could speak for himself—they wanted to hear the defendant defend himself. Despite what the letter of the law said, juries tended to view a refusal to take the stand as an admission of guilt. The late Victorians who sat as jurors were solid law-and-order men, who generally trusted authorities such as William Moresby. They held to that now-discredited notion that a person had nothing to fear and nothing to hide if they were innocent.

Even though he had never argued a case where the defendant took the stand, Morrison was well aware of the jurors' expectations. He also knew that the public—both inside the courtroom and those following the case through the newspapers—was divided over whether Stroebel was innocent or guilty. All the defence attorney had to do was get a similar split in the jury, and it was with that in mind that he called his client to the stand.

Stroebel limped across the courtroom and settled into the witness stand, his workman's hands resting on the railing. He wore prison trousers and a collarless shirt, along with a shabby dress jacket and vest, both unbuttoned. His skin had grown even paler in prison, his eyes duller, but he still sported a lopsided grin as his lawyer approached. What Morrison needed most from Stroebel was a clear, credible narrative of his movements for the evening and early night of April 19. Stroebel began by stating that the testimony of William Blair, William Porter and Archie Baxter, covering that day up to 6:00 p.m., was accurate. He then described his movements in the crucial period that followed: walking to the railbed after milking Porter's cow; passing Baxter when he turned north to pick up some salmon eggs he had stored a few days earlier; turning back south to retrieve the fishing rod he had stashed that morning; fishing his way up the creek that ran between the escarpment to the west and the rail line to the east; picking his way to the railway grade; then returning to the City Hotel.

"How long did you fish that evening?" Morrison asked.

"I should say I fished about two and a half hours, or more, maybe." He continued, saying that on returning to the rail line and turning south, he passed three strangers who were walking the opposite way. Glancing over his shoulder, he slipped and bashed his bad leg on the rail track. He then sat and nursed the leg for a spell before returning to the City Hotel, arriving there around 9:15 p.m.

Asked by Morrison to account for all the cartridges he had possessed, Stroebel explained: "I shot the gun only twice myself. The time on the hill after I chased Eyerly, and down Harrison street with Elizabeth Bartlett." Four bullets were fired in these two incidents, a fifth cartridge was accidentally fired by George Hilliard the Sunday before the murder, and the final two, loaded cartridges were stowed under Stroebel's bedding.

Stroebel showed a rare flash of anger when asked about Eyerly's confession: "All I have got to say is that every word of it he made up himself. Either Schofield or the boy made it up, I don't know which." He did not see Eyerly on April 19, did not go looking for him that night or at any other time. In fact, he did his best to avoid the bullyboy. "I didn't go on the street hardly of a night without getting hit on the side of the head with a rock or brick. He was after me all the time."

As he sat down, Morrison thought he had done the best he could in this uncharted territory. He had never before questioned a defendant in court. Theodore Davie had, just the week before, when he kept Ben Kennedy on the stand for most of an afternoon. Relishing another chance to grill a defendant, Davie approached the stand and his first question was aimed directly at the key matter of Stroebel's gun and cartridges.

"Where did you get the cartridges for your revolver?"

"There was five in the gun when I got it from Bill Rowe. Then I took two away from Mr. Bartlett one night. He was drunk and threatened to do some dirty work."

"That made seven cartridges?"

"Yes, sir, that made seven cartridges I had altogether."

The Attorney General then asked how many of the cartridges had been fired off. Stroebel repeated his story of the two shots he fired on the hill after chasing Eyerly before moving on to the accidental firing of his gun on April 16.

"How did that latter bullet get into the gun?"

"There was one fitted the gun tight. I took them all out in the evening before but this one. There was one cartridge in the revolver and four in under the quilt on the foot of the bed." Stroebel's own testimony revealed he had four loaded cartridges left as of the Sunday before the murder. Earlier, the Attorney General had tried to shake Elizabeth Bartlett's testimony to show that the two Harrison Road shots on Tuesday never happened. He wanted the jury to reach the conclusion that those two bullets ended up in Marshall's body.

Davie then turned to what he labelled Stroebel's "fish story," narrowing in on its key weakness, Stroebel's claim that he had been fishing for "two and a half hours or more" starting at 6:00 p.m. He asked in disbelief: "So you fished till half-past eight?"

"I would not say it was half-past eight. I quit just before dark, it was just getting dusk."

"What time did it get dark at the time of the year?" Davie knew the answer: the sun set at 7:03 p.m. on April 19, and the heavy clouds moving in made it completely dark by 7:30.

"It got dark between seven and eight o'clock," Stroebel admitted reluctantly.

"Well, if you were out there for two and a half hours, you must have been fishing for an hour in the dark?"

"I may not have been there for two and a half hours. I just took a rough guess at it." With desperation in his eyes, Stroebel backpedalled further, explaining he must have returned to the rail line by the time it got dark. Davie nodded: he had forced Stroebel to contradict himself on how long he had been fishing and blown a gaping hole in his time-line.

Davie pressed Stroebel to explain what had happened in the hour and a half or more from the time it got dark to the time the defendant returned home. Stroebel replied he had been held up by the injury he sustained falling on the railway: "It detained me pretty near an hour."

"You must have hurt yourself pretty badly to have done that?"

"Yes, sir." The Attorney General nodded and made a mental note: his witness Frank Warnock had seen Stroebel just before 10:00 p.m., "walking quite fast" toward the City Hotel.

Stroebel had been on his feet for over three hours, two of those under a relentless cross-examination, and despite the blows Davie had landed, reporters in the courtroom judged that Stroebel had held his own. One wrote, "The Attorney General cross-examined the prisoner most searchingly upon all the evidence in chief, to which the answers were given in a straight-forward and apparently truthful manner." Another commented that Stroebel responded to the marathon grilling by "giving an amusing account of his fishing experiences, contradicting himself once or twice, but adhering to his story in the main." Many in the public gallery agreed, but of course it was the jury's opinion that mattered. Had the defendant done well enough to plant seeds of doubt about his guilt in their minds?

❖

As Davie returned to the Crown's table, Louis Ekstein stood and began his case for David Eyerly. Ekstein's task was straightforward: discredit the statement his client had given to Moresby and Schofield that implicated the two defendants. George Hillhour was the first of two witnesses to provide Eyerly with an alibi for the time covered by the confession. Hillhour, who tended bar at the Dunn and Warmsley tavern, testified he saw Eyerly just before 9:00 p.m., then again at 9:05: the boy was standing on a bridge in Sumas City, talking with the owner of the Kennedy mill. Eyerly's father, Orrin, then testified that he spoke with his son in his bedroom at 9:15. Even if Orrin had fallen asleep right away, David could not have snuck out undetected until after 9:30, too late for him to have joined Stroebel for the robbery and shooting of Marshall.

Ekstein then turned directly to his client's confession. Called to the stand, Charles Brown stated that Eyerly had admitted to him that the statement he gave Moresby and Schofield was a lie. The boy had concocted the story because he thought after hearing it, Moresby would bring him to New Westminster, put him up in a hotel and pay him $3.50 a day.

David Eyerly himself was up next and he stepped pertly into the witness box, his face lit by a cocky grin. Ekstein's questioning of his client was short and sweet.

"You heard Mr. Moresby and Mr. Schofield give evidence as to the confession made by you?"

"I did."

"Was that confession true or false?"

"False."

Davie rose for the cross-examination and what followed was a half-hour of chaotic, at times nonsensical, back and forth. As the Attorney General tried to pin him down, Eyerly constantly changed his testimony, contradicted himself and treated the whole experience as a running joke. In one exchange, Davie asked the boy about the brick-throwing incident in the alleyway that ended with Stroebel firing his revolver.

"I heard the shots. Stroebel put his hand up like that. He wanted to show that he was after me," Eyerly explained.

"When was this?"

"The day before the murder."

"*The day before the murder?*"

"Yes, sir."

"Are you sure about it being the day before the murder?"

"I am. It was on Tuesday or Thursday. One of them."

"The day before the murder?"

"No, that was not the day before."

"I asked you several times, and you said the shots were the day before the murder."

"No. It was about six weeks, to the best of my knowledge."

The Attorney General grew ever more frustrated as he ploughed through the questions he had prepared. Finally, he threw up his hands and returned to his seat. Ekstein then closed the case for the defence and the court broke for supper.

Over the recess, a growing crowd of spectators thronged to the New Westminster courthouse, drawn by rumours that the trial was nearing its end and a verdict was imminent. The halls filled and many stood outside, shivering in their coats as the thermometer dropped. Inside the heated courtroom, the jury wearily returned to their seats and foreman Ross asked McCreight if it was possible to finish proceedings that evening, a Saturday. The court did not sit on Sundays, so if the trial went any further, it would have to pick up on Monday. Ross said that some jurors risked losing their jobs, while others were having to pay for substitutes to take their place at work. McCreight responded that the two sides still had to call their rebuttals, then the Crown, defence and himself give their closing statements. The jurors sagged visibly; after six long days, with more than a score of witnesses and a confusing mass of testimony, the fates of Albert Stroebel and David Eyerly had yet to be decided.

REBUTTALS, CLOSINGS AND VERDICT

In late Victorian courts, a rebuttal period was squeezed in between the end of the defence case and the beginning of the closing statements. Going first, the Crown could recall witnesses, or even introduce new ones, to respond to anything presented or argued by the defence. The defence then could do the same in response to anything the Crown had just presented in rebuttal. If the defence called no rebuttal witnesses, it was allowed to give its closing statement after the Crown; if it did call witnesses, the Crown had the advantage of closing after the defence.

Davie's first gambit in rebuttal was to reintroduce the brief letter allegedly written by Stroebel that John Bartlett had pilfered and given to David Lucas. The Attorney General had tried to do this earlier in the trial, but was unable to prove the note was in Stroebel's handwriting. He now called on William Falding, the butterfingered registrar of the New Westminster supreme court, to act as a handwriting expert. Davie passed the letter to the registrar, along with the April 22 note written by Stroebel requesting clothes from his room. Falding responded with his opinion: "I have compared them already. I have no hesitation at all in saying they are written by the same person."

Having matched the rolled letter to a verified piece of Stroebel's handwriting, Falding then tried to decipher it. The paper was creased and frayed at the edges, and the writing was in a crude hand and in pencil, which had been smudged by repeated handling.

" 'Sumas City, April.' I cannot read the date, but I think it is '22'—'April 22/93'," Falding commented as he went along. "It is addressed to no one, and there is no signature. 'I have got myself into a hell of a scrape. Old Marshall was shot here last Wednesday, and the people think that I did it, and I guess that they will take me down to New Westminster and try me on the guary down there.' I suppose it means 'jury'. It is spelt 'g-u-a-r-y'."

Falding stayed at the ready as Davie sprang an eleventh-hour surprise: the signed statement that David Lucas had wrung from Margaret Bartlett. Falding had received the document from Superintendent Moresby in May, but the registrar had tossed it into a tin box in his office, then promptly forgot about it. He had found it only that morning and was now presenting it to the court. After McCreight overruled an objection from Morrison, the registrar read the statement to the court. It contained nothing that directly incriminated Stroebel, and the fact that the document had been lost and then mysteriously found at the last minute only made the Crown look bad.

The Crown's next rebuttal witness only made things worse. David Lucas strode to the witness box, was given the Bartlett statement, then launched into a combative defence of it. Morrison approached on cross-examination and pointed to one paragraph of the document, asking Lucas to read it out loud. The defence lawyer stood back while half a minute ticked away. Lucas sat in stony silence amidst snickers from the public gallery.

"Can you read it, Mr. Lucas?" Morrison pressed, but the marshal stayed mute as another half-minute passed.

"Haven't you got that upside down?" Morrison asked with a devilish smile, and a wave of laughter chased Lucas out of the witness stand.

Morrison then called Wellington Miller as a defence rebuttal witness. The New Westminster constable testified to meeting Lucas in the city in summer 1892. Lucas told him that he had once been a policeman in San Francisco: "He said that in arresting a man there at one time, he was in danger of being killed and had shot a man. He had to stand trial for the murder and was acquitted, but lost his position through that."

Davie put Lucas on the stand to deny Miller's account, but this only gave Morrison another shot at the marshal. The defence attorney

Constable Wellington Miller (standing, first from left) posing with colleagues from the New Westminster police department. Miller had a conversation with David Lucas in which the Sumas City marshal admitted to killing a man in San Francisco. New Westminster Archives, IHP 9129

reviewed Lucas's chequered career as a lawman and private detective, casting doubt on the marshal's methods and integrity. As for Miller's testimony, Lucas claimed first he had never met the constable, then that he had met him, but that he did not recall saying anything about killing a man.

"Do you say you never said that to him?"

"I say that I don't remember."

"You might have said that?"

"A man is liable to say anything," the marshal snapped back.

"I know of lots of men who are not, Mr. Lucas," Morrison replied evenly. As the defence lawyer turned and looked knowingly at the jury, Lucas fumed in the witness box, his credibility in tatters.

A sinking feeling in his stomach, Davie declared that the prosecution's case was closed, then informed McCreight that "at this stage it is my intention to direct the officer of the Court to enter a *nolle prosequi* against the prisoner Eyerly." A *nolle prosequi* was a legal declaration by the Crown that it would proceed no further with the charges against the defendant. Of course, the dismissal of charges against Eyerly was a serious blow to the Crown's case, for the latter had argued that Stroebel had conspired with Eyerly to rob Marshall, and that the murder had resulted from that robbery attempt. However, the Attorney General had little choice: the only way to salvage a conviction against Stroebel was to separate his case from the discredited evidence attached to Eyerly.

The long trial wearing on his nerves, McCreight peered over at Morrison and asked, "Is that all?"

"Yes, my lord."

"Then evidence is closed."

❖

Day six of the trial sat well into Saturday night, adjourning at 10:30 p.m., and as the weary jurors trudged back to their hotel, they looked forward to their beds and the opportunity to sleep in. Sunday brought a return of the season's grey skies, rain and cold, a day to stay inside. Jurors returned to their familiar seats when court reconvened at ten o'clock the following morning.

Because he had called a witness during rebuttal stage, Aulay Morrison rose first to deliver his closing statement. The defence lawyer stated gravely that "The evidence in this case is purely circumstantial, and the jury must be satisfied—not have the slightest doubt—of the defendant's guilt before convicting." There was no room for error: a guilty verdict would lead to his client's execution; a mistaken conviction could not be undone. Morrison argued that the Crown had presented no direct evidence even on so key a question as when the murder took place. The aging trapper Ira Airheart had heard a dog barking from Marshall's place, but the dog could have been barking at any number of things. Morrison dismissed David Lucas's testimony evidence as "worthless," and ruthlessly attacked his reputation. He reminded the jurors that the marshal had admitted to killing a man in San Francisco and pointed out that the lawman could not even read the statement he had connived out of Margaret Bartlett.

Curiously, Morrison did not raise an issue that could have been even more damaging: Lucas's questionable handling of the core pieces of evidence in the Crown's case. There was a two-week gap between the time Lucas obtained the evidence and the time he handed it to Superintendent Moresby at the preliminary hearing. During that fortnight, the marshal had stored Margaret Bartlett's statement, Stroebel's rolled note, the two empty shells and the two loaded cartridges in a locked trunk at his home. There was no way of knowing whether Lucas had tampered with any of the material while he had possession of it.

As the court broke for lunch, spectators were impressed with Morrison's performance, the *Daily Columbian* reporting, "It was admitted on all sides that he had made a hard and masterly fight for his client." When the court returned, all eyes turned to Theodore Davie, and the Attorney General quickly cut to the centre of the Crown's case: the time from six to ten o'clock the evening of the murder. No one had seen Stroebel during those four hours, and the defendant's own account of them "was unreliable and contradictory." A week earlier, in his closing statement in the Ben Kennedy trial, Davie had noted a fundamental problem with accepting the testimony of a defendant charged with murder. When a less serious crime was involved, the threat of a perjury charge and the stiff punishment that went with it worked to ensure the defendant testified truthfully. "But in the case where a man's life hangs upon his own testimony, what matters one more crime to a man if thereby he save his life?"

The Attorney General moved from Stroebel's testimony to the physical evidence: the revolver, cartridges, and slugs from Marshall's corpse. Putting the most optimistic spin on Samuel Webb's testimony, Davie proclaimed dramatically, "The bullets taken from the head of the murdered man exactly correspond with those used in the prisoner's revolver." Davie then came to the defence of a key witness. "David Lucas has been called a sleuth hound and a murderer"; a sleuth hound, yes, but that just showed he was "an industrious, vigilant, faithful officer of the law"; a murderer, no. The marshal may have "killed a desperado in San Francisco," but he had done so while carrying out his lawful duties. It was no different, Davie argued, than a lawman defended by Judge McCreight himself two decades earlier. Then a young defence lawyer, McCreight had won the acquittal of Police Superintendent J.D. Sullivan, who was on trial for killing two suspects he was trying to bring in. McCreight argued that Sullivan had only been doing his duty, and the jury agreed.

As for Stroebel's motive, Davie continued, it was as old as the ages: money and love. The defendant was penniless, with no vocation or steady job, and had fallen behind in his rent. Stroebel had found himself trapped: "Desirous of satisfying his landlady on the one hand, and on the other hand, burning with a desire to marry the landlady's daughter. There you have a direct motive for the crime charged." The Attorney General concluded that the Crown had proven "a perfect chain of circumstances," leaving no reasonable doubt that the defendant was guilty. "Give your verdict according to your conscience, and so help you God."

One final set-piece remained before the case was handed over to the jury. The judge's closing instructions carried much weight in the minds of the farmers, tradesmen and shopkeepers who sat on late Victorian juries. Unschooled in matters of law and evidence, and faced with a mass of evidence and conflicting arguments from Crown and defence, they looked to the judge for guidance. In theory, the judge was the impartial finder of law, the jury the finder of fact: it was the jury who decided what evidence to believe, what conclusions to draw. In practice, judges of the time exercised a great deal of latitude in analyzing the evidence and drawing conclusions, up to and including declaring a defendant guilty or innocent.

McCreight was no exception, and as he leafed through the trial transcript, the judge rejected Stroebel's defence piece by piece. Warnock's testimony that he saw Stroebel walking swiftly back to the City Hotel showed the defendant had not been hurt on the rail line, casting his whole alibi into question. Stroebel contradicted himself in telling Porter what hour he had returned home the night of the murder, giving him one time one day and a much later time another day. The judge also stated his belief that one or both of the incidents of Stroebel firing off shots did not happen. This point was crucial "as upon it depends the accounting for the cartridges known to have been in Stroebel's possession."

Yet the most damning evidence, McCreight continued, came out of Stroebel's own mouth. From the time of his arrest through his lengthy trial testimony, Stroebel tried to talk his way out of trouble, only to be caught in his own contradictions: "It is remarkable that criminals as a rule after committing a crime cannot keep their tongue still about it." This explicit statement of the defendant's guilt was followed by a defence of David Lucas. Rising to Davie's bait, Mc-Creight cast his memory back two decades to his heroic defence of Superintendent Sullivan. Resurrecting the same defence he had used then, the judge argued that Lucas's actions—including the lies he told to get Stroebel to hand over his revolver—were justified, because he was only doing his duty.

The judge concluded with words that echoed the Attorney General. The Crown had presented a convincing "chain of circumstantial evidence." Stroebel's guilt was sealed not by any single or particular piece of evidence, "but by the whole combination so skilfully collected and laid before you." McCreight commended the jury for its patience through a trying week of testimony, then added, "the most painful part of your duties is now about to begin."

❧

Wisely, the jury decided to take advantage of a new regulation that permitted them to have dinner before beginning their formal deliberations. At 6:40 p.m., the jury filed out and the court adjourned to await its decision. As the evening progressed, the crowd gathered in and around the courthouse swelled to over a thousand. One reporter wrote: "the benches and aisles in the courtroom were packed as close as sardines in a box, and the overflow in the corridors extended some distance out of hearing range. Inside the bar were nearly all the members of the legal profession and a score or more of ladies and their escorts." An overflow crowd waited outside in the cold drizzle, with some adventurous souls climbing onto the window sills and peering into the courtroom.

At 8:45 p.m., the side door in the chamber opened and the jurors resumed their seats, a breathless silence falling over the room. Instead of delivering a verdict, though, foreman Ross asked the stenographer to read out the transcript of Stroebel's testimony covering the period from when he left Porter on the afternoon of the murder up to his arrival back at the City Hotel. The testimony was read, the jury retired, deliberated for another hour, then returned to the courtroom for the final time. Stroebel nervously eyed the jurors as they filed in, some of them looking back.

"Have you agreed upon your verdict?" McCreight asked.

"We have not," Ross replied, pausing from weariness. "Neither is there any possibility of our ever doing so." This was the last thing McCreight wanted to hear: defying the judge's instructions, the jury had failed to bring in a guilty verdict. The expense and efforts of a seven-day trial had come to naught.

"Are you quite sure you can't agree?" he demanded sharply.

"Absolutely certain, my lord."

"I can do nothing else than discharge the jury."

As McCreight hurried out of the room, the court erupted into a cacophony of voices. Elizabeth Bartlett clapped her hands in glee, and Stroebel turned to her with a beaming smile, both believing he would now be set free. These hopes were immediately dashed as the defendant was handcuffed and rushed outside to an awaiting carriage, then transported back to his prison cell. The hung jury was not an acquittal; the indictment passed by the grand jury at the beginning of the assize still stood, and the Crown could proceed with the same charge at a new trial, with a new jury. When Davie and Morrison appeared in front of McCreight the next morning, the Attorney General informed the judge that the Crown would go ahead with a fresh trial. Davie requested the new trial be held at the Victoria district court, which was just opening its fall assize; otherwise, the case would have to wait another six months for the spring assize in New Westminster.

Morrison objected to the venue change and snap trial, noting that it was an established legal principle that any proceedings were to be tried in the judicial district where the alleged crime took place.

Morrison's unspoken reasoning was that a trial six months down the road in New Westminster was better for his client than one in Victoria in two weeks. There had been blanket coverage of the trial in the New Westminster newspapers, with much briefer reports in Victoria. A large segment of the mainland city's reading public was already convinced that the evidence did not support a conviction, and it was from this public that a New Westminster jury would be chosen. There was also the chance that some witnesses would not be available to make the trip to New Westminster to testify in six months, or that their memories would have faded. This would harm the Crown more than the defence, because the former relied on far more witnesses than the latter.

Judges at the time possessed a great deal of leeway in deciding whether to move a trial to a new location. Given that McCreight was convinced Stroebel was guilty, it is not surprising that the judge gave the Attorney General a change of venue and quick trial. The second trial of Albert Stroebel for the murder of John Marshall was set to begin in Victoria on Wednesday, December 6.

Albert Stroebel had come closer to being set free than it might first appear. One correspondent covering the proceedings reported that the jury had split right down the middle, six men decided upon conviction and six holding out for acquittal. None of the men, it was reported, would budge from his position. However, if McCreight had wanted to force a verdict out of the jury, he could have kept the jurors sequestered until they had reached a decision, as judges sometimes did in that era. Desperate to gain their own freedom, it is easier to see the men reaching a consensus that reasonable doubt existed as to Stroebel's guilt than them all agreeing that the Crown had proved his guilt beyond a doubt. The sobering fact that finding Stroebel guilty would send the young man to the gallows raised the bar for a guilty verdict even higher. Alternatively, the jurors might have struck a compromise, as juries in other cases of the time had done, returning with a guilty verdict but guilty of manslaughter, not murder.

Aulay Morrison had done a masterful job defending his client. The quick-witted, often acerbic attorney was a natural defence lawyer, a pitbull that tore strips out of the Crown's case. Nowhere was this more artfully done than in Morrison's unmanning of David Lucas.

However, the failure to convict Stroebel was due less to Morrison's skills than to mistakes made by the Crown. The "experts" who commented on the Crown's physical evidence—Boggs on medical forensics, Webb on ballistics, Falding on handwriting—were not compelling enough. David Lucas was responsible for producing the most important pieces of evidence, but his flamboyant performance on the stand and the damage Morrison inflicted on his reputation weakened the marshal's testimony. And Theodore Davie himself did not bring his A-game. The Attorney General had risen from his sickbed to prosecute Ben Kennedy, then, with just a single day's rest, had thrown himself into the Marshall case. Davie performed well enough in court, but the organization of his case suffered: the string of Crown testimony did not produce the clear, unbroken chain of evidence needed to convince the jury.

The biggest mistake of all was trying Eyerly alongside Stroebel, thereby making the boy's confession a central part of the Crown's case. When he first received Eyerly's statement from William Moresby, Davie no doubt thought it gave him a slam-dunk case. Yet Eyerly retracted his statement in full, months before the trial and to Moresby himself, and there was ample evidence the boy himself was too unbalanced to stake anything on his word. Moresby ignored the bright warning signs and stubbornly clung to his conviction that the confession was credible. The Attorney General relied on the superintendent's judgment in the matter, so Moresby must bear the larger part of the responsibility here. As the evidence against Eyerly crumbled, the case against Stroebel weakened. By the time charges against the former were dropped, it was too late to repair the damage done to the case against the latter.

SECOND TRIAL: INTERMISSION

The deadlocked decision in Albert Stroebel's first trial caused a sensation in the province. Hung juries were rare a century and more ago, as were second trials. The story of John Marshall's murder and the prosecution of his alleged killer had already been newsworthy—the latest twists were making it even more so. "Great surprise was evinced on every side" declared the *Daily Columbian* under the headline "NO VERDICT":

> The agony in the Stroebel case is over for the present, but will be immediately resumed again in Victoria. The desperate fight made by the defence and the unusual length of the trial combined to raise public interest in the issue to a point far beyond the ordinary in such cases.

The *Daily Colonist* labelled the trial "an interesting case of circumstantial evidence which has excited considerable interest," and which had failed to come to a decision despite costing "the country a great sum to prosecute."

Government officials and legal authorities were disappointed as well as unsettled. They feared the court's failure to reach a decision after a seven-day trial reflected badly on BC's justice system. They did not doubt that Stroebel was guilty, and few wanted to think about the nightmare scenario in which the defendant got off altogether in a second trial. To reassure the public, authorities and the press played on a widely held belief that justice in the province represented the very best in British law and order. The *Daily Columbian* boasted that

BC owed its existence "to the law-abiding and orderly genius of the British people, who formed the nucleus of the early settlement in the country." The purported superiority of British justice was a founding myth of BC's White immigrant society, and like all founding myths, people clung to it no matter how much it clashed with reality.

And the reality was that, in the decade and a half preceding John Marshall's death, the province's justice system was plagued by a series of missteps, foul-ups and outright travesties involving crimes of the most brutal violence. The most infamous case in BC history was one of those. In March 1880, a special sitting of the New Westminster assize convicted Alexander Hare and the three McLean brothers for the brutal murder of police Constable Johnny Ussher. Three months later, the BC Supreme Court justices stunned the province and nation when it threw out the convictions on the grounds that the trial had not been authorized by them. The decision was one skirmish in the ongoing civil war between the justices and the provincial government. Appointed in colonial times, judges Matthew Begbie and Henry Crease claimed that Victoria had no jurisdiction over them because their authority predated the existence of the provincial government itself. Hidebound, arrogant and brooking no challenges to their power, Begbie and Crease insisted that they, not Victoria, determined the rules of the court, such as when a special assize could sit.

The provincial government scrambled to avert disaster, for the prospect that Johnny Ussher's killers might get away with his murder horrified both the public and those in power. Official claims of the superiority of British justice rang hollow, and some of the province's lawyers privately thought the unthinkable: that Hare and the McLeans could not be tried again because of the principle of double jeopardy. The authorities forged ahead, however, putting Hare and the McLeans on trial for a second time at the regular sitting of the fall assize in November. With John McCreight pressing the Crown's case, the four defendants were convicted and, on January 31, 1881, duly executed.

The administration of justice in BC received more body blows over the following years. In 1884, a vigilante mob riding up from Sumas

City lynched a fourteen-year-old boy named Louis Sam, a Sema:th from the Sumas Indian Reserve. The vigilantes accused Sam of killing a shopkeeper south of the border, even though evidence points to members of the mob itself as the true killers. The murder of Louis Sam took place in BC, but provincial authorities made no serious effort to locate and prosecute those responsible.

Two years later, Robert Sproule was tried and convicted for the murder of a fellow miner in the Kootenay district. After the trial, key witnesses recanted their testimony, and a number of jurors swore affidavits declaring they were no longer certain of Sproule's guilt. A spirited campaign led by Victoria's mayor called for clemency, and Sproule's lawyer, Theodore Davie, worked tirelessly to overturn the sentence. There was even pressure from the British and American governments to stay the execution and revisit the case. Deaf to all pleas, the BC government was hell-bent on Sproule's execution. On October 29, 1886, he was hanged in the Victoria Gaol yard, leaving many in the province convinced an innocent man had been judicially murdered.

Another case damaging to the reputation of BC justice was that of Alexander Houston, the son of one of the first White settlers in Langley. In June 1890, he was convicted of manslaughter in the death of an eighty-year-old Kwantlen woman. The judge imposed a fourteen-year sentence, saying he believed Houston had raped the woman, and that she had died from the assault.

In March 1892, Houston escaped from the New Westminster penitentiary, and for seven months found refuge across the line in the mountains outside Sumas City. He regularly visited the town and no doubt Albert Stroebel had heard of him, had maybe even met him. He also snuck into Langley to see his family, and on one such visit, he shot at some local residents but was captured and disarmed by them. His second trial was held at the shortened spring assize of 1893, where he was acquitted of attempted murder but convicted and sentenced to three years for his jailbreak. The judge ruled the new sentence could be served concurrently with his manslaughter sentence. Houston thus paid no penalty for his seven-month holiday from prison nor for the shots he had fired at his captors. During that whole time, authorities proved incapable of finding the escaped killer of a helpless old woman, even though he never left the area, and his presence appeared to be an open secret. When at last he was captured, it was not by the police, but by members of the public.

❖

In the bustle of events that marked the end of his first trial, a confused Albert Stroebel was bundled up and returned to his cell in the New Westminster Gaol. Two weeks later, on December 5, Stroebel was woken early, handcuffed and carted down to the government wharf along the city's riverfront. Accompanied by an armed William Moresby and a guard, he boarded a steamer for the three-hour trip across Georgia Strait to Victoria. Stroebel was used to the cuffs and constant guard so, despite the dreary weather and low clouds that blended into the grey of the water, he felt a certain excitement. It was his first trip across Georgia Strait, and he kept a keen eye open, hoping to catch a glimpse of the whales he had been told swam through its waters.

Another black carriage awaited the party at the Victoria dock. Stroebel, Moresby and the young guard ducked into the coach and started the climb to Victoria Gaol. As the jail came into view, the prisoner was reassured by its resemblance to the New Westminster Gaol, his home for the past seven months. Both were constructed on the same design but, built atop a rocky outcropping, the Victoria jail lacked the flowerbeds, rows of trees and climbing ivy that softened the brick façade of its twin on the mainland.

Passing through the prison doors, Stroebel's vital statistics were recorded anew: 5'4" in height, crippled in the right leg; light grey eyes, fair complexion, full face proportions; Presbyterian, American nationality; literate and temperate, a barber by trade. Issued his Victoria prison garb, Stroebel was led to the familiar U-shaped block and entered a six-foot by nine-foot cell. The prisoner was not allowed to settle into the routine of his new home. Early the following morning, December 6, he was escorted from his cell and taken by carriage to the Victoria courthouse two miles away for the first day of his second trial; at the end of the day, he was transported back. This would be his routine for the following fortnight, with the exception of two Sundays when the court did not sit.

❖

There was a buzz of excitement in Victoria's main courtroom as the fall assize reassembled that dreary Wednesday morning. The assize had opened on November 27 and sat for only three days, the light docket consisting of two cases of theft and a charge of manslaughter. After dispensing with these, Justice George Walkem adjourned the session for a week so the lawyers, witnesses and defendant in the much-anticipated Stroebel trial could make their way to the province's capital. At 11:00 a.m., December 6, the main chamber was filled with spectators, packed together behind the low railing that bisected the room. In front of the railing, reporters and members of the Victoria bar crowded against the wall across the room from the jury seats. Stroebel looked anxiously about him at the sea of new faces before his glance settled on the familiar form of Theodore Davie, who again appeared for the Crown, and the reassuring presence of his counsel, Aulay Morrison.

The courtroom fell silent as Justice Walkem took his seat behind the bench. Short and trim, Walkem was a study in contrast with his counterpart in New Westminster, John McCreight. Walkem's owlish eyes peered through a pair of pince-nez, his mouth was downturned, framed by a white walrus moustache, and his chin creased upward; there was a sense of sadness about his look. Temperamentally, he was known for his strong emotions and sometimes violent outbursts rather than his legal erudition. Like McCreight, sixty-year-old Walkem was an Irishman who had been at the centre of BC's early politics, serving two terms as premier and Attorney General. Upon his retirement from politics in 1882, he was appointed to the Victoria district court.

After a dozen years on the bench, very little surprised Walkem, yet he was momentarily rattled when Davie rose to inform the court

Justice George Walkem, another former premier, repeatedly intervened in the questioning of witnesses during Stroebel's second trial, most notably during the examination of the defendant himself. Royal BC Museum and Archives, F-08418

that the indictment against Stroebel had been lost. The defendant's first trial ended with no decision, so the true bill passed at the New Westminster assize was still valid. Davie explained that the indictment had not been found among the documents sent over by New Westminster court registrar William Falding. At the earlier trial, the indictment had been handed to the jury foreman as the jurors retired to deliberate, and Falding had failed to get it back.

The Attorney General tried not to show his embarrassment and anger. This was the second time in as many trials that Davie could not produce a valid true bill in a murder trial, and the second time he had to meekly ask the judge that a new one be approved. Morrison half-rose to object, but, realizing a motion to dismiss the charges would be denied, he settled back into his seat and shook his head in disgust. Walkem too was annoyed by the incompetence, yet he approved Davie's request, and a fresh indictment was handed to the grand jury. The latter sat through the afternoon and returned with a true bill against Stroebel just before suppertime, at which point Walkem adjourned the court until the following morning.

❖

The Crown's second attempt to prove Albert Stroebel guilty of the murder of John Marshall had gotten off to a bumbling start. An entire day of court time was wasted because the existing indictment against Stroebel could not be found. This was not the first slip-up in the case for Registrar Falding, who was responsible for safekeeping exhibits, evidence and legal documents presented in the New Westminster district court. During Stroebel's first trial, he had misplaced a statement from Margaret Bartlett, finding it just hours before the trial closed. The registrar also left the bed and mattress from Stroebel's room dangerously exposed to the public. Superintendent Moresby had seized the items during his investigations, sending them on to Falding at the New Westminster courthouse. For four days, the items sat in the hallway just outside the door of the main courtroom, the daily crush of people passing by.

Born in England and trained as a bookkeeper, thirty-four-year-old Falding had lived a chequered life. In 1883, he was fired from his job as accountant and storekeeper at the BC penitentiary, presumably for incompetence. After working in the private sector, he found a job at the federal government's customs station in New Westminster, and in 1888 he was appointed registrar of the New Westminster district court. Even as he and his wife made room for a growing family, he struggled with alcoholism and a compulsive desire to spend beyond his means. As Falding's personal problems became more dire through the fall of 1893, he stopped keeping proper accounts of the money received by the courts and began using some of it to pay his escalating bills.

This situation went on for two more years, a reflection of the loose oversight that existed at the time. Then, in late August 1895, the registrar vanished. The provincial police alerted authorities across the continent and even called in the Pinkerton detective agency. After a dramatic railway chase, Falding was arrested in Spokane, Washington, and brought back to New Westminster. Criminal charges of theft were dropped when an investigation found that his misdeeds owed more to incompetence than malfeasance. Relieved, he quietly moved his family to the Kootenays, where he found work as an accountant.

In yet another turn of an already twisted plot, Falding had fled on the same day in August 1895 as James Prevost, registrar of the Victoria district court, had. Prevost was registrar during Stroebel's Victoria trial, so he had been responsible for receiving and safekeeping evidence and documents sent out by Falding. The son of a knighted admiral in the Royal Navy, Prevost embezzled thousands of dollars from estates held in probate by the court. He fled just as authorities stumbled upon his crimes, and his flight triggered Falding's. Prevost was caught and charged that September. He pleaded guilty to three counts of theft and was sentenced to four years in the BC penitentiary. Upon release, he left the province and country in disgrace.

THE CASE FOR THE CROWN

With their jury summons in hand, four dozen men shuffled into the Victoria courtroom on day two of the Stroebel trial. The men had shown up first thing the previous morning, Wednesday, and waited in the hallway just outside the chamber door. Their patience wore thin as the hours dragged on. Court officials brought out chairs and coffee to try to placate them, but a collective grumble rose up when the court adjourned at suppertime and they were told to return Thursday morning.

Now, standing in front of Judge Walkem, they looked on in confusion as one after another of them was dismissed. In the great majority of trials, jury selection was completed quickly, with defence and Crown counsel setting aside a handful of candidates before the required twelve men were chosen. However, Morrison and Davie were being picky. Twenty of those called were set aside by the defence lawyer, thirteen by the Attorney General. The notoriety and press coverage of Stroebel's first trial made it difficult to find jurors who came in with a completely open mind, and each side wanted to weed out anyone who might have already formed an opinion against their case. At last, with only a couple of candidates left in the jury pool, a dozen men were selected, and H.B. Rendall was sworn in as foreman. The sole indictment charging Albert Stroebel with the wilful murder of John Marshall was read and the defendant asked how he pled. Anxious to get the trial underway, the defendant replied with a rushed "Not guilty."

Theodore Davie wasted no time in launching into the Crown's opening statement. The Attorney General had visibly changed since the trial in New Westminster. Any lingering effects of illness were gone, his fierce dark eyes were clear, and his jaw was set in determination. In the two weeks between the trials, he had worked furiously to improve the Crown's case—he knew he could not fail to obtain a conviction a second time.

Drawing the jurors' attention to the sprawling map of Sumas set out on a table before them, Davie walked them through a detailed chronology of the events of April 19 and 20, focusing on Stroebel's movements. As he did so, he drove home the two points at the heart of the Crown's case. First, the handgun owned by Stroebel and later obtained by David Lucas "was a .38 calibre revolver, carrying a missile *precisely similar* to that which killed Marshall"—expert witnesses would be called to prove this point beyond reasonable doubt. Second, the barking of Marshall's dog placed his death at 9:00 p.m. on the nineteenth—and between 6:00 and 10:00 p.m. that night, "Stroebel was not seen by any living person." With a disdainful wave, Davie dismissed Stroebel's account of those lost hours, given at the previous trial, as "absurd and palpably untruthful."

Davie moved smoothly to his first witness, Ira Airheart, who replayed his account of April 19 and 20. Davie asked, "When did you first hear Marshall's dog barking on the nineteenth? When did it start barking?"

"I heard it around nine o'clock. But I don't rightly know when it started. I couldn't hear outside too good, on account of the crackling of the fire and me cooking. And my door was shut."

At the New Westminster trial, Airheart did not qualify his testimony in this way. During the earlier court's visit to Sumas, he did mention the crackling fire and closed door to jurors assembled on Marshall's trestle, but that was to explain how he might not have heard any gunshots the night of the murder. Now, under oath again, the trapper admitted that Marshall's dog might have been barking earlier than 9:00 p.m. and he just did not hear it. This was significant, because it is on Airheart's testimony that the Crown based its claim that the murder occurred at nine o'clock or shortly thereafter. The possibility that the barking and shooting occurred earlier opened the Crown up to questions about its timeline.

A view inside the main courtroom of the Victoria Courthouse in 1895. This photograph shows a full sitting of the BC Supreme Court. In a criminal trial such as for Stroebel, only one judge presided. The robes and gowns worn by the judges and lawyers were worn for all trials. Royal BC Museum and Archives, D-00808

Through the next four witnesses—William Blair, William Porter, Archie Baxter and Frank Warnock—Davie established Stroebel's movements on the nineteenth. There was nothing new in Blair and Porter's testimony. Baxter, who saw Stroebel walking north toward Marshall's house a few minutes before 6:00 p.m., added that the defendant walked the rail line, "sometimes with his lame foot on the rail. For a lame man, he is a fast walker." Warnock stated that, when he encountered the defendant just before 10:00 p.m. in Sumas City, "he was going south, walking quite fast."

Seventeen-year-old George Hilliard then took the stand. Hilliard again described the events of Sunday, April 16, including the morning's accidental shooting and the afternoon visit to Marshall's house. Hilliard explained: "We talked to Mr. Marshall about his girl. He said he was going to buy her a new dress and that he had the money to buy it." With that, the farmer took out a long purse and tipped out half a dozen gold coins. While the witness did not mention it, later testimony from Charles Bartlett revealed that Hilliard then told Stroebel about the visit and Marshall's bag of gold.

Hilliard looked anxious and pale as Morrison rose to cross-examine him. After two harmless questions, the teen "got sick and nervous and was taken out." Hilliard's collapse drew a disapproving glare from Judge Walkem and caused a stir in the courtroom; it also raised the question whether the youth knew more than he was willing to say. In Hilliard's version of their conversation, Marshall did not identify "his girl," the one he was going to buy a dress for. It is possible the farmer did identify her as Elizabeth Bartlett, or perhaps no name was mentioned, but Hilliard understood she was the one the older man was talking about. If Hilliard mentioned this to his friend Stroebel, it would have given the latter a solid motive for attacking Marshall. Moreover, when Hilliard told Stroebel about Marshall's gold coins, the pair may have swapped dreams of what they would do with that kind of money. Hilliard's talk of gold may have planted the seed of an idea that grew to robbery in his friend's mind. The pair might even have gone so far as to discuss ways they might get their hands on the money. This is speculation, of course, but intriguing speculation.

❖

Aside from George Hilliard's nervous swoon, day two of the Victoria trial produced little drama, and Aulay Morrison stayed uncharacteristically quiet. Day three began in similar fashion when the Attorney General called Flitcroft Evans to the stand. Evans was a bookish, thirty-five-year-old Englishman who had been the official stenographer for the New Westminster trial. Davie handed the stenographer a copy of Albert Stroebel's testimony at the trial, which Evans had transcribed, and asked him to read it.

Morrison shot to his feet, objecting that Stroebel's prior testimony should not be admitted as evidence "on the ground that it being optional whether or not the accused takes the stand, it was not proper in this trial to use the evidence given by the accused when a *voluntary* witness at a former trial." Morrison pointed out that the new Criminal

Code made no provision for such an action, nor was there precedent or case law to fall back on, since defendants had never testified before.

"Everything the defendant said in all previous examinations can be used against him at any subsequent trial," Walkem shot back, then ordered Evans to proceed. The stenographer spent the next three hours reading Stroebel's testimony in full.

The decision to admit Stroebel's New Westminster testimony was as questionable as it was arbitrary. Untroubled by the deeper legal issues it raised, Walkem gave no reasons for his ruling, acting as if the old rules concerning statements from defendants still applied. In allowing the accused to testify, the new code greatly expanded the opportunity for defendants to incriminate themselves, yet it provided no safeguards to protect the accused against self-incrimination in these new legal waters. The barring of testimony from previous trials would be one of the key safety provisions that would be developed in subsequent decades.

Walkem's peremptory ruling was a major victory for Davie. Even before the transcript was admitted, Stroebel's first trial testimony had given Davie the advantage of hearing what the defendant's alibi would be. With it included as evidence, Davie was handed even more ammunition, while Morrison was constrained in the defence he could mount: the defendant and his lawyer could not stray from or contradict the account or risk having Stroebel deemed a liar. Moreover, it ensured that Morrison would call his client to the stand, to explain the defence he had given in November—and with Stroebel in the box, Davie would be able to unleash a well-planned attack on cross-examination.

❧

As day four of the trial opened at the Victoria courthouse, the building's radiators hissed with steam from a central boiler set on high to fight the damp winter cold. The second trial in John Marshall's murder had captured the public's attention as much as the first one had, so the courtroom was packed on this Saturday in December. Collars were loosened and hats used as fans, but one member of the public found the stifling atmosphere too much to bear. Sweating profusely and struggling for air, the unidentified man let out two groans "so horrible that a momentary sensation was caused in the court," then fell to the floor in a dead faint. Frowning at the interruption, Judge Walkem ordered the man removed and called for more window transoms to be opened. With calm restored, Walkem instructed the Attorney General to proceed with his case.

Called to the stand, Dr. Boggs repeated his autopsy findings as if by rote, identifying the two slugs pulled from Marshall's body, which were entered as Exhibits A and B. Boggs testified that the shot to the back of Marshall's neck (bullet A) would have been instantly fatal, while the shot to his forehead (bullet B) would not have been. He also repeated his contention that the former came first, the latter second.

Morrison rose, smiled tightly, and asked, "So, doctor, can you explain to the jury how a body would fall if shot from the back, and how if shot from the front?"

Boggs paused, caught off guard with the shift in questioning: "The man if shot first in the neck, from the back, would not have moved beyond falling forward, on his face. If shot first in front he would have fallen backward."

"This is your considered opinion?"

"This is the prevailing medical opinion, although there are other authorities who think otherwise."

Morrison then asked whether, if the victim were walking forward, "the probabilities are stronger still that he would fall forward with a shot from behind?"

"Yes, sir, exactly."

Morrison did not press further, but the same could be said for a person walking forward who is shot in the front by a small calibre pistol: that he would generally fall forward. It is the walking—the motion or momentum of the body—not the bullet that determines how a body will fall. A cheap, small-calibre pistol such as Stroebel's delivered a light bullet at very low velocity; the momentum that bullet transferred into its target would be negligible. If the victim were not moving when shot, he would fall straight down, yet Marshall's body was fully laid out on the veranda, not crumpled in a heap, signifying he was moving, not standing, when shot. Since his head was propped against the doorsill and his feet were hanging over the veranda edge, he must have been walking back into the house when the first bullet hit him.

In both the first and second trials, Davie did not attempt to reconstruct the shooting of Marshall. He and Superintendent Moresby had their theories about what had happened, but they never aired them in court. Moresby came up with his working scenario within days of the murder: after finishing supper with his killer, Marshall went to the veranda and bent down to feed his dog. The killer followed him to the door and, standing above him, shot him in the back of the neck. Davie developed a similar theory, working from Moresby's conclusions and Boggs's testimony. After supper, Marshall was walking from his kitchen table to the door, showing Stroebel out, when the younger man shot him from behind. Marshall fell flat on his face, breaking his nose, and Stroebel then turned him over and shot him in the forehead.

We can see why Davie did not present either scenario to the jury. In attempting to account for Marshall's fall, they failed to explain how Marshall's body came to be fully stretched out on the front porch, feet off the veranda and head toward the door. Moresby's theory was inconsistent with the downward angle of the frontal shot, and Davie's scenario would leave Marshall's body with head pointing out of the house and legs pointing in, spun 180 degrees from the way he was actually found. Airing either scenario in court would have opened them up to stiff questioning from Morrison, who no doubt would have seized on the weaknesses in the accounts. Such questioning could only have sown confusion in the jurors' minds, and in that confusion, doubt would grow.

The Attorney General knew it was better to focus on more tangible, easily understood evidence, given to them by a trusted source such as William Moresby. The superintendent entered the witness box and described his investigations in the murder again, then identified and explained the key Crown exhibits: Stroebel's revolver, the empty and loaded cartridges, and the pouches of money found in Marshall's home. The jury listened closely as Moresby described the condition of Stroebel's gun when Lucas gave it to him: two chambers fired, two chambers greasy from unfired cartridges, one chamber clean.

However, another significant piece of testimony went largely unnoticed. Moresby explained that, when he first examined Marshall's body, he had grabbed it by the shoulders to turn it over and found that "the body wasn't warm, but quite stiff and cold." Nobody in the courtroom was surprised by this—the victim was found outside on his veranda, where night and early morning temperatures hovered just above freezing. What those in court did not know was that the corpse's stiffness was caused not by external temperatures, but by the internal process of rigor mortis.

Immediately after death the body's muscles are soft and relaxed; the muscles start to stiffen within a few hours, reaching full rigor from twelve to eighteen hours after death, depending on the conditions. The damp cold of the Sumas night would have slowed the stiffening in Marshall's body somewhat. If rigor was complete by the time Moresby handled the corpse at around 2:00 p.m. on April 20, then Marshall died anywhere between 8:00 p.m. on April 19 and the early hours of April 20; if rigor was not complete, those times would be later. Only a modern pathologist could have determined whether that time stretched past dawn on the twentieth, right before Marshall's body was found.

❖

Davie did not have access to modern pathologists or forensic scientists. Even so, the Attorney General was convinced he could demonstrate the one thing that would make his case: that the bullets extracted from Marshall's body were fired from the revolver of Albert Stroebel. To prove this point, Davie called up not one but two gunsmith experts. As we have seen, ballistic experts at the time matched markings on a fired bullet to the build-up of rust in a gun's barrel—not to the incised rifling unique to each barrel, as is done today. Samuel Webb's first trial testimony had been hesitant and confusing. This time, Davie made sure the New Westminster gunsmith came better prepared. Once again on the stand, Webb identified Stroebel's .38 calibre revolver as "of the cheapest kind," much more likely to rust.

"How does rust affect the bullets such a gun fired?" Davie asked.

"Rust causes the 'leading' of a barrel, namely, a piece of the bullet is likely to adhere to the rust"—bullets fired from that barrel take on grooves in just that spot.

Davie then presented Webb with Exhibits A and E. Bullet A was taken from Marshall's neck; bullet E was produced when Webb test-fired one of Stroebel's loaded cartridges from the defendant's revolver into a sack of flour.

"Exhibit A shows a great similarity to bullet E, with the same scooped and irregular grooves," Webb explained. "Both show the effect of rust and both were fired from a weapon equally rusty."

"Can you say that Exhibit A and E were fired from the same gun?"

"Well, bullet A has a groove near the base that is precisely the same as one from bullet E." Davie then passed the two bullets to the jurors who, with the aid of a magnifying glass, examined the grooves for a good quarter-hour.

The confidence Webb had displayed to that point was shaken by Morrison's cross-examination.

"You say the defendant's gun is a .38 calibre revolver. What do you mean by 'calibre'?"

"I mean a .38 calibre revolver takes a .38 calibre cartridge," Webb answered defensively.

"What do you mean by 'calibre'?"

"It means a decimal."

"A decimal of what?"

"I don't know." Webb's ignorance baffled Morrison and the jurors, for the answer to the question was a simple one. On a .38 calibre gun, the diameter of the barrel was .38 of an inch, just over one-third.

Davie turned to his second gun expert to clear up any confusion left by Webb. John Barnsley was a gunsmith from Victoria who ran a sporting goods shop that specialized in English and American firearms.

As Barnsley stepped into the witness box, the Attorney General handed him Exhibits A and E.

"What can you tell us about these two bullets?"

Barnsley replied with authority: "There are marks of similarity which would lead me to say, but not positively, that they had been fired from the same revolver. The marks are occasioned by the roughness of the inside of the barrel caused by rust or bad workmanship." Each slug had angular grooves on two sides that matched those on the other slug, although the length of one groove on bullet A was slightly shorter than that on bullet E.

Under Morrison's aggressive questioning, Barnsley conceded that the large majority of revolvers in private hands had rusty barrels. The gunsmith also admitted that when a barrel became badly leaded or fouled, "no two successive shots leave the same marks on the bullet."

The last statement was potentially fatal to the Crown's efforts to prove that bullet A came from Stroebel's gun. On re-examination, Davie gave Barnsley the chance to repair the damage.

"To be clear, what can you say about Exhibits A and E?"

Compensating for his slip-up, Barnsley went further than he had in his initial testimony: "I should judge bullets A and E were fired from the same revolver. The difference in one groove length could be caused by a number of things." The Attorney General had, at last, obtained the definitive match he was pressing for.

❧

Despite some glitches, day four had ended well for the Crown. However, Theodore Davie looked ahead to day five with some apprehension, because it was David Lucas's turn to take the stand. Lucas's performance in the first trial—his swagger and shiftiness, Morrison's devastating cross-examination—had hurt the Crown's case at least as much as it had helped it. Yet the marshal had obtained the most important pieces of physical evidence against the defendant. On the stand again, the marshal ran through the three days following Marshall's death, which he spent "knocking around" Sumas City collecting evidence:

the revolver he tricked Stroebel into handing over; the two empty cartridges he found in the alleyway below Stroebel's window; the two loaded cartridges found in Stroebel's bed.

In reply to Davie's question about finding the two empty shells, though, Lucas went off script: "I found two empty shells lying in the mud, just beyond a pool of water. I went to this place because, I may as well tell you, I dreamt the night before that the shells were near water."

Davie hurried past the point, but the marshal's surreal tale could not be untold. Morrison saw the strange story as further proof that Lucas had planted the incriminating shells. If the marshal were to be believed, the shells sat atop a muddy pool below Stroebel's window for three days without anybody spotting them, clear as day and clean as new.

"Tell the court again, what made you think of searching that spot, at that time?" Morrison demanded.

"I dreamt the night before about finding the cartridges, but I didn't go to the place because of the dream."

"You saw them in a dream!" Morrison paused, letting the idea sink in. "Did you put those cartridges there?"

"No, sir, I did not."

"Mr. Lucas, what is your religion?"

"Well, it is hard to tell. I used to try to be a Christian. I am not a spiritualist, nor a free thinker, nor a believer in dreams. I belong to the Odd Fellows." The admission shocked the jurors, spectators and even Justice Walkem.

Morrison then asked about the trickery by which Davie had obtained Stroebel's revolver, drawing a confession: "I admit that I lied when I told him the wound on Marshall was from a .44 calibre."

"And you lied when you said you weren't trying to arrest him or fix him up, then lured Stroebel across the line and had him arrested?"

"Yes, I lied."

Continuing to press the witness, Morrison revisited the first trial testimony of Wellington Miller, who had described a conversation with Lucas in which the latter talked of killing a man in San Francisco, but being acquitted of his murder at trial.

"I acted as a special constable in San Francisco," Lucas scrambled. "I never told Officer Miller I murdered a man there." With Lucas glaring angrily at him from the stand, Morrison handed the witness a letter signed by the San Francisco police chief, P. Crowley.

"Can you read that letter to the court?"

The illiterate Lucas stayed mute, his anger brewing.

"Is that the signature of San Francisco's chief of police?"

"I don't know who the police chief is." Morrison shrugged at the obvious lie and took the letter back, leaving the jury to wonder what incriminating evidence it might have contained.

❖

David Lucas was not the only Crown witness subjected to Morrison's aggressive tactics. Others called up by Davie also faced questions laced with insinuations and accusations of wrongdoing. After Frank Warnock confirmed that he had seen Stroebel at 10:00 p.m. on April 19, Morrison attacked the bookkeeper's integrity. When Warnock explained he lived in BC but did most of his work in Sumas City, Morrison asked pointedly, "Have you ever been suspected of smuggling?"

"I have heard of my being accused of smuggling opium. But no steps have been taken against me." Warnock's ambiguous answer hung in the air, and Morrison hoped the jury got the point—where there's smoke, there's fire.

The defence lawyer posed the same question to Frank Black and Frank Carpenter. Black heatedly denied that he used his position as railway station master in Sumas City to smuggle goods across the line; Carpenter was more evasive.

"I suppose living on the boundary line affords opportunities for making money?" Morrison asked suggestively.

"Yes, I suppose so." It was another ambiguous answer that left doubts in the jurors' minds.

Morrison's insinuations about smuggling were not pulled from thin air, for Sumas City had gained a reputation as a smugglers' haven, where drugs, alcohol and illegal immigrants moved across the porous border. No one was more touchy about this reputation than the city's mayor, Phillip Lawrence. Testifying for the Crown, Lawrence defended Carpenter and spoke of Stroebel's lack of money. Morrison then went to work: he dangled suggestions of political cronyism (in Lawrence's relationship with David Lucas) and professional misconduct (in the way the lawyer charged his clients). He then accused Lawrence of "contravening Canadian Customs laws by coming into Canada to fish." The mayor sputtered a reply as chuckles rippled through the room.

Morrison also sought to portray Crown witnesses as a collection of gamblers and crooks. The defence lawyer had heard that Frank Carpenter was involved in a number of petty scams. He asked the barber if he ever ran a game called thimble-rigging, the nutshell and pea game where through sleight-of-hand the operator fools a betting player who tries to guess the pea's location. "I ran a nutshell and pea game," Carpenter replied lamely. "I don't know nothing about no thimble-rigging."

The defence counsel then went after a juicier target. After Davie called up Charles Moulton to testify about Stroebel's financial woes, Morrison asked on cross-examination: "You are a sporting man, are you, sir?"

"I occasionally indulge in betting. And I keep a racehorse, a slow one."

"Have you bet on the result of this trial, with other witnesses staying at Holbrook Hotel?"

"I have not," Moulton replied indignantly. "I don't remember any of the witnesses betting on it. I talked to some about the result, but no money was put up."

Morrison nodded, then pressed Moulton on his ties to the Sumas Bank and the shifty deals it was involved in. At first, Moulton denied he was a partner in the bank and insisted he received no money from it, but in the face of sharp questioning, he admitted he had acted as an agent for the bank and had been paid for his services.

"You are proprietor of the Huntingdon Hotel and its saloon, are you not? Where is that located?" Morrison shifted topics.

"Yes. The hotel is about two hundred feet north of the border. There's nothing but underbrush between it and the line."

"And the saloon, no doubt it serves smugglers' whisky?" Moulton gave no reply and was released from the box.

Morrison's aggressive questioning left a string of wounded witnesses in their wake and lit Judge Walkem's short fuse. In the midst of wrangling over some procedural issues, Walkem unleashed a heated diatribe: "Defence counsel has adopted a very dangerous line of defence. He has practically accused a half-dozen witnesses for the Crown of being smugglers, pickpockets, thimble-riggers, or criminals of other types. And this without any evidence to show the slightest justification." The judge informed the court that some of these witnesses, led by Phillip Lawrence, had written a private letter to complain of the abuse. Reaching the height of his outrage, Walkem concluded: "To continue in this course toward the witnesses would make this, not a court of justice, but a court of injustice and torture."

Morrison withstood the harangue from the bench, a look of feigned innocence on his face, then responded that "unless His Lordship stops me, I should follow the course I have so far been pursuing and take my chances with the jury."

❖

At the New Westminster trial, Attorney General Davie had spent little time discussing Stroebel's alleged motive for killing Marshall. He had mentioned it only in his closing statement, arguing that Stroebel had committed the crime for money and love. The law did not require that the Crown prove motive, only that it show the accused had formed the intention to commit the crime, then went ahead and committed it. However, the reality was that juries were very reluctant to convict someone unless they could see why the defendant would commit the crime he was accused of committing. This was especially true in a death penalty case. For the late Victorians, the idea of a motiveless crime was an oxymoron—it could not exist. Man was both a rational and moral being, who could choose between right and wrong, good and evil. The criminal chose to do wrong and chose it for a reason.

In the second trial, the motive attributed to Stroebel remained the same as in the first trial, money and love. But now Davie called up a string of witnesses to demonstrate that the defendant was in dire need of money to set himself up in business so he could marry the young girl he loved. The Attorney General's questioning of Margaret Bartlett revealed that Stroebel had been a month behind in his rent payments. Phillip Lawrence testified that when Stroebel came to him for help in dealing with David Eyerly, the defendant admitted "I have no money to pay for advice or to prosecute him." Frank Carpenter stated that the defendant had desperately wanted to buy his barbershop because he was getting married. The barber never saw any of the $250 Stroebel offered for the shop, and the $500 the latter claimed to have in the bank was a delusion. William Porter corroborated Carpenter's testimony, saying the defendant had told him he planned to purchase the barbershop. Finally, Charles Moulton and his lawyer, Grey Myers, described in minute detail the land deal that had gone sour, leaving a hapless Stroebel without assets or money.

The picture Davie painted was bleak: a young man, physically disabled, uneducated and penniless, in debt and lacking a steady job; a young man engaged to be married, who needed to find the means to support a wife and family. So when George Hilliard told Stroebel of the money in Marshall's house, it planted the seed of an idea—here was a way out of all his problems, if only he could get his hands on that purse of gold. Driven by his need for money and carrying a loaded revolver in his pocket, the defendant went to Marshall's house the evening of April 19 to rob him. Whatever happened next, the night ended with Stroebel shooting Marshall dead, the shooter fleeing into the dark, and the farmer's money still safety hidden away.

As day six of the trial came to an end, the Attorney General met the eyes of each juror and liked what he saw. Turning to Judge Walkem, he declared, "The case for the Crown is closed, my lord." And with that, the court adjourned until the following morning.

The Case for the Defence

Residents of Victoria have long taken great pride and comfort in the fact that they have the mildest winters in Canada. Even compared to BC's Lower Mainland, their winters are drier, sunnier and warmer. The provincial capital sits on the lee side of westward mountains, which absorb rain coming in from the Pacific Ocean. At the same time, moderating ocean currents keep the temperature safely above freezing. But December 1892 was an unusually cold, wet month for the city, a fitting backdrop for the legal battle grinding away in the capital's courthouse. The sun seemed to have disappeared along with any chance that the trial would end soon. Attorney General Davie had taken nearly a week to lay out the Crown's case, and now it was Aulay Morrison's turn.

Morrison opened the case for the defence on the morning of day seven with a direct, economical statement. "There is no direct evidence that the accused committed this crime," he declared, and the circumstantial evidence presented by the Crown was inadequate to send the young defendant to the gallows. Nor was there proof that the murder had occurred between 9:00 and 10:00 p.m. on April 19, "but there was a strong probability it was committed between 4:00 and 5:00 the next morning." Other men were more plausible culprits than young Stroebel. The victim lived on a "tramps' highway. Tramps very frequently passed there and had ample opportunity to commit the crime." As for the defendant, he would take the stand and account "for every moment of time between leaving Porter on the afternoon of the nineteenth and arriving at Bartlett's hotel." Finally, the Crown had failed to establish what motive might have driven Stroebel to kill his friend. It alleged robbery, yet no money or gold was ever found on the defendant or in his room.

As the stenographer struggled to keep pace with Morrison's rapid-fire delivery, the defence lawyer turned and called up Oliver Ackerman. The family remained steadfastly in Stroebel's corner, and Oliver once again took the stand to describe the investigations he had undertaken on behalf of the defendant. Ackerman's main function, though, was as the defence's sole expert on guns. Ackerman agreed that rust in a revolver's barrel created markings on the bullets it fired, but he rejected claims that you could prove that "any particular bullet came out of any particular gun, from marks on the bullet caused by rust." He then offered a detailed comparison between Exhibits A and E, concluding that they showed both similarities and marked differences. In the midst of this testimony, Ackerman made a telling point: the condition of Stroebel's revolver in September (when it fired slug E) could very well have been different than it was in April (when it allegedly fired slug A). It was not unreasonable to suppose that the rust build-up in the gun's barrel might have grown during these five months. Because the telltale rusting of a barrel could and did change over time, it could not be definitively proven that two bullets fired five months apart came from the same barrel.

This finer point was lost amidst the detailed and contradictory testimony given by Crown and defence gun experts. Meanwhile, on cross-examination, Davie was able to chip away at Ackerman's credibility. Under stiff questioning, Ackerman conceded that most of his experience with firearms dated back to his service in the Union Army, three decades earlier. At this earlier time, revolvers still fired paper-sided cartridges rather than the metallic ones in use by the 1890s. Ackerman also admitted he had worked closely with Morrison to build the defence case. It was he who told Morrison about the alleged cases of smuggling and other wrongdoing by some of the Crown's witnesses. He had heard these reports from a number of Sumas City residents, including John Bartlett and Peter Strumm, a newly married Swedish immigrant who knew Stroebel and Elizabeth Bartlett.

Justice Walkem joined in the attack on Ackerman's credibility. Walkem had berated Morrison for using rumours and innuendo to impugn Crown witnesses, so Ackerman's admission that he had been the source for the defence lawyer's aspersions set the judge against him. Walkem interrupted the questioning of Ackerman to charge that his testimony was "certainly contradictory." Later, in his closing statement, the judge would go so far as to label Ackerman a perjurer and serial liar. His voice dripping with scorn, Walkem declared that "this man in the most confident and jaunty way" had repeatedly and intentionally tried to mislead the jury on cardinal points.

Asa Ackerman followed his brother into the box, and he too would be rebuked by Walkem. After Asa described his journey home from a neighbour's house between 9:00 and 10:00 p.m. on April 19, when the only dogs he heard barking were his own, Walkem stepped in sharply: "You say you were outside at 9:00 p.m.?"

"No, it was more like 9:30. I didn't want to leave the impression it was nine."

"You must be more careful. You certainly gave the impression that you were out earlier."

The Ackermans' nephew Elmer Jesseph was next. Morrison asked him to describe the tramp he and his brother Frank met along the rail line a half-mile north of Marshall's on the evening of the nineteenth.

"He was tall and light complected, with hard looking clothes."

"Is it extraordinary to meet strangers along this road?"

"No, sir, strangers are passing every hour in the day, nearly so. It is a tramps' reserve, that track."

Earlier in the trial, Morrison had drawn a similar reply from Archibald Baxter, the CPR section man who passed another tramp on the trestle opposite Marshall's gate at about the same time. Baxter worked the line from Huntingdon to Mission every day, and he stated he regularly met people walking along the railbed.

"Tramps and so forth?" Morrison asked.

"Yes, lots of them."

❖

As day eight opened, Elizabeth Bartlett picked her way across the crowded courtroom and delicately sat down on the wooden chair in the witness box. Justice Walkem had ordered a chair be brought in for the use of the trial's two female witnesses, Elizabeth, and her mother, Margaret. The other witnesses, all male, had to stand—even the crippled defendant, who would spend nine hours on his feet testifying.

In a voice raised just above a whisper, Elizabeth repeated her account of April 18 (the couple's walk on Harrison Road) and the night of April 19 (when Stroebel arrived home). Davie pressed the twelve-year-old girl on cross-examination, but once again she stood her ground. As the Attorney General returned to his seat, Judge Walkem looked down paternally and asked Bartlett about her feelings toward the defendant.

"I am very friendly with Stroebel, very. He hasn't bought me a ring yet, that's all."

"There's probably a little love. Well, I am not surprised that you should try to defend him." Of course, with this statement the judge completely dismissed Bartlett's testimony—she would, he intimated, say anything to defend the man she loved.

Wellington Miller took the stand next, to contradict the earlier testimony of David Lucas. The New Westminster constable described the conversation he had engaged in with Lucas in which the marshal said he had killed a man in San Francisco and was tried and acquitted of murder. Once again Judge Walkem jumped in, this time sternly. Morrison and Davie looked on, dumbfounded, as the judge moved to throw out Miller's testimony. The question Morrison had asked Lucas was whether he had told Miller he had murdered a man in San Francisco, Walkem argued. Miller's testimony did not speak directly to that question because what Lucas described to him "was not a case of murder, but of homicide in the discharge of his duty. The evidence must be excluded."

Recovering his voice, Davie responded that he had no objection to the constable's testimony, and it went ahead. On cross-examination, the Attorney General drew a reply from Miller that echoed Walkem: "Lucas said he had shot a man in the discharge of his duty, and not that he had murdered a man." On this point, both Walkem and Miller were splitting hairs. In the first trial testimony that gave rise to Morrison's question, the constable had stated that Lucas said "he was in danger of being killed and had shot a man; had to stand his trial for *the murder* and was acquitted." Morrison watched with concern: the fact that the judge and one of his own witnesses spoke against him was a setback; the fact the judge was becoming increasingly hostile and intrusive was cause for deeper concern.

❖

As spectators filed back into the courtroom after the lunch recess, their excited whispers blended into a single, rising hiss. Judge Walkem entered and the whispers stopped, but the feeling of anticipation remained. Morrison paused to take in the expectant air, then called Albert Stroebel to the witness stand.

The chair had been taken from the box, and Stroebel settled as comfortably as his leg would allow, his cane propped against the banister and his workman's hands resting atop the rail. A guileless smile tugged at the corner of his mouth as his blue-grey eyes scanned the courtroom. Stroebel was eager to testify. He was confident the jury would believe him, and that all he needed to do was explain his version of events, what he had done and not done. Aulay Morrison had warned him to be careful; the jury had heard his testimony from the first trial, read out from the transcript, and he could not contradict it now.

At Morrison's prompt, Stroebel began to describe his movements on April 19 from the time he awoke in his room at the City Hotel. A few minutes into the testimony, Justice Walkem pushed Morrison aside and took over the questioning. The judge walked Stroebel through the events of the day. When the defendant arrived at the crucial period between 6:00 and 10:00 p.m., the questioning became even more rigorous as Morrison looked on helplessly. Stroebel explained how he fetched his fishing pole and salmon roe after milking Porter's cow.

"Then I fished along upstream close to the east side of the foothills. I was there till near dark. I got to McQuee's bridge. I sat on the bridge with the rod hanging over the edge, and whittled some time." In the semi-dark, he then picked his way along a trail past his old house to the rail line. Walking south, he turned as he passed three strangers, lost his footing and fell, bashing his crippled leg on the steel track. After resting some time, "I got up and walked on slow towards Sumas," arriving home sometime after 9:00 p.m.

The court broke for supper recess, and when it returned, Morrison tried to take back control of the witness. With his own counsel posing the questions, Stroebel had the chance to deny testimony presented by Crown witnesses. He rejected Lucas's accounts of the conversations they had had, and insisted he never told William Porter he had arrived home between 5:00 and 6:00 p.m. on the nineteenth.

Walkem then cut in and returned to his direct questioning of the defendant. The judge grilled Stroebel on the rolled note allegedly written by him on the twenty-second. As the young defendant tried to explain himself, Walkem rudely interrupted, "What was that? Speak a little louder." The judge then pressed Stroebel over his statement that he knew others thought he might have killed Marshall, asking "At what time did you hear others suspected you?"

"From the time I was going out to Marshall's, I understood I was suspected. From about 9:00 a.m. on April 20." To Walkem's mind, Stroebel's wariness so soon after Marshall's body was discovered was proof of a guilty conscience.

As Morrison struggled to get his own questions in, Walkem continually interrupted, even returning to matters dealt with earlier in Stroebel's testimony. Throughout the entire direct examination period, which was supposed to be when the defence counsel questioned his own client, the judge effectively mounted his own cross-examination of Stroebel. There is little doubt that Walkem's actions harmed Stroebel's ability to defend himself on the stand—the defendant was not given an unimpeded chance to present his own version of events. The judge could get away with this because the move to allow defendants to testify was so new. No one knew what should and should not be allowed, and no provisions had been put in place to ensure that defendants could say their piece without bullying or trickery from the judge or Crown.

❖

Enduring the questioning of his own attorney and an arbitrary cross-examination from Judge Walkem, Albert Stroebel was kept on his feet in the witness box from early afternoon until 11:00 p.m. He returned to the stand at 11:00 the following morning, day nine, to face the proper cross-examination from Theodore Davie. The defendant would be kept there for most of the day.

Beginning with the question of motive, Davie set out to show that Stroebel was in desperate need of money to buy Frank Carpenter's barbershop. Carpenter had testified that Stroebel offered to pay him $250 for the business, and William Porter recalled the defendant saying he planned to buy the shop. Davie pressed Stroebel on this, but the defendant insisted he "had no intention of buying Carpenter out," that he had only been joking.

To further demonstrate Stroebel's money problems, Davie brought up his land dealings with Charles Moulton and John Loughran, president of the Sumas Bank. Through his own brother's blunders, Stroebel was left with the deeds on two Vancouver properties along with the $250 mortgage owing against them, which Loughran had supplied. Stroebel agreed to sell the property to Loughran for that amount, with the money going to pay off the mortgage. We can see that this settled the matter. Stroebel, however, did not understand why he had ended up with no properties and no money—he believed Loughran should have paid the money from the sale to him.

"He owes it to me yet," the defendant stated plaintively. Davie let the jury connect the dots. The $250 Stroebel claimed to be owed was the money he planned to use to buy Carpenter's barbershop. When he realized he would not be getting the money, Stroebel decided on a more drastic course, robbing his friend John Marshall.

The Attorney General then moved on to the crux of Stroebel's defence—his account of those missing hours between 6:00 and 10:00 p.m. on April 19. For a good hour, Davie grilled the defendant on every detail, demanded an accounting of his every move: ten minutes to get from Porter's cow to the rail line; five minutes to wash his hands;

twenty minutes to retrieve his rod; ten minutes to get the salmon roe; then more time fishing along the creek up to McQuee's bridge.

"And how long did you fish for?"

"Until just before dark."

"At the last trial you stated, 'I should say I fished about two and a half hours, or more.' Did you say that?"

"I believe I said that. But I could not have fished that long. It would have been too dark, and I quit before dark."

Stroebel agreed that it was dark that night by 7:30, and he admitted he must have returned to the railbed just after that. Davie now pressed the defendant to explain what happened in the two hours between then and just before 10:00 p.m., when Frank Warnock saw him walking briskly into Sumas City. Stroebel replied that he had slipped and banged his crippled knee on the tracks.

"That held me up for some time. And then I had to walk home slow."

Pulling together all of the defendant's inconsistencies and contradictions, Davie drove home his point that the whole "fish story" was an elaborate lie: "When you gave your testimony at the last trial, you had not calculated the time, then. You did not see that two and a half hours of fishing would mean you fished an hour in the dark?"

"I just guessed at it," Stroebel replied weakly.

Davie had made devastating use of the defendant's first trial testimony to blow a hole in the defendant's alibi. On a string of other questions, the Attorney General confronted Stroebel with his November testimony, contrasting it with what he was saying now in December. "You said in December you fired the shots at David Eyerly six weeks before Marshall's death, now you say three weeks—Then you said Porter's testimony was all true, now you say it was not—Then you said Lucas asked you about cartridges and you answered you had none, now you say he never talked to you about any cartridges."

To each of these contradictions, Stroebel could only stammer, "I don't remember saying that. I might have said it, but it was untrue."

"How did you come to tell us an untruth there at New Westminster?"

"I don't know. I don't remember whether I said so or not."

Stroebel was visibly flagging under the Attorney General's relentless questioning, and as the afternoon wore on, his answers grew more muddled. At one point, Judge Walkem admonished Stroebel to be clearer in his answers, not to hide behind "I don't think so" or "I don't remember."

Morrison rose for re-examination with the hope he could undo some of the damage inflicted on his client. At his prodding, Stroebel wearily went over the basic elements of his alibi. However, even here, Walkem would not permit the defence lawyer to have the witness to himself, sharply interrupting on nearly every question. Then, after nine hours spread over two days, Stroebel was released from the witness box. Ashen and spent, he hobbled back to his seat as Morrison declared the case for the defence closed. The courtroom fell silent as the jurors and spectators alike slumped in exhaustion, worn down from watching Stroebel's ordeal on the stand. Relief greeted Walkem's declaration of a well-deserved recess.

❖

Morrison knew he had to recharge his case, and quickly. As the court reassembled for the evening session, and Davie opened the Crown's rebuttal, the defence lawyer returned to what he did best—playing offence. Davie called up Phillip Lawrence to corroborate the testimony of Frank Carpenter. On cross-examination, Morrison went straight for Lawrence's sore spot, asking the Sumas mayor if he had been behind the letter sent to Judge Walkem complaining of the defence attorney's treatment of Crown witnesses. When Lawrence admitted he had been, Morrison asked what the mayor's complaints were.

"For one, your insinuation related to contingency fees, that lawyers south of the line who take them are guilty of pettifoggery."

"Well, anything else?"

"Your insinuation that I gave free legal advice in exchange for support in municipal elections."

Morrison needled Lawrence further, asking why the mayor had not made his objection known from the witness box rather than going "round the back" to the judge.

"Because I had seen the way others were treated in the witness box," Lawrence replied.

Morrison let a smile grow on his lips before saying coyly, "If I may say, sir, you are the most sensitive lawyer I have ever known."

By this point, Davie had had enough of Morrison's witness-baiting and called on Walkem to put a stop to the defence attorney's "reign of terror." The judge balked, saying he did not want to be criticized for impeding Morrison's ability to defend his client on a capital charge. This argument was hypocritical coming from Walkem. The judge had impeded Morrison's ability to defend his client in a much more serious way by taking over the initial questioning of Stroebel. Because of Walkem, the defendant never had an unhindered opportunity to defend himself. Concerning Davie's objection to Morrison's witness-baiting, Walkem had already vented his spleen over the matter and was tired of the whole mess. He just wanted the day over. With the legal fireworks over, he adjourned court until the following morning.

CLOSINGS AND VERDICT

Day ten, Saturday morning, opened with Aulay Morrison calling his own witnesses on rebuttal. Theron Ackerman took the stand and testified that the Saturday evening a week before, Peter Strumm had spoken to him at their hotel.

"Strumm said, 'It's a damned shame the way these men are swearing; and if I wasn't afraid of being stabbed in the back, or having some depredation committed to my property, I would go on the stand and swear I wouldn't believe Lucas under oath.' " Thinking nothing of the conversation, Ackerman had not informed Morrison of it until Friday evening.

John Bartlett, who along with Stroebel was a friend of Strumm's, then told the court of a conversation he had with Strumm that Friday afternoon. Strumm wanted Bartlett to tell Morrison that if he, Strumm, got called to the stand, "he didn't want to say anything against Lucas, or be on bad terms with him." Morrison's aim in airing these behind-the-scene conversations was clear: to further sully the reputation and credibility of David Lucas. Given what we know of the marshal, Strumm's fears were justified. There existed in Sumas City a widespread feeling that Lucas was willing and able to exact revenge on anyone who crossed him.

The Strumm affair was the last bit of drama in the trial's witness phase. A few rebuttal witnesses were called to clear up some minor points, but they were finished by mid-afternoon. Rather than move into closing statements, Judge Walkem decided to adjourn and start afresh the following Monday. After a relaxing Saturday evening and church services the next morning, the jury spent its second Sunday sequestered in their hotel. It was also a second Sunday of leaden skies and cold rain, so even though they had been cooped up in a stuffy courtroom for a week and a half, the jurors had little desire to venture outside.

Monday morning brought more of the same weather. The jurors shuffled into their seats, wiping the sleep from their eyes and stifling yawns. The only bright spot was the belief that the trial would be over that day—surely the closing arguments would not last longer than that.

Once again, because he had presented witnesses during rebuttal, Aulay Morrison gave his closing statement first. Morrison had fought tooth and nail through every day of the lengthy trial, and he was showing signs of tiring. Keenly aware that his client's young life was on the line, the defence lawyer gathered every ounce of his remaining energy. Rising to his feet, he spoke for two hours through the morning session, then another three after the lunch recess.

Morrison opened by reminding the jury of the solemn duty they bore. Considering what was at stake—the life of a man "in the prime of his youth"—a guilty verdict "should only follow the most positive evidence." The Crown had failed to present that positive evidence, relying instead on "inferior circumstantial evidence." Foreseeing Davie's argument about the "chain of evidence," Morrison cautioned that "if even the slightest link were weak, the chain of evidence against the prisoner would not be complete or justify conviction."

Morrison then argued that the Crown had failed to establish any motive for Stroebel to commit the crime. Playing to the beliefs of the jury rather than the letter of the law, Morrison declared that "it is an axiom that there could be no crime without a motive. It is like an effect without a cause." The Crown alleged that robbery was the motive, yet there was no evidence that any money had been taken from Marshall's house, and no money was ever found on the defendant. Stroebel may have been a little short of funds, but in this year of the great economic crash, so were many others, including Airheart, Lucas, even Loughran at the Bank of Sumas. No one had suggested that they had a motive to kill Marshall.

Edging onto thinner ice, the defence lawyer asserted that his client did not have the "exclusive opportunity" to commit the crime. It was upon this principle, Morrison argued, that the infamous Borden case had been decided just six months earlier. Lizzie Borden was tried and acquitted of the brutal axe murders of her father and stepmother in her New England hometown. In the face of strong circumstantial evidence, Borden's lawyer had shown that on the day of the murders, there were fifteen minutes during which someone other than Lizzie could have entered the Borden house and killed her parents; this had been enough for an acquittal.

There was no shortage of people who could have confronted and killed Marshall at his home, Morrison continued: "The deceased lived on a tramps' highway, along which the offal of humanity daily passed." Archibald Baxter, Elmer Jesseph and Stroebel himself had all seen tramps in the vicinity of Marshall's farm around the time of the murder, and many other strangers could have been there unseen. It was the theory of the defence that one of these tramps killed Marshall, not the night of April 19, but just after dawn on April 20.

"In the morning, the tramp first laid out the dog with a heavy blow from a club. When Marshall came to the door to see what was happening, the tramp fired once and then again to finish the work. He intended to rob Marshall, but the approach of Airheart frightened him off before he secured the money."

Morrison then attacked the weakest link of the Crown case: "Airheart's testimony that he heard Marshall's dog barking before 10:00 p.m. was the only indication presented by the Crown of the time the crime was committed." Yet it was never proven that this was Marshall's dog, and if it was, why he was barking. Asa Ackerman lived closer to Airheart than Marshall did, and his dogs barked through much of that night. In rural Sumas, "there was nothing unusual about a dog barking."

Morrison continued his attack on the Crown's case with undiminished energy: one by one, he dismissed the testimony of Crown witnesses as untrustworthy. From Porter and Boggs to Moresby and Webb, Crown witnesses were "overzealous in their desire for conviction." Of course, Morrison was most critical of David Lucas; all the evidence the marshal had produced had been in his possession for some time and could easily have been altered by him. The empty cartridges found in the alleyway could only have been planted by Lucas. Acting on a "dream story," the marshal found them atop a muddy puddle days after the murder, clean and in the open.

Addressing an unspoken unease over the youth of Elizabeth Bartlett, Morrison argued that there was no proof that she and Stroebel were properly engaged. However, even if they were, "it would be no disgrace, for it would show there was affection in the heart of the boy. And the action of the girl spoke volumes for her in following the case from one end of the province to the other."

Morrison concluded by reminding the jurors again that a guilty verdict would cost Stroebel his life. They could convict "only where the evidence was most clear-cut and convincing. A mistake against the Crown might be rectified, but against the prisoner never." The defence lawyer held the jury's gaze for several moments as his last words sank in, then returned to his seat.

Walkem glanced at his pocket watch, which registered a few minutes before five o'clock. The judge doubted the Crown's closing statement could be squeezed into an evening session so, not wanting to interrupt Davie's summation midway through, he adjourned the court to the following morning.

❖

The twelfth and final day of the trial opened to a packed courtroom. At 10:00 a.m., Justice Walkem called the court to order and nodded to Theodore Davie, who stood and launched into the Crown's closing argument. Davie began with another defence of the reliability of circumstantial evidence. He rejected Morrison's argument that such evidence was inherently inferior, insisting that in many ways it was superior to "the direct evidence of supposed actual witnesses." Witnesses often were mistaken in what they thought they saw, or intentionally lied or misled in describing events: "But in the case of a long chain of circumstantial evidence, where twenty or thirty facts were joined link by link, there was less liability of error through perjury or otherwise."

The Attorney General also rejected Morrison's argument that unless it could be proven the defendant had the "exclusive opportunity" to commit the crime, he had to be acquitted. No such principle existed in the law—indeed, if it did, "no one would ever be convicted." In the Lizzie Borden trial, the defendant was acquitted because her lawyer presented positive evidence that the murder might have been committed by a third party, who then escaped the scene. No such evidence was produced by Stroebel's counsel: the defence provided no evidence to support its theory that a passing tramp murdered Marshall. On the contrary, the evidence before the court demonstrated that the killer was known to Marshall, as the remnants of a shared supper showed.

Davie then walked the jury through the events of April 19, quickly homing in on the time between 6:00 and 10:00 p.m.: "The facts show that the homicide occurred about 9:00 p.m., and the prisoner's whereabouts are unaccounted for from 6:00 to 10:00 p.m., except by himself."

Davie highlighted the contradictions between Stroebel's account of these hours given at the first trial with that of the second trial. In the former, Stroebel had stated he had gone fishing for two and a half hours after he was last seen on the rail line at six o'clock. Since the sun set at 7:03 p.m., and it was fully dark by 7:30, in this first account "he must have fished for a least one hour in pitch darkness." Recognizing the contradictions, Stroebel told a different "fish story" in the second trial, in which he claimed he had stopped fishing and was back on the rail line by 8:00 p.m. For more than an hour he was delayed by an injured leg, during which no witnesses saw him. Davie drove the point home: both accounts, both alibis, were "palpable untruths" that were undermined by their own contradictions and by conflicting evidence from other witnesses.

The Attorney General was equally emphatic and forceful as to motive. The defendant was penniless, owning no assets and was "in urgent need of money." The money he claimed to have in a New Westminster bank, the land he claimed to own in Sumas and Vancouver—these were mere fables. He had no steady income and no vocation, and even the prospect of a ditching contract with William Porter did not solve his problem since he would not get paid for two months. He also owed rent money to his landlady, who was also his future mother-in-law. Stroebel dreamed of buying Frank Carpenter's barbershop, to provide the vocation and livelihood he lacked, but he had no money to pay for it.

Driving all the defendant's dreams and schemes was his "burning desire to possess the girl he loved." To marry Elizabeth Bartlett, he needed first to pay her mother what he owed in back rent, and second, to satisfy both daughter and mother that he had the means to support a young wife. Davie's voice grew ominous: "It was in this time of terrible temptation that Stroebel heard his friend Hilliard's story of the twenty-dollar gold pieces, held by Marshall in a leather pouch." The defendant came back to the farmer's house the evening of April 19 to rob him. Robbery escalated to murder after Stroebel pulled a loaded revolver from his pocket and shot his friend dead.

Davie spoke for nearly three hours through the morning session and continued for another hour after lunch recess. The Attorney General then turned to the gun and cartridges he asserted were responsible for Marshall's death. "Marshall was killed by a .38 calibre Smith & Wesson bullet fired from a cheap trade revolver with a highly rusted barrel." Stroebel was in possession of cartridges of the same calibre and make, which he kept hidden in his bed. On the very day of the murder, Stroebel carried a cheap trade revolver, the barrel of which was thick with rust. And the bullet extracted from the neck of the victim was "precisely similar" to a bullet later test-fired from the defendant's gun.

Davie then tried to repair the damage done to one of his key witnesses. David Lucas's testimony "was not of the nature to most strongly impress the jury, but there was no foundation for the vicious attack upon his character." The Attorney General even claimed Lucas's evidence could be thrown out in its entirety without harming the Crown's case. Of course, this might have been true for the testimony Lucas gave, but it was not true for the physical evidence the marshal had produced. Davie concluded by once again addressing the nature and quality of the Crown's evidence: "The chain of circumstantial evidence about Stroebel that night is complete and the evidence not contradicted. Indeed, never was a case more clearly brought home to anyone, by evidence both circumstantial and direct."

As the Attorney General returned to his seat, the heavy responsibility he had carried throughout the trial seemed to lift from his shoulders. His case had been disciplined and exhaustive, and his closing—in the words of one reporter—"clear, concise and manifestly fair on every point."

❖

It was now the turn of Judge Walkem to present his instructions to the jury. Jurors placed great store in the instructions given them by the judge, and late Victorian judges did not hesitate to express their thoughts on a defendant's innocence or guilt. Walkem began by asserting his right to do just that: "It is the duty of the judge to advise the jury more or less strongly at his discretion. From this duty I do not intend to flinch."

Over the next two and a half hours Walkem stayed true to his word. The judge had grown increasingly hostile toward Morrison and his defence witnesses as the trial progressed, so it came as no surprise when his charge to the jury went strongly against the defendant, agreeing with the Crown on all the points that mattered. He declared that the defendant's motive was well proven: "He wanted money, and he knew from Hilliard's talk that Marshall had money." Stroebel's alibi for the night of April 19 was "a strange account" that varied from one telling to the next, made all the less credible by his off-putting "appearance and general demeanour in the dock." The cartridges and shells discovered in Stroebel's bed and below his window were incriminating. The fact that the shells were found after Lucas dreamed of them was of no relevance. Elizabeth Bartlett's efforts to defend Stroebel should be dismissed: "lover-like she came to his rescue. I ask the jury not to blame the poor little thing."

In Walkem's mind, the single most important question was whether the slug extracted from Marshall's neck matched the slug test-fired from Stroebel's revolver: "If the jury thought the bullet taken out of the neck could not have been fired from the prisoner's revolver, there was little doubt that the prisoner would be free. But if the bullet fired into the flour sack and that taken out of Marshall's neck were shown to be so alike that they almost assuredly were fired from the same revolver, then the case for the crown would be almost completed."

Walkem made it clear he thought the latter was the case, speaking of the "wonderful similarity" of the bullets in question. He also praised the Crown's ballistics experts as disinterested and credible, then excoriated Oliver Ackerman, the defence expert, as biased and untruthful, a man who brazenly set out to mislead the jury.

The judge concluded that "in addressing the jury, I have spoken just as I felt. I have sought to avoid acting the part of the advocate and not the judge." No doubt, Walkem piously believed this, but no impartial observer of the trial could have agreed—he persistently and forcefully tilted the court against the defence. The judge gathered himself together and delivered what he intended as his final word: "If the jury found that there was a doubt in favour of the prisoner, they must give it to him. But that doubt must be a substantial one, not based on shadows."

The courtroom clock struck 6:00 p.m. and Walkem declared the court adjourned until nine o'clock. Rather than taking their supper in the hotel restaurant as they usually did, the jurors had their meals sent up to the jury room, where they could eat and deliberate at the same time. When the court reconvened at 9:00 p.m., the air was heavy with anticipation. Instead of asking the jury if it had reached a verdict, though, Walkem announced he had more instructions he wished to give the jury. The judge used the next forty-five minutes to rebut the defence theory that Marshall was killed by a passing tramp on the morning of April 20. The tramps seen by Elmer Jesseph, Archibald Baxter and the defendant "appeared to be innocently there," and there was no reason to believe they were armed. The actions of Marshall's dog also pointed against the tramp theory: the dog's barking was heard late on the nineteenth and he barked again when Ira Airheart approached the house the next morning. It surely would have barked at any tramp approaching Marshall's house and attacking its master before Airheart's arrival, yet no barking was heard.

With that, Walkem dismissed the jury again, and the court settled in for another wait. Having already deliberated over suppertime, the jury quickly came to a decision and the judge was summoned back. Before the jury returned, Morrison shot to his feet and stated that if the verdict were to go against his client, he wanted to place a number of objections into the record. First, Judge Walkem's charge to the jury "was not confined to instruction on points of law and a presentation of the evidence adduced, but contained expressions of his Lordship's opinions, impressions and convictions." The objection was well-founded, but Walkem replied tersely, "Refused, on obvious grounds." Second, "the jury was recalled and charged a second time, notwithstanding that they had not asked for further, or any instructions." Another valid point, but Walkem dismissed this objection as well.

The jury entered at 10:05 and filed into their seats. Jury foreman H.B. Rendall remained standing to field Walkem's question: "Do you find the defendant guilty or not guilty?"

"We the jury find the prisoner at the bar guilty of the wilful murder of John Marshall." Half the courtroom gasped with relief while the other half unleashed hisses of protest. In her front row seat, Elizabeth Bartlett collapsed into her mother's lap and wept.

Regaining control of the court, Walkem instructed Stroebel to stand, then asked if he had anything to say before sentence was passed.

"Well, I still hold I'm innocent."

"You have had a fair trial?"

"I have."

"You have had able counsel?"

"I have."

The judge fixed a stern gaze on Stroebel and shook his head. How could someone so young commit such a barbarous crime and be so impassive in the face of the law's punishment? Mastering his emotions, Walkem proclaimed the terrible sentence: "Albert Stroebel, you have been found guilty of the wilful and malicious murder of John Marshall. I hereby direct that you be taken from here to your prison cell, and from there to a place of execution, and that on the 30th day of January, 1894, you be hanged by the neck until dead. And may God have mercy on your soul."

The court erupted in a swirl of voices and motion as Walkem fled to his private chambers. Stroebel remained standing, his broad face emotionless and pale—he felt a lightness in his head and his body swayed slightly. Then two burley constables grabbed hold of his arms, shackled his wrists and pushed him toward a side door. The condemned man's composure broke, and he hurled back a string of oaths, screaming madly, "I don't care! It won't bother me! I don't care!"

❖

The second trial in the murder of John Marshall was the largest and costliest held in the province during the Victorian era. It tied up twelve days of court time and brought a total of forty-three witnesses to the stand: thirty-four for the Crown, nine for the defence. The first trial lasted seven days with thirty-two witnesses: twenty for the Crown, twelve for the defence. In total, it took the Crown nineteen days, two judges, a half-dozen lawyers and seventy-five witnesses to find Albert Stroebel guilty of Marshall's murder. One newspaper estimated the total cost to the public purse at $10,000, the equivalent of $300,000 today; two-thirds of this was spent on the second trial alone.

There is little doubt that Theodore Davie's performance in the second trial was superior to that of the first. Not distracted by the mess surrounding David Eyerly, Davie constructed a more disciplined and exhaustive case, focused solely on Stroebel. The Attorney General was also in much better health, having shed all traces of the illness that had confined him to bed in early November.

For the defence, the trial brought out both the strengths and weaknesses of Aulay Morrison. The kind of sharp-edged combativeness Morrison showed toward Crown witnesses is what we today expect in a defence attorney. In nineteenth-century Canadian courtrooms, however, counsel for both the Crown and the defence were supposed to act with more decorum. Morrison's hardball tactics proved off-putting to the jury and turned the judge actively against the defence. Moreover, Morrison made a mistake in not coming up with a ballistics expert of his own, relying solely on Oliver Ackerman. A sympathetic gunsmith with more up-to-date expertise could have shown that the ballistics evidence so central to the Crown's case was not as strong as Davie claimed. The .38 calibre trade revolver was the most common firearm around; cartridges for it were plentiful and available to anyone; barrel rust plagued nearly all of these handguns; and rust build-up changed over time. Given all these factors, it was difficult, verging on impossible, to take two bullets fired five months apart and say definitively that they came from the same barrel.

As it stood, the single most damning piece of physical evidence in the trial was the slug taken from the neck of John Marshall. With Stroebel's revolver and loaded cartridges entered as exhibits, Davie's gun experts were able to convince the jury that the neck bullet was fired from Stroebel's gun. It was the first case in BC jurisprudence where such weight was placed on the ability to match one bullet to one gun. Yet if Stroebel had not handed his revolver to Lucas, after being tricked by the marshal, no such match could have been made and the defendant might have walked away free. Today, no Canadian court would have accepted the revolver as evidence. It was obtained under false pretence, on foreign soil, by someone without any clear legal authority. The same could be said for the loaded cartridges, empty shells and rolled note allegedly belonging to Stroebel.

Yet, despite how important the gun and bullets proved to be, it is debatable whether the physical evidence alone would have convinced all twelve jurors that no doubt existed as to Stroebel's guilt. If in his nine hours of testimony, Stroebel had given a convincing account of his actions during the evening and night of April 19, the defendant might have avoided a death sentence. However, during six hours of relentless cross-examination, Theodore Davie tore gaping holes in Stroebel's alibi. The Attorney General himself thought the defendant's testimony was decisive. Speaking to the provincial legislature just days before Stroebel's scheduled execution, Davie expressed his doubts "whether the man could have been convicted if he had not gone into the box and got himself tangled up in a mass of contradictions."

Morrison's decision to put his client on the stand cannot be faulted, though, for he really had no choice. Juries expected to see a defendant defend himself now that the law gave him the chance to do so. And once Stroebel's testimony from the first trial was admitted into evidence in the second, the defendant had to take the stand to explain it. Given Stroebel's intellectual limitations, it is surprising how well he performed, maintaining a degree of consistency in delivering a complex alibi. To the end, Stroebel remained convinced of his own cleverness, confident he could talk his way out of a bind if given the chance. Davie knew otherwise—if he kept the defendant talking, exposing the young man's alibi to external facts, the tale so neatly woven in Stroebel's mind would fray and, eventually, fall apart.

AFTER THE VERDICT

Inside the main chamber of the Victoria courthouse, the guilty verdict handed down to Albert Stroebel brought a sharply divided reaction from the public gallery, murmurs of support competing with hisses of disapproval. Outside, public opinion in Victoria, New Westminster and the province as a whole was equally divided. For many, the province's justice system had worked as it should; after an "exhaustive and admittedly fair trial," the murderer of John Marshall had been duly convicted and his just sentence set. For others, "a good deal of popular doubt" remained. The evidence presented against the defendant was seen to be purely circumstantial, not strong enough to warrant a guilty verdict and death sentence. The day after the verdict, supporters began circulating a petition calling for the sentence to be commuted "on the ground that the evidence was not satisfactory." In Sumas valley, residents on both sides of the border were "divided into two bitterly hostile camps"—some of its most respected citizens lined up behind Stroebel, while others welcomed his conviction.

The province's newspapers were not at all divided. Without exception, they welcomed the guilty verdict. During the trial itself, the papers had been refreshingly even-handed in their reporting, with witness testimony from both sides quoted at length and correspondents resisting the temptation to editorialize. The occasional assessments made of the trial's progress were generally favourable to the Crown, but the comments were brief and restrained. Once the verdict and sentence were handed down, newspapers shed their editorial restraint. Trumpeting "STROEBEL CONVICTED" on its front page, the *Daily Colonist* declared "a peaceful, unoffending citizen was wantonly murdered at his own door... and that miserable man, Stroebel" had been justly found guilty of the crime. Likewise, the *Daily Columbian* led with the story that Stroebel had been "SENTENCED TO HANG." The condemned man had met the verdict and grim sentence with an eerie composure, lacking any show of emotion or remorse and "unimpressed with the solemnity of the occasion." His poor victim had been "an inoffensive, elderly man who lived by himself in an isolated and lonely cabin."

Newspapers welcomed Stroebel's conviction as a vindication of the province's justice system, particularly in the wake of the first trial's hung jury. The *Daily Colonist* crowed, "the people of BC are to be congratulated that in their province justice is firmly and effectively administered." The Victoria trial demonstrated "the fairness, thoroughness, and promptness of British justice." Not to be outdone, the *Daily Columbian* stated that the lengthy trial and just verdict upheld the province's "high reputation for the strict and impartial administration of the criminal law."

❧

The province's newspaper editors believed the final scene in the drama of John Marshall's death had been written. Albert Stroebel was sent to his new cell on death row, where he would await his inevitable date with the gallows. However, even as the ink was drying on the papers' congratulatory headlines, the condemned man introduced a new twist to the plot, taking everyone by surprise.

On the morning of Wednesday, December 20, Elizabeth Bartlett approached the front doors of the Victoria Gaol, tightly gripping her mother's arm for support. Elizabeth shivered from fear and the damp cold as a guard opened the heavy doors to let her and her mother in. Standing in the front office, the Bartletts were met by the warden, R.J. John, and the provincial police superintendent, Frederick Hussey, who delicately escorted them the short distance to Stroebel's cell.

The condemned man rose to greet the visitors, casting a sheepish grin at his young fiancée. A minute of tense silence was broken by Elizabeth's girlish voice: "Al, I want to ask you about this," she swallowed, her mouth dry. "And I want you to tell me straight—was it you who did it?"

Stroebel struggled with his answer, finally stammering, "Yes, I did kill him. But it, but it was over you!"

"Oh, Al, how was it over me?"

"Well, me and old Marshall was at the dinner table and got to quarrelling. He called you a rotten name. I couldn't stand that, not from any man."

"You should have, Al. It would have been better to have got out and not had any fuss."

Stroebel then explained how Marshall attacked him, first with a chair, then with an axe the farmer got from a woodpile outside: "So I drew my pistol and shot him, as I was crippled and had to protect myself. Then I guess I shot him again. I was so mad I didn't know what I was doing."

The young couple stood in stunned silence, staring at each other through the iron bars. For Elizabeth, the shock of Stroebel's confession was nearly as great as the shock of the jury's verdict. She had believed him innocent from the very start, and her faith in him had never wavered. Now he was saying he had killed Marshall, but only to defend her name, and in self-defence. She could make no sense of it. Elizabeth let herself be led away into a small room where Superintendent Hussey presented her with a handwritten statement. Hussey had written down what Stroebel had just said to her. The superintendent asked the girl to read the notes over and sign them, which she did in a daze. "It's all so horrible," she said weakly. "If only none of this had happened, we would be married now."

As Elizabeth and Margaret Bartlett were ushered from the jail, prison officials sent word to Aulay Morrison that his client had confessed to killing John Marshall. Morrison arrived at Stroebel's cell after lunch, and the prisoner explained to his attorney how he came to shoot Marshall. After arriving at Marshall's around 6:00 p.m. on April 19, "we was just talking, everyday stuff, while he made supper." Sometime after eight o'clock, as the men finished eating, the conversation turned to Elizabeth Bartlett.

"Old Marshall said he wanted to marry her, and when I told him we was engaged he got furious and threatened to kill me. Marshall then fetched an axe from outside and came at me. I drew my revolver and fired twice." Stroebel paused to catch his breath. "It was in self-defence. And Marshall was a Portuguese, he had a terrible temper."

Morrison nodded, his thick brows knit together, then said: "I need to think this over. We must see if there is a way for us to present your confession to Judge Walkem. For now, do not say anything about the matter to anyone. I will talk to you tomorrow."

Stroebel watched his attorney turn and walk away, his spirits lifted by a glimmer of hope. Sometime after supper, the prisoner frowned as another visitor approached his cell. Hearing word of Stroebel's confession from sources in the jail, a *Daily Colonist* reporter had finagled his way to death row. Stroebel insisted he could not talk. He had given his lawyer all the facts and was hoping to present his statement to the judge.

"Don't you think it's too late for that?" the reporter asked. "It would have been better to tell the truth before."

Stroebel thought for a moment. "I guess it don't much matter now. I know that I didn't murder him. If I did kill him, I shot him in self-defence." The young prisoner then repeated the account he had given Morrison: the dinner, the argument, Marshall attacking him, the shooting. Then, Stroebel added, he fled the scene and returned to the rail line, and as he made his way home, he stopped several times to think.

"I knew no one could swear I did the killing, but I feared my story wouldn't be believed. That's why I told the story I did. But they were all off about robbery, money had nothing to do with it. Old Marshall threatened to kill me and tried to do it. I shot him to save myself."

While the condemned man was giving his third statement of the day—this one to a reporter—Morrison was in contact with Attorney General Davie, requesting a hearing in front of Justice Walkem. Morrison wanted his client brought into court to give his new account of what happened the night of Marshall's death. The hearing was granted, set for the following afternoon.

At 2:30 p.m. on Thursday, December 21, Walkem strode into a packed courtroom. Nearly every attorney in the city was in attendance, and the public gallery was filled to the walls. The judge frowned at the two men standing in front of him: Davie's deputy, A.G. Smith, for the

Crown, and Stroebel himself, alone at the defence table.

"Where is Mr. Morrison?" Walkem demanded. Smith answered that the attorney was no longer acting for the convicted man. Walkem's anger rose as he declared he "had no earthly power" to hear any statement from the defendant. The latter had been convicted and duly sentenced, and when given a chance to speak at the end of his trial, had said nothing. Moreover, the convicted man was without counsel, and it would be hazardous for him to say anything—"Men in this awful position do not really know the effect of what they say." Walkem was clearly rattled and fatigued. The stress of the two-week trial, the weight of the public's attention devoted to it, and the grim duty of condemning a young man to death had taken their toll. "I am now writing up my notes," the judge said plaintively. "This case has cost me sleepless nights—I have no taste for it."

With that Walkem closed the irregular hearing, and Stroebel was hustled out of the courtroom and into the police station next door. He met briefly with Aulay Morrison and agreed to reinstate the lawyer as his counsel; he also agreed to obey Morrison's second order not to speak to anyone else.

The defence lawyer had initially arranged the hearing in front of Walkem so he could control where and how his client's confession came out. However, when the *Daily Colonist* published Stroebel's Wednesday evening confession as its lead story Thursday morning, Morrison decided that his client should not make any more statements to anyone, including Justice Walkem.

Stroebel broke his second promise not to speak to anyone just as he had the first. Hussey had stood behind Elizabeth Bartlett on the twentieth, recording what the prisoner had said to his fiancée. Revisiting the cell block, Hussey shrewdly played on Stroebel's misguided confidence in his own cleverness, his belief he could talk his way out of any mess. Now, within a week of his initial string of confessions, Stroebel found himself seated across a table from the superintendent, giving yet another account of the fateful night.

Stroebel admitted that he was at Marshall's that evening, and that he and the farmer were finishing supper when an argument broke out:

"Marshall said, 'Now you can go back to Sumas and turn in with Lizzie Bartlett.' I said I don't do anything like that. He said, 'You might as well, as everyone else is doing so'."

The heated words quickly escalated to physical violence: "Marshall ran outside and got a three-pound axe and came toward me. I was at the front door and tried to pass him, but saw I could not. I drew my gun and shot him in the forehead." The farmer fell forward and struck his nose on the doorsill, coming to rest face down.

"I turned him over and was going to put him in his bed. The second shot in back of his neck was accidental as in the excitement the pistol went off." The prisoner finished by saying the only reason he lied about that night was he did not want his brothers and sisters thinking he was guilty of murder.

Hussey completed his handwritten notes of the confession, dated and signed it. Belatedly remembering Morrison's instructions, Stroebel refused to add his signature. The damage, though, had been done. The superintendent of the provincial police himself had taken down his freely given confession. Hussey returned to his office, had his secretary type up copies of the statement, then sent it off to Attorney General Davie. Stroebel's confession was now officially on the record.

❖

The string of confessions made in the week after his conviction were Stroebel's instinctive reaction to the guilty verdict and death sentence. Before the conviction, he did not believe he could be found guilty of Marshall's murder; after it, he did not accept that he would be executed for it. Stroebel was convinced that if he came clean, admitted he had killed John Marshall but explained it was in self-defence, then Judge Walkem and the others would believe him and change the verdict or at least reduce his sentence. The condemned man failed to understand that the justice system did not work that way. Stroebel's trial was lengthy, exhaustive and deemed fair by the standards of the time, despite Justice Walkem's biased, heavy-handed interventions. There were no flagrantly violated points of law that might form the basis of an appeal, no surprise evidence that appeared after the verdict—and even if there had been any of these, Stroebel's own confessions would have made them moot.

Stroebel did not yet know, but would soon find out, that there was only one legal way for him to escape execution. At the time, every capital conviction in Canada was automatically reviewed by the federal cabinet and the Governor General, who would decide whether to go ahead with the execution or commute the sentence to life in prison. The formal capital case file sent to Ottawa would have to convince the cabinet and Governor General that Stroebel was worthy of clemency. Yet Stroebel's own actions undercut the chances of this happening. In the wake of his post-conviction confessions, public sympathy for him evaporated, and the petition that had been gathering signatures in support of commuting his death sentence was dropped.

In the press, Stroebel's name was blackened further after his confessions, with newspapers crowing that his statements proved they had been right all along. The *Daily Columbian* dismissed the condemned man's confessions as "shot full of falsehoods," the biggest being his claim that the shooting was in self-defence. The one fact the statements got right was that Stroebel shot Marshall dead. The paper concluded triumphantly that the confessions "will relieve any lurking fear in the public mind that an innocent man may have been convicted of the terrible crime of murder." The *Daily Telegram* poured salt on Stroebel's self-inflicted wounds.

> Had Stroebel kept his mouth shut after his condemnation, a remnant of doubt of his guilt might have lingered in many minds, in spite of all the circumstantial evidence brought against him. But Stroebel sealed his own fate after his sentence by hastening to confess that he had killed Marshall, although in self-defence.

Not a single newspaper expressed sympathy for the convicted murderer or suggested that, in light of his confessions, the authorities should reconsider the sentence of death handed down to him.

DEATH ROW

The very words *death row* send a chill down the spine. There is the physical image they conjure up: a row of whitewashed cells, each penning a solitary condemned man who stares out with hopeless eyes. The only sounds are the echoing clop of a guard's heels on a tiled floor and the jangle of his key chain. Then there is the fear behind it, the worst of all terrors: a man knowing the day and hour of his death. The condemned man is not just a prisoner of four walls but also a prisoner of time, of the ominous, grim and inevitable march of time. Nothing can stop or slow the days, and, just as terrifying, nothing can hasten them, bring that last morning to now while a man still has the courage to face it. As Albert Stroebel was brought to Victoria Gaol for the final time, facing this terror would be his last trial.

Physically, at least, death row at the Victoria Gaol was not what our imaginations conjure up. For all its dour greyness and crude accommodations, the jail did not have a purpose-built wing to hold those sentenced to death. Between its opening in 1886 and Albert Stroebel's conviction in 1893, the prison housed only three condemned prisoners. Two of them were duly executed, while a third committed suicide in his cell. In the late nineteenth century, the time between conviction and execution was relatively short, six weeks on average, so there was never more than one prisoner at a time on Victoria's death row. The practice was to isolate a condemned man from the rest of the inmate population kept in the regular cell block, which was in the eastern wing of the jail. Thus, upon his return from court on December 19, Stroebel was moved into a single cell in the prison's central wing, where he could be watched more closely.

Perversely, as a convicted murderer facing death, Stroebel received a level of attention and special treatment he had never seen in life. Penned in his isolated cell, he was exempt from many of the rules that applied to regular prisoners. He was spared the stubble-length haircut given to others and was not placed on the mandatory work details that kept inmates busy six days a week, rain or shine. He was allowed a short stroll in the prison yard on occasion, but never when other prisoners were there. Inmates on the regular block were supposed to adhere to a policy of strict silence between themselves and with their guards (although the rule was not strictly enforced). Stroebel could talk freely with his guards, whom he got to know well, and while other inmates rarely saw anyone from the outside, he received a parade of visitors.

We might expect that the people who most wanted to see him would be his family and legal counsel. However, through to the end of 1893, Stroebel's family was conspicuous by its absence. They had not visited him during the seven months he spent in New Westminster Gaol, had stayed away from both trials, and throughout December left the young man alone on death row. In his December 27 confession to Frederick Hussey, Stroebel mentioned that his brothers and sisters were close by. With naïve optimism, he told the superintendent that "my father is in Oklahoma and I expect he is now on his way to Victoria." Stroebel wrote George Sr. a number of times, pleading with him to come, but heard nothing back from him.

On New Year's Day 1894, George Jr. made the first of three visits to his younger brother. The pair talked for some time under the vigilant gaze of guards, and when George rose to go, Albert embraced him in an awkward hug. George returned four days later for another brief visit, and this time, Albert grasped his brother's hands as the elder Stroebel stood to leave. A day later, on January 6, Aulay Morrison saw his client for the first and only time. Morrison helped Stroebel write a statement to be included in the capital case file sent to the federal cabinet and Governor General.

The majority of Stroebel's visitors, though, had never met him before his time on death row. These were Christian ministers and church members concerned not with the condemned prisoner's legal plight but with the fate of his soul. At the time, pretty much any established religious figure who requested death row access was granted it by prison officials. Stroebel's religious affiliation was not clear, aside from being a Christian. He was not an active member of any church, partly because there were no churches on Sumas prairie. While their German-born father was originally Lutheran, the Stroebel siblings identified themselves as Presbyterians on the 1891 census. Albert did the same on his prison identification card for Victoria Gaol.

For this reason, the first clergyman to contact Stroebel after his conviction was John Campbell, the forty-eight-year-old minister of First Presbyterian Church in Victoria. The latter was one of the two most influential churches in the provincial capital, the other being the Anglican Christ Church Cathedral. A heavy-faced man of haughty bearing, Campbell was a prominent member of the city and province's elite, who boasted BC Supreme Court Justice Sir Henry Crease as his next-door neighbour.

Campbell led the clerical campaign to save Albert Stroebel's soul. From his first appearance on December 27 to his last on January 19, the reverend visited the condemned man's cell seven times. The message he brought was a stern one: there was no hope for Stroebel's body; he must admit his guilt and accept the just punishment of the God-ordained authorities. The only hope lay for his spirit. The grace of God may have predestined his soul for salvation, but Stroebel could pray to God for mercy, that this grace would deliver him to heaven.

Campbell was not the only clergyman to visit Stroebel's death row cell, with Methodist ministers S. Cleaver and Joseph Hall each seeing him once. The Methodists were the pre-eminent evangelicals of the time, with their greatest support among the middle classes. They brought a more hopeful message of personal forgiveness and salvation, gained when the sinner accepted Jesus Christ as his saviour. A delegation of nine Methodist women followed up on Cleaver and Hall's visits. The delegation was led by Mrs. Florence Siddall, wife of Victoria's deputy sheriff, James Siddall, who had arranged the visits. The women first saw Stroebel on January 12, his twenty-first birthday, when they crowded around his cell to sing Wesleyan hymns and pray. The women came again a week later, and their visits lifted Stroebel's spirits. The singing was sweetness to his musical ears, and the women's sympathy pulled at the heartstrings of a young man who had lost his mother and dearly missed his sisters.

John Campbell pressed Stroebel hard through this same week, meeting with him four times, but the reverend's stern message fell on deaf ears. On the nineteenth, the young prisoner shocked Campbell by declaring he had converted to Roman Catholicism. Taking the snub personally, the good reverend left death row and did not return.

Stroebel's conversion had come the day before during a visit from Joseph Nicolaye, a forty-three-year-old priest from St. Andrews Cathedral in Victoria. Both in personal appearance and the message he brought, Nicolaye represented a sharp contrast to the cold righteousness of Rev. Campbell. Even to the jaded eye, the priest's was a kind face, made for listening and forgiving. Nicolaye's message was that there was no sin God would not forgive, not even murder, and this forgiveness and salvation came in very tangible forms: baptism into the Catholic church, celebration of holy mass, and confession to a priest, who could give absolution from sin. These concrete rituals—which Nicolaye performed in the confines of Stroebel's cell—appealed to the condemned man's mind, which had difficulty processing more abstract ideas.

During the last week of January, as the clock ticked down to the scheduled execution, Nicolaye was a constant presence in Stroebel's cell. He visited daily, sometimes twice a day, staying for hours to comfort the condemned man and to perform the soothing rituals of mass and confession. There was, though, more behind Stroebel's conversion to Catholicism than Nicolaye's compassion and commitment. Both of Albert's parents had converted to Catholicism just prior to his mother's death four years earlier. On her deathbed, Elizabeth Stroebel had expressed her wish that her children too would enter the church. Albert wanted to honour her memory by doing so now.

A death row prisoner received more visitors than regular inmates; he also received more attention from guards. The two biggest fears for officials were that the condemned might break out of jail or that he might cheat the hangman by committing suicide. The latter was the greater concern of Robert John, warden of the Victoria Gaol; John had been appointed warden five years earlier, and just a few months into his new job, condemned murderer Chan Ah Heung managed to hang himself in his cell using his own clothing. To prevent Stroebel from doing likewise, John formed a two-man team whose sole job was to watch the prisoner. Each guard worked a twelve-hour shift, then handed the watch over to the other. An extra guard was assigned to the team as the execution date came nearer, in mid-January, so that each man now worked an eight-hour shift.

Warden R.F. John and some of his staff stand outside the Victoria Gaol, built atop a rocky outcrop devoid of vegetation. Months before Albert Stroebel was admitted here, the absence of a proper sewage system led to an outbreak of typhoid fever among prisoners. Royal BC Museum and Archives, D-01778

Given what we know of his temperament, Stroebel was an unlikely candidate for suicide. During his time on death row, guards and the few reporters granted access considered him a model inmate who was adjusting well to prison life. In a pair of articles, on January 1 and 5, the *Daily Colonist* reported that Stroebel "appeared cheerful" and showed a healthy appetite. He spent much time reading and he "writes a great deal." To accommodate this, guards brought a table and chair into his cell, and supplied him with pencils and writing paper. The young prisoner also indulged his "fine ear for music. Warden John says that he is the best player of the mouth organ that he has ever heard." The paper concluded that, from all appearances, Stroebel had come to terms with his fate and was "resigned to the inevitable."

At the time, the *Daily Colonist* reporter was not aware of the real reason for Stroebel's good spirits and alertness, nor that the impression he gave of accepting his fate was just a façade. The truth was just the opposite. Stroebel was determined to do whatever he could to avoid the death sentence. He had hoped his confessions would change the court's verdict or reduce his sentence, but when that hope was dashed, he turned his mind to escape. During the final days of 1893, he made a careful study of his guards' routines and of the jail's physical layout, particularly the central block where he was held and the enclosed prison yard out back. He then set to work crafting an elaborate escape plan, committing it to paper in a lengthy letter written to his siblings. He wrote for hours on end, slowly and with great effort, bent over the cheap, rough paper with his back blocking the view of his guards. Periodically, he would stop to sharpen his pencil or glance up to see whether his minders were watching too closely. The *Daily Colonist* reporter's comment that Stroebel "writes a great deal" was indeed true, but naïve.

"Dear Brothers and Sisters," the prisoner's first escape letter began, "I have got a scheam worked up and I now that it will work all wright if you boys will just help me a little." Stroebel explained his plan over several pages of cramped writing, illustrated by a detailed, annotated map of the jail. First, during a prison visit, George Jr. was to smuggle in a kit of tools—a keyhole saw, gimlet and pocket knife—which Albert would use to escape his cell and make his way to the back of the central block. Then, at 9:00 p.m. the night of the escape, George and his brothers William and Louis would use a ladder to scale the thirteen-foot-high wooden wall surrounding the prison yard. The trio would sneak over to the base of the central block wall and, with the younger boys acting as lookouts, George would chip away at the mortar and brick to make a hole big enough for Albert to squeeze through. All four Stroebel boys would then flee back over the perimeter wall and make their way down to the waterfront, where a boat would be stashed. Albert would escape by water while his brothers ran off into the night.

Stroebel's first escape plan was foiled before it had a chance to begin. In preparation for his older brother's visit on January 1, the prisoner had folded the pages of his escape letter into a small, tight square. As the visit ended and the brothers hugged, Albert slipped the square into his brother's pocket. However, a guard was watching the whole scene, so when George left death row and headed for the prison

Stroebel drew and annotated this map as part of his first escape letter, which he handed to his brother on January 1, 1894. Stroebel spent hours hunched over his prison-cell table, carefully crafting the details of the map and plan, explaining it step by step. A guard confiscated the letter as George Jr. left his brother's cell, before the elder Stroebel had a chance to read it. Library and Archives Canada, RG 13, v. 1428, f. 265A

doors, the guard stopped him and confiscated the letter. George Jr. had not read the pages and stayed ignorant of his brother's plan, nor had Albert seen the confiscation.

On George's second visit four days later, Albert again slipped him a square of paper and again the letter was taken by a guard. The younger Stroebel's second "scheam" was written in haste and was much simpler than his first. Albert asked his older brother to "get a rope about 20 ft long and paint it white so as they cant tell it from the fence." Overnight, George would throw the rope over the fence and the next morning, on one of his exercise days in the prison yard, Albert would make a sprint for the rope and use it to scale the wall. Albert would then run for a horse tied up a short distance away and meet up with his brother some miles outside the city.

Albert Stroebel's two escape letters provided a fascinating look into the condemned man's character and his state of mind as he faced the prospect of his own execution. For one, they demonstrated that Stroebel had not accepted the dire situation he was in, and that he was willing to do anything to escape the gallows. For another, they revealed much about Stroebel's personality and his capacity to commit the crime for which he had been convicted. The two letters are the only surviving documents where he expressed himself at any length, freely and honestly; he was not defending himself in court, confessing to an authority, or making a plea for clemency.

Though cramped and shot through with spelling and grammatical errors, the letters' handwriting was surprisingly well-formed for a man with so little formal education. Also, there were sections where Stroebel's thoughts and plans were clear and plausible, but others where he drifted into fantasy. An example of the latter was Stroebel's belief that if the authorities did not find him that winter, "they will give up hunting for me." In the summer, "I can have my leg cut of and get a cork leg and then they couldent tell me from any body else." The siblings then could all be together and life would go on as before.

The escape letters also presented further proof of Stroebel's love and affection for his "dear" brothers and sisters. He told his three brothers they were the only ones he could turn to for help, and he pleaded with George Jr. to get their sisters to visit him before the planned escape, "so as I can see them and tell them not to feel to bad." Yet Albert could not see that his willingness to involve his younger brothers was absolute folly, as selfish as it was irresponsible. William was thirteen years old and Louis twelve: if they were caught helping a convicted murderer escape from prison, their young lives would be ruined before they had a chance to begin.

More darkly, the letters showed that Stroebel was unrepentant over killing a man, did not consider it murder at all but self-defence, and could not accept his death sentence. In short, he did not see himself as guilty, writing emphatically: "I wont let them put a rope around my neck. I don't deserve it." An even more sinister fact was that Stroebel was willing to use lethal violence to escape. As part of his first escape scheme, he requested that a Winchester lever-action rifle be stowed in his getaway boat, "to keep clear of them if they was to find where I was." At one point, Albert conceded that his brothers might think it was too risky for them to do what he was asking of them. If that were the case, he instructed George Jr. to place a revolver in the tool kit the older brother would smuggle into the prison. Albert insisted he would not shoot anyone: "I promise you all faithly that I wont use it a tall only to scare them with if there is to many of them for me [to] handle." However, the most likely result of pulling a gun on prison guards would be that he would have to shoot the guards or be shot by them. Stroebel admitted as much, writing that, even if things did not go as planned, "I will die trying to get out my self."

Last Days

From his post-conviction confessions to his schemes for escape, Albert Stroebel spent the first half of his time on death row trying desperately to elude the hangman. With the confessions backfiring and the escape plans thwarted, he was left with one final chance to save his life. In the 1890s, every death sentence in Canada needed to be approved by the federal cabinet and Governor General before it could be carried out. After a murder conviction, the trial judge put together a formal capital case file, which included the judge's trial notes, his recommendations regarding the sentence, material from the Crown counsel, a statement from the convicted defendant, and any public petitions supporting the death sentence or calling for commutation. The case file was sent to the justice minister in Ottawa, who reviewed it and came up with a recommendation either to let the execution proceed or to commute the sentence to life in prison. The minister presented the dossier and recommendation to the federal cabinet, which usually approved the minister's decision. Finally, the file and cabinet decision were forwarded to the Governor General, who signed the official order to put the decision into effect—authorizing the execution or commutation of the sentence.

In spite of the Victorian era's reputation as a time of rigid, eye-for-an-eye justice, the commutation rate for convicted murderers in BC was surprisingly high. In the eight years prior to Stroebel's scheduled execution, the federal cabinet reviewed twenty-two capital case files from the province. Twelve of these resulted in executions; the remaining ten were commuted to life imprisonment. Officially, the two overriding considerations in a commutation decision were the extent to which the Crown relied on circumstantial evidence to gain a conviction, and the presence or absence of mitigating factors in the crime. Unofficially, the weight of public opinion and the political optics of the case were often just as important.

These unofficial factors weighed against Stroebel's chances for clemency. Stroebel's case file arrived in Ottawa at a bad time. The previous November, as his first trial in John Marshall's murder was unfolding a few blocks away, the Chehalis Elder known as Jack and his son Peter were convicted for the murder of Albert Pittendrigh, with their execution scheduled for January 15 in New West-

The executive order-in-council from the federal cabinet, approved by the Governor General, which authorized Sheriff James MacMillan to carry out the death sentence on Albert Stroebel. A frantic MacMillan did not receive the document until the evening before the planned execution. Library and Archives Canada, RG 13, v. 1428, f. 265A

minster. The post-conviction dossier sent to Ottawa included letters from Methodist minister Charles Tate and local band Elders that cast doubt on the pair's guilt. The area's Indian Agent also expressed his opinion that clemency should be applied. Other officials involved in the case opposed calls for commutation, but Ottawa announced on January 9 that Jack and Peter's death sentences had been changed to life in prison. Local newspapers and residents protested "that executive clemency was not merited, and that it is a mistake to extend leniency to Indian criminals." New Westminster papers had portrayed Pittendrigh in glowing terms and the White public was outraged that his killers were getting away with murder.

The unpopularity of the decision to commute Jack and Peter's sentences made it difficult to do likewise for Stroebel, lest the federal government appear soft on violent crime. The condemned man's own actions only made things worse. During his two trials, a large part of the public had felt sympathy for Stroebel and harboured doubts about his final conviction; a petition for clemency began circulating the moment the verdict was announced. This sympathy and doubt vanished overnight with Stroebel's post-conviction confessions, and the petition vanished with them. Even members of the Ackerman family, who had put their substantial resources and reputations on the line, withdrew their support.

Thus, when Stroebel's capital case file was sent to Ottawa in mid-January, there was not a single statement from family, friends or neighbours appealing for commutation. Nor did anyone testify to his good character, even though both Crown and defence witnesses at his trials acknowledged he had a reputation as an honest, obliging, hard-working young man. Instead, William Porter, James Schofield, James Silverthorne and three other neighbours swore out affidavits stating they had known Marshall as "a quiet, peaceful and good-tempered man, the last man to pick a quarrel with anyone." Stroebel's dossier also contained the damaging confessions and escape plans he had produced. Attorney General Davie saw to it that typewritten copies were produced of Elizabeth Bartlett's statement to Superintendent Hussey on December 20 and of Hussey's own transcription of the confession Stroebel made a week later. Davie also included the handwritten originals of the prisoner's two escape letters, complete with annotated map.

Stroebel's own submission to the file was the sole document speaking in his favour. The statement was completed on January 7, a day after Aulay Morrison visited his client to counsel him on what to write. This was Morrison's only contribution to his client's commutation appeal. Over five pages of legal-sized paper in Stroebel's cramped handwriting, made more legible because he used ink, the condemned man made one final plea for his life. He began with an awkward appeal to sentiment: "It is not for my self altogether that I am to ask you for mercy. It is principly for my dear Brothers and Sisters." His two sisters and two of his brothers were younger than he, aged twelve to nineteen years. "The day I am to be executed is a day that they will never forget"—he begged the Governor General to spare his siblings the horror that day would bring.

Stroebel then proceeded to explain the events of April 19. This final confession followed the general lines of his earlier statements, with one or two important changes. Here, again, it was Marshall who started an argument by accusing Stroebel of sleeping with Elizabeth Bartlett: "After finishing supper I was a going to go home... when Marshall said that I would go home and sleep with this girl, which was only fourteen years old. I replied that I wasn't that kind of man and then he said that I might just as well for all of the boys in Sumas was and that you are to."

Stroebel angrily protested that this was a lie, and Marshall came at him with a chair, but the young man fended him off. The farmer rushed outside, retrieved an axe and was stomping back across the veranda when Stroebel met him at the door: "I took out my revolver and pointed it at him and told him to drop the axe. He hit the revolver with his hand and it exploded."

Marshall fell toward him, face down on the doorsill, and as Stroebel scrambled over the body to escape, he tripped on the axe and the revolver fired a second time, into the back of the older man's neck. The shooter threw the axe on the woodpile and fled down the rail line, stopping a few times to cry and think. He wrote, "I made up my mind not to tell anybody I done it. I thought if I did I would be hung for it."

This latest explanation of how he fired two bullets into Marshall was the most significant part of Stroebel's third and final confession. In Stroebel's first confession, both shots were fired intentionally but in self-defence. In his second confession, the first shot was in self-defence, the second was accidental. In this last confession, both shots were accidental, fired in self-defence. Authorities reading his file could and did compare Stroebel's changing accounts, noting their inconsistencies.

The final and weightiest piece of Stroebel's capital case file was produced by Justice George Walkem. In the majority of cases, documents provided by the presiding trial judge were the most decisive material considered by the justice minister, the federal cabinet and the Governor General. For Stroebel's dossier, Walkem had his extensive trial notes typed up and included. To this he added a twenty-one-page typewritten statement in which he argued forcefully that Stroebel's guilt had been proven beyond any doubt, by both circumstantial and physical evidence. The judge argued further that the rolled note written by Stroebel and picked up by John Bartlett was an admission of guilt, that the motive for the crime was clearly shown to be robbery, that the testimony of defence witnesses was unreliable, and that Stroebel's own fishing alibi collapsed from its own contradictions. Physical evidence was the final, decisive proof, for the Crown had demonstrated "that the bullet found in Marshall's neck had been fired from the prisoner's pistol."

Walkem then laid out the reasons why the death sentence he handed down to Stroebel should be carried out. The condemned man had shown no emotion over Marshall's death and demonstrated no remorse for his part in it. He had testified with "great nerve" and cunning at his trial, and he had accepted his sentence "with the utmost composure and indifference." Walkem returned to the shooting itself for the single most decisive fact: "Whether a struggle occurred or not between him and the prisoner, or whether Marshall was aggressor or not, the last bullet fired into the back of Marshall's neck seems to have been a *needless and merciless act*, for Marshall must have been completely stunned, either by the blow on the nose, or shot under the forehead, or by both combined."

Walkem's concluding statement was remarkable in ways the judge never intended it to be, for on key points concerning Marshall's shooting, it contradicted the theory of the Crown and lent support to Stroebel's account of events. In his statement, the judge granted the possibility that a struggle occurred between the condemned man and Marshall, and that the latter might have been the aggressor, neither of which the Crown had conceded. He also reversed the order of the shots from what the Crown had argued: the frontal shot to the forehead came first, the shot to the back of the neck second. Walkem's purpose here was not to raise doubts about Stroebel's culpability. Rather, he argued that, even granting these possible scenarios, the answer to the question in front of him was clear: Albert Stroebel was

guilty of the wilful murder of John Marshall and justice demanded he
be executed for it.

❖

The Department of Justice in Ottawa received the capital case dossier
for Stroebel on January 15. The justice minister reviewed the file's
contents and decided the execution should proceed. The minister rec-
ommended this to the federal cabinet, which gave its approval. On
January 23, the Governor General signed the official order that the
sentence of death was "to be carried into execution on Tuesday, the
30th day of January."

Late in the afternoon of January 24, a telegram was received by
Sheriff James McMillan at the Victoria Gaol. It stated: "Governor
General in Council orders that law be allowed to take its course in the
case of Albert Stroebel. Letter by mail." McMillan was a sixty-eight-
year-old native of Ontario, a printer by trade, who had been appointed
high sheriff of Victoria a decade earlier. Of the many duties entrusted to McMillan, the most unsettling involved prisoners sentenced to
death. The sheriff was responsible for overseeing the prisoner while
he sat on death row, organizing the logistics of his execution, and
ensuring the execution was properly carried out. Stroebel's execution
would be McMillan's fifth, and no matter how necessary the grim task
was, it never got any easier. The sheriff would visit death row daily in
the weeks prior to the execution and could not help getting to know
the condemned prisoner. When the day came, his duty was to escort
the prisoner to the gallows, then give the signal that sent the pinioned
man plunging through the trapdoor to his death.

Finishing his tea, McMillan slipped the January 24 telegram into
his jacket pocket and marched to death row. The sheriff stood uneasily
in front of the cell door as Stroebel rose to face him.

"Al, it's the news we expected. The law is to take its course." The
condemned man opened his mouth to speak, but words failed him, and
he sat back down on his bunk.

Over the next week—the final one of his life—Stroebel went
through a dramatic transformation. Shedding the oddly upbeat façade

he had maintained since coming to death row, he became quiet and withdrawn, spending his time huddled with Father Nicolaye or the priest's colleague, Father Van Goetham. When not in prayer, the priests kept Stroebel busy copying out long sections of the Bible in his unschooled handwriting.

The Saturday evening before the Tuesday execution, Stroebel was visited by his brother George and his sister Ida. The pair had travelled up from Everett, Washington, where eighteen-year-old Ida lived, to say a final goodbye. As the pair rose to go, Albert collapsed onto his bed sobbing, all the emotions and tensions of the last weeks bursting out. It was the last Albert would see of his beloved siblings; the next day, George and Ida boarded the steamer home.

❖

Monday, January 29, dawned with the faint hope of sunshine. To the west, narrow breaks were showing in the leaden clouds that had shrouded the province's capital for most of the month. Rain came down in a fine mist, almost too soft to feel. Up the hillside at Victoria Gaol, the machinery of death was rising from the rocky prison grounds behind the central block. Sheriff McMillan arrived at the jail early that morning, tense and fretful as he always was before an execution. McMillan walked into the prison yard and spotted John Burgess, the local builder and contractor who was directing the crew erecting the gallows. The sheriff had employed Burgess in the jail's last two executions, of Robert Sproule in 1886 and Ah Fat in 1888. This time, the work was quicker and quieter. Burgess had built the scaffold at his factory, taken it apart, then moved the pieces by dray to the jail. Bolts instead of nails were used in reassembling it. The scaffold could be dismantled just as smoothly, and the provincial government planned to use it in future executions.

The structure itself was built to a proven design, although with some peculiar twists. Wooden stairs led up to a planked platform ten feet off the ground, in the middle of which lay a two-panel trap door. A lever to the side released the bolt holding the panels closed. Bracketed posts supported a beam ten feet above the platform, and an iron hook was screwed into the beam immediately above the trap door to hold the noose rope. Someone had decided to paint the structure a dark green, in the vain hope it would disguise the machine's true purpose. Also, on three sides, Burgess had installed shutters that ran from the platform down to the ground to save spectators the sight of the hanged man's body.

The scaffold was completed by mid-afternoon, and Sheriff McMillan, accompanied by the hired hangman, climbed onto the platform to perform a trial run. The hanging rope was slipped onto the hook in the overhead beam, a large sandbag the same weight as Stroebel was attached to the noose end, and the trap door was released. The weight dropped the designated eight feet, then was left to hang for some time to stretch the rope fully, as any play in it would bounce the hanged man and possibly tear his head off.

Although satisfied with the hardware, McMillan was unsure of the hangman. The slight man, pale and skittish, had not been the sheriff's first choice for the job. There was no designated executioner in the province, and the sheriff had complete discretion over whom to hire for the task, but finding a capable executioner was a hit-or-miss business. In 1885, the man McMillan had hired to hang Charles Rogers bungled the job. The inexperienced hangman placed the knot of the noose at the back of Rogers's neck rather than behind his left ear; the condemned man's neck was not broken, and he slowly strangled to death. In 1886, McMillan hired William Jones, a Victoria bartender, to execute Robert Sproule. The execution went as planned, and the sheriff rehired Jones eight years later to hang Stroebel. It was established policy to keep the identity of the hangman secret, so Jones was sequestered in a local hotel for the days leading up to January 30. However, either nerves or alcohol—or most likely a combination of the two—got the better of Jones and he bailed out.

The sheriff scrambled to find a replacement. From the few applications that had come in for the job, McMillan picked that of James Dupen, a forty-three-year-old tailor from Calgary. Dupen had no experience as a hangman, but McMillan reckoned that, with two decades of service in the Royal Navy, the former seaman was no stranger to rough justice. Now, on the eve of Stroebel's execution, the sheriff worried that his initial confidence in the man had been misplaced.

The fear that Dupen would make a mess of the hanging was not McMillan's only worry. The sheriff had heard nothing from Ottawa in the five days since receiving the telegram on January 24 that informed him the execution was to go ahead. The telegram had promised that a duly signed letter would follow, but none had arrived—and the letter, not the telegram, was the legal document the sheriff needed to proceed. As the afternoon light began to fade on the twenty-ninth, McMillan fired off a frantic telegram: "Re Albert Stroebel letter. Not yet arrived. Execution fixed for tomorrow morning." Ottawa's telegraphed response simply repeated its message of the twenty-fourth, then primly criticized McMillan for not acknowledging receipt of it. No mention was made of the required letter. In a panic, the sheriff raced to Warden John's office. The pair were deep in conversation when a guard entered with the evening's mail, and with it the letter signed by the Governor General authorizing Stroebel's execution. McMillan sighed with relief as he handed the letter to John, then walked over to the sideboard and poured two generous glasses of whisky.

Meanwhile, on death row, the last hours and minutes of Albert Stroebel's life wound down, painfully slow yet unstoppable. Fathers Nicolaye and Van Goetham sat with the condemned man in his cell, doing their best to distract him. At their urging, he wrote a long letter to his brothers and sisters, which Nicolaye promised to mail. He also gave a short statement to his guards in which he again confessed to shooting Marshall. At midnight, the two priests departed and Stroebel stretched out on his bed for the last time. He fell into a stupor that was half-sleep and half-waking, the terror of the waking bleeding into the sleep.

❖

The death-row guard checked his pocket watch against the clock on the wall as it clicked to three o'clock on the morning of January

30, five hours before the allotted time of execution. Stroebel stirred in bed, then sat up quickly, fully awake. He had barely slept, but he was not tired. He had not eaten since yesterday afternoon, but he was not hungry. The guard greeted him and, seeing the panic in the prisoner's eyes, coaxed him into playing his mouth organ. Stroebel squeezed out a few listless bars before letting the harmonica drop into his lap.

At 6:00 a.m., Nicolaye and Van Goetham entered his cell, and Stroebel stood to greet them. The prisoner's eyes were almost colourless, his skin a yellowish grey. The priests could see that Stroebel was already leaving this life, even as the minutes to his death counted down. The condemned man knelt and meekly received mass, then spent the next hour in prayer, managing a shaky "No, sir" when guards offered him breakfast.

At 7:30, Sheriff McMillan led the official party onto death row. McMillan cleared his throat and said simply, "It's time, Al." Dr. J.S. Helmcken, the prison surgeon, slipped into the cell, opened a small leather case and extracted a hypodermic needle filled with a milky liquid. While the others turned away, Helmcken cradled Stroebel's left arm; the prisoner's veins had all drawn inward from fear, and it took the doctor a few agonizing moments to find one close enough to the skin. Stroebel's eyes fluttered, and he let out a sigh as the morphine sulfate entered his bloodstream. A guard stepped forward to steady him as Stroebel slipped a faded tuxedo jacket over his collarless shirt—the jacket so improbable and out of place, lent to him for a photograph three weeks earlier. Fumbling with the unfamiliar buckles, James Dupen bound the condemned man's arms behind him.

Outside, the morning was clear and cold, the first of its kind in weeks. At 7:45, the rays of the sun struck the whitewashed walls as the prison bell began to toll. A crowd of more than seventy men was gathered at the foot of the gallows, chilly, restless and expectant. These were officials, reporters, professionals and other city notables who had accepted invitations to the event. Scores of uninvited boys and men perched atop the prison fence or scurried to gain a vantage point higher up the rocky hill.

Just before 8:00 a.m., heads turned as the door to the central block opened and the official party filed out. Sheriff McMillan led the way, trailed by Helmcken and the two priests. Stroebel followed, his normally crippled walk loose and smooth, his face and neck flushed red. A guard stayed close behind, with a black-masked Dupen farther back. At the back were Superintendent Moresby, who had come across from the mainland, and Warden John. Moresby and John stopped at the foot of the scaffold stairs, while the rest of the party climbed to the platform.

As the others shuffled into place, Stroebel looked out over the crowded prison yard and gasped. All eyes locked on him; all voices fell silent. The sun warmed his right cheek as he lifted his gaze past the outlying streets of Victoria, past the rolling farmland, to the shimmering blue of Haro Strait. Stroebel blinked as Sheriff McMillan broke the spell.

"Al, have you anything to say?"

The condemned man nodded and replied in slow, measured words: "I can only say this much. I'm very thankful to everybody, for the kindness they've shown me. No one need have no fear but that you're hanging a guilty man. I don't hold no grudge against nobody."

Stroebel paused for a moment, sinking under a wave of morphine, until a few whispered words from Nicolaye brought him back to the surface: "The reason I say this is to free the jury's conscience in thinkin' they've done anything wrong. The jury done their duty all through, and everybody else has."

Stroebel swayed and fell silent. Dupen edged forward and drew the condemned man back onto the trap door, pinioned his legs and draped a white hood over his head. With trembling hands, Dupen placed the noose around Stroebel's neck and cinched it tight, the knot sitting just behind the left ear. Nicolaye and Van Goetham dropped to their knees in prayer as the hangman moved to the trap door lever. A tense moment stretched out, the silence broken only by the murmur of the priests' prayers and Stroebel's rasping breath.

McMillan chopped his arm down, but Dupen did not move. The sheriff cursed, then repeated the signal, more emphatically, and this time Dupen grunted as he pulled the lever. Stroebel shot through the trap door and out of sight. McMillan heard the telltale crack of the hanged man's neck breaking and the gurgle of his strangled breath. A small stream of blood trickled down from behind Stroebel's ear where the rope bit in, and a yellowish-purple stain quickly spread across the back of his neck from his dislocated spine. It was 8:05 a.m.

A guard stepped toward the flagpole in front of the centre block and ran up a black banner as the prison bells ceased, the last toll echoing in the hills beyond. Stroebel's body was left to hang for half an hour before Dr. Helmcken stepped forward, checked for vital signs and pronounced him dead. Guards wrestled the corpse to the ground and placed it in a crude pine coffin, nailing the cover shut. The coffin lay under the gallows, shuttered from view, until later that afternoon. Four figures emerged in the dying light, lifted the coffin and carried it to the far side of the prison yard, then lowered it into an unmarked grave. The remains of Albert Stroebel—alone and unclaimed by family and friends—had found their final resting place.

ENDINGS

No headstone marked Albert Stroebel's grave, no etched words mourned his death or eulogized his life. One local newspaper provided a solitary, sombre epitaph: "Life had been a failure in his case." Finding nothing to praise in his short life, some observers did find a glimmer of redemption in the way Stroebel died. His execution was big news in the province's newspapers, with reporters providing pages of dramatic copy. The papers agreed that Stroebel had met his death well, doing what was expected of him. The *Victoria Times* reported approvingly: "He made a speech on the gallows, freely acknowledging his guilt, exonerating all who had to do with his conviction and execution, and expressing the hope that he would meet all in heaven." The *Daily Columbian* and *Daily Colonist* ran Stroebel's gallows confession in full and commended him for it.

Yet there is reason to be skeptical that the words attributed to Stroebel on the gallows were his. Reporters routinely misquoted confessions from the gallows, writing what their readers expected to hear. For the last week of his life, Stroebel was heavily under the influence of Father Nicolaye, who helped compose and rehearse the gallows speech with him beforehand. The condemned man was also high on morphine from the injection Dr. Helmcken had given him. Sleep-deprived and with no food in his stomach, Streobel would have felt the full effect of the potent opiate as it coursed through his body. None of these messy details mattered, however, to the public, press and authorities. What mattered was that the story of this young man's failed life had come to a just and proper end, and the story could now be filed away as a sad but cautionary tale of a life gone wrong. So, after gripping the public's attention for months, the case of Albert Stroebel quickly disappeared from view.

While quickly forgotten by most, the trials and ignominious death of Stroebel altered the lives of others. John Marshall was, of course, the first to fall victim. A lean, vigorous man of thirty-eight years, he had still held out hope of marrying and starting a family. He would have expected decades of life ahead of him and could look forward to a modestly prosperous future on his successful farm. Sadly, there was no one around to mourn him, and it is unlikely his family back in the Azores were notified of his death, as nobody in Sumas knew his real name. What remained was his name on a creek that flows through his old property, and a forgotten gravesite in a hillside cemetery, unmarked and overgrown, its headstone long since gone.

Aside from Marshall, no one was more directly and immediately affected by Stroebel's troubles than Elizabeth Bartlett, and no one was less able to protect herself. After bidding a final goodbye to her fiancé, just days after her thirteenth birthday, Elizabeth told a reporter "but for the murder, we would have been married." By this time, she had gained an unmerited reputation as a precocious *femme fatale*. Picking up a story from the newswire, newspapers across Washington state reported that "Miss Lizzie Bartlett, of Sumas, is only about 14 years old, but one man has been shot and another to be hung on her account." The day of Stroebel's execution, Nanaimo's *Daily Telegram* heaped scorn on her as "a girl of no character, but of insufferable conceit. She gloried in the fact that 'Al' had 'told her all about it'."

The unearned notoriety and stress of the previous months were too much for the thirteen-year-old. She could not settle back into her old life, and in August 1894, she was arrested as she entered a brothel on the outskirts of New Westminster. A local newspaper reported: "Learning of the new life she had chosen, Chief of Police Huston gave her notice to leave the city at once, strongly advising her to return home. Lizzie left the city, but where she went is not known." Fortunately, Elizabeth was able to turn her life around. In May 1895, she married a twenty-two-year-old tradesman named George Crosby and settled in Sedro Wooley, Washington.

Unlike Elizabeth Bartlett, Oliver Ackerman was protected by money, gender and social standing, but he too was damaged by his efforts to help Stroebel. During the trials, Attorney General Davie subjected him to gruelling cross-examinations and Judge Walkem explicitly labelled him a devious liar who had set out to deceive the jury. Stroebel's post-conviction confessions made matters worse; Ackerman had staked his money and reputation on the lad's protestations of innocence, only to be betrayed by the young man he had tried to help. Ackerman took a couple of weeks to clean up his business affairs in BC, then moved his family back to Petaluma, California, where he still owned property. Ironically, this was where he had first crossed paths with the Stroebel family and befriended George Sr.

For the Stroebels, Albert's troubles were the latest tragedy pulling the family apart. George Sr. made no effort to come to his son's aid, no matter how many times Albert wrote to him, pleading for help. The father never returned to claim the property west of Sumas prairie he left behind. He remained in the Oklahoma Territory throughout the 1890s, then moved into a nursing home for Civil War veterans in Leavenworth, Kansas. George Jr., after thrice visiting his brother on death row, left for Everett, Washington, where he stayed with his sisters. The property he had owned in BC was gone, and he too never returned to the province, living out his days in northern Washington. In July 1894, Stroebel's younger brother William died at the age of fourteen in the Sedro Wooley hospital. Consumption had taken him, just as it had taken his eldest brother, August, and, most likely, his mother. With young William gone, three of the five sons born to Elizabeth Stroebel had died premature deaths.

Sisters Ida and Hattie did their best to keep hold of what family ties remained. Hattie had lived with her sister in Everett until she married in August 1893, while Albert was still in prison. After their last visit to Albert, Ida and George Jr. returned to Ida's home in Everett, before George moved out on his own. Louis, the youngest of the Stroebels, stayed with Hattie for a number of years before he too married. The two sisters and youngest brother stayed close, settling in the lower Puget Sound area. In 1904, the siblings arranged for their father, by then sixty-six years old and crippled by rheumatism, to be admitted into the Orting nursing home for veterans, just outside Everett. At long last, the dream of Albert Stroebel had been realized—what remained of the Stroebel family had come back to each other.

❖

Stroebel was convicted of murder at his second trial because the Crown convinced the jury of two things: first, that the slug taken from Marshall's neck matched another test-fired from Stroebel's revolver; and second, that Stroebel's alibi for the night of Marshall's death—he was not at the farmhouse, but spent the crucial hours fishing—was not believable. As the jury filed out of the Victoria courtroom to deliberate, it was fairly obvious it would return with a guilty verdict. However, looking back over the whole drama from Marshall's death to Stroebel's trials, there was nothing inevitable about how it would end. Stroebel might have saved his life, been convicted of a lesser crime, or even been acquitted altogether, if he had played things differently.

In the days after his conviction, Stroebel sealed his fate by reversing his story and confessing to the shooting, actions that killed any chance he had of receiving a commutation of his death sentence. Looking back further, to the days surrounding Marshall's death, we can spot a number of careless mistakes he made that led to his arrest and conviction. While ditching with Porter the afternoon of April 19, Stroebel removed his revolver and threw it atop his coat. Porter's sighting of the gun caused suspicion to fall on the younger man within hours of the discovery of Marshall's body. By the afternoon, investigators had zeroed in on him as their sole suspect. Three days later, Stroebel left a scribbled note to his sisters in the open for John Bartlett to pick up; at trial, the Crown presented the letter as an admission of guilt. And in a breathtaking blunder, Stroebel voluntarily handed his revolver to David Lucas, gifting the Crown a decisive piece of physical evidence.

The most fateful decision of all, though, was made in the minutes after Stroebel shot John Marshall. As the *Daily Telegram* noted:

If Stroebel had made his confession before his trial, that he had killed Marshall in self-defence in a
quarrel he had with his victim, and thrown himself
on the mercy of the Crown, he would undoubtedly
have escaped with his life. His sentence would at
most have been penal servitude for the rest of his
days, and he might possibly have got off with even
a lighter sentence.

What if, upon rushing out of Marshall's house, Stroebel had gone
to one of the neighbours or to James Schofield at the Huntingdon
train depot, and told them he had shot the farmer in self-defence?
There were no witnesses to the crime to contradict him, no physical evidence to prove he had intentionally killed Marshall. The two
decisive arguments the Crown used to convict him would have been
nullified: evidence matching the slug from Marshall's neck to his gun
would prove nothing beyond what Stroebel himself admitted; and he
would not have needed to invent the "fish story" that served as his
alibi.

To be sure, Stroebel would have been indicted and tried for killing
Marshall, but in the skillful hands of Aulay Morrison, the defence
could have controlled the narrative of what happened that night.
That narrative would have sketched a positive picture of Stroebel that
played to the strong public sympathy felt for him: his reputation as
obliging, honest and hard-working, who persevered despite a serious
physical handicap; a loving brother who stayed true to his siblings
after the death of his mother and flight of his father; a man young for
his years, thought of as a harmless "boy." By contrast, the picture of
John Marshall would be darker: an old man with no family who lusted
after young girls; a braggart and miser who hoarded his precious bags
of gold coins; and worse, a swarthy foreigner, a Portuguese who could
not control his belligerent temper, who did not fit in and could not
even speak proper English.

The prejudice against Portuguese and other dark-skinned immigrants was deep-seated in Canada through the 1890s, and an aggressive

lawyer such as Morrison could have used it to sway a jury against John Marshall, the purported victim. Stroebel himself appealed to this bigotry in one of his confessions: "Marshall was a man of very savage temper—he was a Portuguese. He threatened to kill me and tried to do it. So I drew my pistol and shot him, as I was crippled and had to protect myself." This tale of self-defence could easily have proven plausible and appealing to a jury; any conviction would then have been for manslaughter, not murder, the sentence given five to ten years. If the jury and judge had believed the further claim that Marshall himself caused the first shot—by swatting at the revolver Stroebel raised in self-defence—that sentence would have been lighter.

Another piece of this alternative narrative would have made Stroebel's case even stronger: his claim that he was defending not just himself but his fiancée, Elizabeth Bartlett. By the 1890s, an "unwritten law" that had swayed juries on the American frontier had spread its influence north of the border. This informal but prevalent rule held that a man was justified in killing anyone who tried to seduce or dishonour a girl or woman—a daughter, sister, fiancée or wife—who was under his protection. According to Stroebel, Marshall was a seducer. The farmer wanted to marry the young Elizabeth, and when Stroebel countered that he was engaged to her, the older man flew into a rage and attacked him. Marshall also cast a vile slur against Bartlett's honour: he said she was sleeping with all the boys in Sumas, and that Stroebel should go home and do likewise. Stroebel was simply defending the honour of his betrothed when he confronted Marshall.

We do not know if what Stroebel claimed here was true, but nobody alive could testify that it was false. Such a claim would have played well with the jury and public, as the *Daily Colonist* recognized at the time:

> In his confessions, Stroebel endeavored to make himself a hero by the allegation that the old farmer had made an insulting reference to Lizzie Bartlett, which he, as the promised husband, was bound to hotly resent.

A jury convinced of this scenario, applying the time's "unwritten law," might have acquitted Stroebel outright, although a more likely outcome was a conviction for manslaughter and a light sentence of a few years.

❖

These what-ifs of Stroebel's case only add to the tragedy—sad and unheroic—that was his life. The death of Albert Stroebel came abruptly, violently and too soon, and all that remained of his life was a story rescued from historical amnesia—a tale of tragedy, yes, but also a tale of mystery. For after all the trials, police investigations and probing newspaper coverage, key questions have remained unanswered, key elements of the plot left unresolved.

The biggest mystery lies at the heart of the case, for we do not know exactly what happened in Marshall's home that dreary night in April 1893. Only two people witnessed the events and both were dead as of January 30, 1894. Marshall had no chance to give his version of events, and Stroebel spent the nine months leading up to his conviction denying he was even there. The string of confessions that followed were self-serving and unreliable. Even after Stroebel's conviction, Judge Walkem himself conceded that he did not know who the aggressor was that night, what the argument was about, or how the first shot was fired. At the same time, the *Daily Colonist* lamented that "the truth in regard to the murder of John Marshall will probably never be known."

So let us take a fresh run at the question: What happened? With the crime scene evidence, trial testimony and Stroebel's confessions, we can piece together an outline of the events from suppertime to the shooting. As Marshall and Stroebel finished eating at the kitchen table, an argument erupted, then escalated into a physical scuffle. The farmer stormed outside to retrieve something and was returning across the veranda when Stroebel met him at the door. The younger man held a loaded revolver in his hand and it fired, the bullet striking Marshall in the forehead. Marshall fell to the floor, face down, and a second shot was fired into the back of his neck. Stroebel turned the farmer onto his back, saw what he had done and fled into the night.

The nature of Marshall's wounds and the position of his body were the two most telling facts here, for they clearly demonstrated that the victim was walking briskly across the veranda toward his front door when Stroebel shot him from the doorway. The trajectory of the first bullet was downward, from the forehead to the inside base of the skull. Stroebel was 5'4" tall at full height, shorter when stooping from his leg injury, yet when he fired the first shot he was standing above Marshall: on the door sill, with the farmer bending forward as he stormed across the veranda. Marshall dropped from the first shot and his forward momentum carried his head to the doorsill. The forward motion also stretched his body out, with his feet splayed back over the front of the veranda.

What, though, caused the argument between these two long-time friends that ended in the younger killing the older? Did they fight over a girl, as Stroebel claimed, or was it a robbery gone wrong, as the Crown and court concluded? Both of these scenarios are plausible. From his first confession to his last, Stroebel was consistent in maintaining that he and Marshall came to blows over Elizabeth Bartlett. Possible corroborating testimony came from George Hilliard; the girl he heard Marshall talk about may well have been Elizabeth Bartlett. If she was, and Hilliard told his friend about it, that could have convinced Stroebel that he needed to protect his fiancée from the older farmer. And even if Marshall's "girl" was not Bartlett, the older man's boasting to Hilliard showed he was not above loose, baiting talk about young girls, the kind of talk Stroebel attributed to him.

We do not know what Hilliard told Stroebel about Marshall's girl talk, or whether the farmer's "girl" was Elizabeth Bartlett—we do know Hilliard told his friend about Marshall's gold coins. We can, indeed, make a very plausible argument that the violence of that night was caused by a botched robbery attempt by Stroebel. The latter needed money badly, he was a frequent visitor at the farmer's house, and he carried a gun. In this scenario, Stroebel arrived at Marshall's the morning of April 19 determined to get his hands on the farmer's gold.

The young man hoped he could find it without his host knowing. Left alone while Marshall escorted Sam Lee to a back field, he searched the farmhouse under the guise of cleaning it, but found nothing. Stroebel returned that evening, and as supper came to an end, he clumsily demanded that Marshall hand over some of the gold, pulling his gun when the farmer refused. The two struggled briefly, Marshall ran outside to fetch an axe or club and rushed back across the veranda, where Stroebel shot him twice. Having already searched the house and with Marshall now dead, Stroebel had no way of knowing where the gold was, so he fled empty-handed.

Whichever scenario we find more convincing, the evidence weighs heavily against Stroebel's claims that there was no premeditation or intention in his actions, that he was only reacting to Marshall's aggression and shot him in self-defence or accidentally. Early in the afternoon of April 19, when Stroebel threw his revolver eight feet out of the ditch he was standing in, the handgun was almost certainly unloaded. Stroebel usually, but not always, carried the gun unloaded and he was well aware of the cheap handgun's tendency to go off when carelessly handled. If it had been loaded, chances are the temperamental revolver would have fired when it hit the ground. Thus the gun was empty when he left Porter later that afternoon, still empty when Baxter saw him on the railbed. Yet, by the time Marshall returned from saying goodbye to Sam Lee to find Stroebel in his house, well before their argument, the young man's revolver had been loaded. Stroebel would have slipped cartridges into his handgun either while waiting for Marshall or just before, when he was making his way from the rail line to the farmhouse.

This meant that, before meeting Marshall that evening, Stroebel had anticipated he might need to fire his gun. He may have planned to confront the farmer about Elizabeth Bartlett: to warn the older man not to be having any designs upon her, as he and she were engaged; or to get Marshall to stop the kind of trash-talk Hilliard told him about. Conversely, Stroebel may have intended to rob the farmer at gunpoint, after an earlier search failed to uncover Marshall's gold. In both of these scenarios, by the time he sat down for supper at the farmer's kitchen table, Stroebel was thinking he might have to shoot Marshall and had prepared himself to do it.

❖

These what-ifs and speculations have taken us some distance away from what we know of Albert Stroebel's life and death, and what we know is enough to tell a good story: at times hopeful, at times pathetic, mundane in most parts, exceptional in others. A fitting, sobering coda for our story takes us back to the prison yard of the Victoria Gaol the morning of January 30, 1894, to return to the scene and imagine what Stroebel felt as he faced the last trial of his life.

The air was sharp with the bite of winter that morning as the first rays of sun hit the fresh green paint of the gallows. Stroebel mounted the staircase in a daze, his arms pinioned to his sides, his legs heavy and sluggish from the morphine. The condemned man shuffled across the platform, recited the words given him and delivered his head to the hangman. He had been given twenty-one years and eighteen days of life: more than his oldest brother, August, who died such a painful death, ashen white and gasping for breath; more than his younger brother William, taken away by the same disease that summer. As the hood was pulled over his head and the noose tightened around his neck, Albert too gasped for breath and his ears filled with the sound of his heartbeat. He felt the platform shudder and the floor disappeared beneath his feet, then all went black—the trials of Albert Stroebel had come to an end.

SOURCES

BCA British Columbia Archives
LAC Library and Archives Canada
WSDA Washington State Digital Archives
f.   file
v.   volume

PRIMARY SOURCES
Archives
BCA, GR 2: Victoria Gaol, Warden's Diaries
BCA, GR 308: Victoria Gaol
  v. 12: Record and Description List of all Prisoners Received into Victoria Gaol
  v. 46: Warden's Daily Diary
  v. 56: Visitors' Book
  v. 60: Gaol Surgeon's Journal
BCA, GR 309: New Westminster Gaol
  v. 1: Record and Description list of Prisoners Received
BCA, GR 312: BC, Dept. of Lands and Works, Sumas Land Applications
BCA, GR 419: BC, Attorney General, Document Series
  f. 1893/77a: Reg. v. Stroebel
BCA, GR 429: BC, Attorney General Correspondence
  f. 674/90: Rules to be observed in the Victoria and New Westminster Gaols
  f. 1571/93: Albert Stroebel murders John Marshall
  f. 200/95: James Dupen wants job as executioner for BC
  f. 3401/01: Rules for Executions
BCA, GR 606: BC, Supreme Court: Regina v. Stroebel and Eyerly
  Plan to Illustrate Stroebel-Marshall Case
  f. Inquisition
  f. Depositions
  f. Case for the Crown
  f. Case for the Defence and Rebuttal
  f. Evidence, v. 1
  f. Evidence, v. 2
  f. Evidence, Sketch Map
BCA, GR 1327: BC, Attorney General, Inquisitions
  #5/90: George Rutherford
  #6/90: Edward Hall

#7/90: John Seagerd
BCA, GR 1422: BC, Supreme Court, Probate Files
    f. 277/1901: John Marshall
BCA, GR 1727: BC, Judiciary, Bench Books
    v. 20: G.A. Walkem
    v. 332: J.F. McCreight
    v. 752: G.A. Walkem
BCA, GR 1818: New Westminster Assizes, Minute Books
    v. 1: Minute Book for Criminal Cases
BCA, Vital Statistics
LAC, RG 13: Capital Punishment Case Files
    v. 1423–24, f. 210A: Robert E. Sproule
    v. 1428, f. 265A: Albert Stroebel
WSDA, Censuses
WSDA, Historical Newspapers
WSDA, Vital Statistics

Newspapers
Bellingham Reveille
Chilliwack Progress
Daily Colonist (Victoria)
Daily Columbian (New Westminster)
Daily News Advertiser (Vancouver)
Daily Telegram (Nanaimo)
Daily Times (Victoria)
Daily World (Vancouver)
Pacific Canadian (New Westminster)
Seattle Post-Intelligencer

Published and Online Sources
British Columbia. *Sessional Papers*. Victoria, 1886–96.
Canada. *Census*. Ottawa, 1881–1901.
Canada. *Criminal Code, 1892*. Ottawa: S.E. Dawson, 1892.
Center for Bibliographical Studies and Research. California Digital Newspaper
    Collection (cdnc.ucr.edu).
Church of Jesus Christ of Latter-Day Saints. Family Search (familysearch.org).
Henderson's British Columbia Gazetteer and Directory. Victoria, 1890–97.
United States. *Census*. Washington, 1850–1900.
Williams, R.T. *British Columbia Directory*. Victoria, 1883–99.

SECONDARY SOURCES

Bell, Suzanne. *Crime and Circumstance: Investigating the History of Forensic Science.* Westport, CT: Praeger, 2008.

Boyd, Neil. *The Last Dance: Murder in Canada.* Scarborough, ON: Prentice-Hall, 1988.

Butts, Edward. *Murder: Twelve True Stories of Homicide in Canada.* Toronto: Dundurn, 2011.

Clark, Cecil. *British Columbia Provincial Police Stories.* 3 vols. Surrey, BC: Heritage House, 1986, 1989, 1993.

Dutelle, Aric. *Introduction to Crime Scene Investigation.* Burlington, MA: Jones & Bartlett, 2017.

Flanders, Judith. *The Invention of Murder: How the Victorians Revelled in Death and Detection.* London: Harper Press, 2011.

Foster, Hamar and J. McLaren, eds. *Essays in the History of Canadian Law.* Vol. 6. Toronto: Osgoode Society, 1995.

Friedland, Martin. *A Century of Criminal Justice.* Toronto: Carswell Legal Publications, 1984.

———. *The Case of Valentine Shortis.* Toronto: University of Toronto Press, 1986.

Gray, Charlotte. *The Massey Murder: A Maid, Her Master, and the Trial That Shocked the Country.* Toronto: HarperCollins, 2013.

Halttunen, Karen. *Murder Most Foul: The Killer and the American Gothic Imagination.* Cambridge: Cambridge University Press, 2001.

Jones, Roy. *Boundary Town: Early Days in a Northwest Boundary Town.* Vancouver, WA: Fleet, 1958.

Knafla, Louis, ed. *Law and Justice in a New Land.* Vancouver: Carswell, 1986.

Komar, Debra. *Black River Road: An Unthinkable Crime, an Unlikely Suspect, and the Question of Character.* Fredericton, NB: Goose Lane, 2016.

———. *The Ballad of Jacob Peck.* Fredericton: Goose Lane, 2013.

———. *The Lynching of Peter Wheeler.* Fredericton: Goose Lane, 2014.

Kramer, Reinhold and T. Mitchell. *Walk Towards the Gallows: The Tragedy of Hilda Blake, Hanged 1899.* Toronto: Oxford University Press, 2002.

Rothenburger, Mel. *We've Killed Johnny Ussher! The Story of the Wild McLean Boys and Alex Hare.* Vancouver: Mitchell, 1973.

Sleigh, Daphne, ed. *One Foot on the Border: The History of Sumas Prairie and Area.* Deroche, BC: Sumas Prairie and Area Historical Society, 1999.

Stonier-Newman, Lynne. *Policing a Pioneer Province.* Madeira Park: Harbour Publishing, 1991.

Thorwald, Jurgen. *The Century of the Detective.* New York: Harcourt, Brace & World, 1965.

Turner, Frederick J. "The Significance of the Frontier in American History." *Annual Report of the American Historical Association* (1894): 199–227.

Verchere, David. *A Progression of Judges: A History of the Supreme Court of British Columbia.* Vancouver: UBC Press, 1988.